Joint Symposium on Semantic Processing 2013

Textual Inference and Structures in Corpora

Trento, Italy
20-22 November 2013

ISBN: 978-1-62993-539-3

Printed from e-media with permission by:

Curran Associates, Inc.
57 Morehouse Lane
Red Hook, NY 12571

Some format issues inherent in the e-media version may also appear in this print version.

Printed by Curran Associates, Inc. (2014)

For permission requests, please contact the Association for Computational Linguistics at the address below.

Association for Computational Linguistics
209 N. Eighth Street
Stroudsburg, Pennsylvania 18360

Phone: 1-570-476-8006
Fax: 1-570-476-0860

acl@aclweb.org

Additional copies of this publication are available from:

Curran Associates, Inc.
57 Morehouse Lane
Red Hook, NY 12571 USA
Phone: 845-758-0400
Fax: 845-758-2634
Email: curran@proceedings.com
Web: www.proceedings.com

Contents

Keynote Talks

Text Understanding using Knowledge-Bases and Random Walks
Eneko Agirre 1

The Groningen Meaning Bank
Johan Bos 2

Ontology Lexicalization as a core task in a language-enhanced Semantic Web
Philipp Cimiano 3

From Textual Entailment to Knowledgeable Machines
Peter Clark 4

Entailment graphs for text exploration
Ido Dagan, Bernardo Magnini 5

Semantic Textual Similarity: past present and future
Mona Diab 6

Corpus-driven Lexical Analysis: Norms and Exploitations in Word Use
Patrick Hanks 7

Sweetening Ontologies cont'd
Elisabetta Jezek 9

Unsupervised Relation Extraction with General Domain Knowledge
Mirella Lapata 10

Design and Realization of the EXCITEMENT Open Platform for Textual Entailment
Günter Neumann, Sebastian Padó 11

Regular Patterns - Probably Approximately Correct Language Model
Octavian Popescu 12

Computational Frameworks for Supporting Textual Inference
Dan Roth 13

Potential and limits of distributional approaches for semantic relatedness
Sabine Schulte in Walde 14

Long Papers

Towards Compositional Tree Kernels
Paolo Annesi, Danilo Croce and Roberto Basili 15

Detecting Bipolar Semantic Relations among Natural Language Arguments with Textual Entailment: a Study.
Elena Cabrio and Serena Villata 24

Aligning Verb Senses in Two Italian Lexical Semantic Resources
Tommaso Caselli, Carlo Strapparava, Laure Vieu and Guido Vetere . . . 33

Abduction for Discourse Interpretation: A Probabilistic Framework
Ekaterina Ovchinnikova, Andrew Gordon and Jerry Hobbs 42

Word similarity using constructions as contextual features
Nai-Lung Tsao and David Wible 51

Short Papers

Inference for Natural Language
Amal Alshahrani and Allan Ramsay 60

Textual Inference and Meaning Representation in Human Robot Interaction
Emanuele Bastianelli, Giuseppe Castellucci, Danilo Croce and Roberto Basili 65

An empirical classification of verbs based on Semantic Types: the case of the 'poison' verbs.
Jane Bradbury and Ismaïl El Maarouf 70

Quantifiers: Experimenting with Higher-Order Meaning in Distributional Semantic Space
Matthew Capetola 75

Alternative measures of word relatedness in distributional semantics
Alina Ciobanu and Anca Dinu 80

Linear Compositional Distributional Semantics and Structural Kernels
Lorenzo Ferrone and Fabio Massimo Zanzotto 85

On a Dependency-based Semantic Space for Unsupervised Noun Sense Disambiguation with an Underlying Naïve Bayes Model
Florentina Hristea 90

Automatic classification of semantic patterns from the Pattern Dictionary of English Verbs
Ismaïl El Maarouf and Vít Baisa 95

Extending the Semantics in Natural Language Understanding
Michael Marlen and David Gustafson 100

What Do We Drink? Automatically Extending Hungarian WordNet With Selectional Preference Relations
Márton Miháltz and Bálint Sass 105

Comparison pattern matching and creative simile recognition
Vlad Niculae 110

Determining is-a relationships for Textual Entailment
Vlad Niculae and Octavian Popescu 115

Proceedings of the Joint Symposium on Semantic Processing.
Textual Inference and Structures in Corpora

Supported by the EC-funded project EXCITEMENT
(grant FP7 ICT-287923)
and by the B-CROCE project

Endorsed by ACL SIGLEX and ACL SIGSEM

November, 20-22, 2013
Trento, Italy

Organizing Committee

Ido Dagan, Bar-Ilan University, Israel
Elisabetta Jezek, University of Pavia, Italy
Alberto Lavelli, FBK, Italy
Bernardo Magnini, FBK, Italy
Günter Neumann, DFKI, Germany
Sebastian Padó, University of Stuttgart, Germany
Octavian Popescu, FBK, Italy

Program Committee

Enrique Alfonseca, Google Research, Switzerland
Luisa Bentivogli, FBK, Italy
Antonio Horta Branco, Faculdade de Ciências de Lisboa, Portugal
Elena Cabrio, INRIA Sophia Antipolis, France
Dan Cristea, University of Iasi, Romania
Ido Dagan, Bar-Ilan University, Israel
Rodolfo Delmonte, University "Ca' Foscari", Venice, Italy
Liviu Dinu, University of Bucharest, Romania
Eduard Hovy, Carnegie Mellon University, USA
Elisabetta Jezek, University of Pavia, Italy
Alberto Lavelli, FBK, Italy
Alessandro Lenci, University of Pisa, Italy
Bernardo Magnini, FBK, Italy
Simonetta Montemagni, Istituto Linguistica Computazionale, Italy
Alessandro Moschitti, University of Trento, Italy
Günter Neumann, DFKI, Germany
Rodney D. Nielsen, University of Colorado, USA
Tae-Gil Noh, Heidelberg University, Germany
Jan Odijk, Institute of Linguistics OTS, The Netherlands
Constantin Orasan, University of Wolverhampton, UK
Sebastian Padó, University of Stuttgart, Germany
Octavian Popescu, FBK, Italy
German Rigau, Facultad de Informatica de San Sebastian UPV/EHU, Spain
Anne Vilnat, Universite Paris-Sud, France
Rui Wang, DFKI, Germany
Annie Zaenen, Stanford University, USA
Fabio Massimo Zanzotto, Tor Vergata University, Rome, Italy

Symposium Program

Wednesday November 20, 2013

8:30	Registration
9:15	Welcome
9:30-13:00	**Morning Session**
9:30	Keynote Talk: *Computational Frameworks for Supporting Textual Inference*
	Dan Roth
10:05	Keynote Talk: *Design and Realization of the EXCITEMENT Open Platform for Textual Entailment*
	Günter Neumann, Sebastian Padó
10:40	coffee break
11:10	*Abduction for Discourse Interpretation: A Probabilistic Framework*
	Ekaterina Ovchinnikova, Andrew Gordon and Jerry Hobbs
11:30	*Towards Compositional Tree Kernels*
	Paolo Annesi, Danilo Croce and Roberto Basili
11:50	Keynote Talk: *Corpus-driven Lexical Analysis: Norms and Exploitations in Word Use*
	Patrick Hanks
12:25	Keynote Talk: *Regular Patterns - Probably Approximately Correct Language Model*
	Octavian Popescu
13:00	lunch
14:30-18:30	**Afternoon Session**
14:30	Tutorials - part 1
16:00	coffee break
16:30	Tutorials - part 2
20:30	**Social dinner**

Thursday November 21, 2013

9:30-12:45	**Morning Session**
9:30	Keynote Talk: *Entailment graphs for text exploration*
	Ido Dagan, Bernardo Magnini
10:05	Keynote Talk: *From Textual Entailment to Knowledgeable Machines*
	Peter Clark
10:40	coffee break
11:10	Keynote Talk: *Potential and limits of distributional approaches for semantic relatedness*
	Sabine Schulte in Walde
11:45	Panel on Distributional Semantics
12:45	lunch
14:15-18:30	**Afternoon Session**
14:15	Keynote Talk: *The Groningen Meaning Bank*
	Johan Bos
14:50	Keynote Talk: *Ontology Lexicalization as a core task in a language-enhanced Semantic Web*
	Philipp Cimiano
15:25	Keynote Talk: *Sweetening Ontologies cont'd*
	Elisabetta Jezek
16:00	Booster session (12 posters, 2 minutes each)
16:30	Poster session (with coffee break)
17:55	Keynote Talk: *Unsupervised Relation Extraction with General Domain Knowledge*
	Mirella Lapata

Friday November 22, 2013

9:20-13:00	**Morning Session**
9:20	Keynote Talk: *Text Understanding using Knowledge-Bases and Random Walks* Eneko Agirre
9:55	*Aligning Verb Senses in Two Italian Lexical Semantic Resources* Tommaso Caselli, Carlo Strapparava, Laure Vieu and Guido Vetere
10:15	*Detecting Bipolar Semantic Relations among Natural Language Arguments with Textual Entailment: a Study* Elena Cabrio and Serena Villata
10:35	*Word similarity using constructions as contextual features* Nai-Lung Tsao and David Wible
10:55	coffee break
11:25	Keynote Talk: *Semantic Textual Similarity: past present and future* Mona Diab
12:00	Panel on Textual Inference
13:00	lunch

Text Understanding using Knowledge-Bases and Random Walks

Eneko Agirre
University of Basque Country

One of the key challenges for creating the semantic representation of a text is mapping words found in a natural language text to their meanings. This task, Word Sense Disambiguation (WSD), is confounded by the fact that words have multiple meanings, or senses, dictated by their use in a sentence and the domain. We present an algorithm that employs random walks over the graph structure of knowledge bases, yielding state-of-the-art results for WSD on both general and biomedical texts. We also show that the same algorithm can be successfully applied to Word Similarity and to enrich texts with related concepts, yielding improvements in Information Retrieval.

The Groningen Meaning Bank

Johan Bos
University of Groningen, The Netherlands

What would be a good method to provide a large collection of semantically annotated texts with formal, deep semantics rather than shallow? In this talk I will argue that (i) a bootstrapping approach comprising state-of-the-art NLP tools for semantic parsing, in combination with (ii) a wiki-like interface for collaborative annotation of experts, and (iii) a game with a purpose for crowdsourcing, are the starting ingredients for fulfilling this enterprise. The result, known as the Groningen Meaning Bank, is a semantic resource that anyone can edit and that integrates various semantic phenomena, including predicate-argument structure, scope, tense, thematic roles, animacy, pronouns, and rhetorical relations. A single semantic formalism, Discourse Representation Theory, embraces all these phenomena by taking meaning representations of texts rather than sentences as the units of annotation.

Ontology Lexicalization as a core task in a language-enhanced Semantic Web

Philipp Cimiano
University of Bielefeld, Germany

In order to provide language-based access to the growing amount of knowledge published in Semantic Web formalisms, e.g. as part of the so called Linked (Open) Data cloud, ontologies and vocabularies used to describe data need to be enriched with information about how classes and properties modeled therein can be expressed linguistically, also in different languages.

In this talk I will discuss the vision of a language-enhanced Semantic Web in which information about linguistic realization is modeled in Semantic Web languages and forms part of the Linked Data itself, thus becoming retrievable by standard Semantic Web search engines and indexing services as well as queryable and browseable using Semantic Web standards. This ecosystem of ontologies enriched with linguistic knowledge can then be exploited by a number of NLP applications across applications, avoiding duplication of work by people aiming at supporting language-enhanced access to the Semantic Web.

There are three important ingredients to make this vision feasible.

First of all, we need vocabularies that allow to model lexical and linguistic knowledge using Semantic Web vocabularies. In the last years, we have been developing the lemon model for this purpose that has formed the initial input for standardization activities carried on in the context of the W3C Community Group on the ontology-lexicon interface.

Second, we need practical approaches that ease the effort of creating such ontology lexica. I will present current efforts in this direction aiming at semi-automatically supporting the creation of ontology lexica by human users by exploiting a domain corpus. I will present results of experiments in which we use Wikipedia to automatically induce a lexicon for the DBpedia ontology.

Third and finally, we need people to recognize the value of ontology lexicalization so that they have incentives to contribute to the development of lexica for their favourite ontologies, and we need efficient and tested (collaborative) methodologies which incorporate semi-automatic support allowing people to develop such lexica effectively and efficiently. I have unfortunately no solutions so far for this third challenge to present.

From Textual Entailment to Knowledgeable Machines

Peter Clark
Allen Institute for Artificial Intelligence

Project Halo is a long-term endeavor to create "knowledgeable machines", systems containing large amounts of general and domain-specific knowledge in a computable form. As a medium-term target, our goal is to have the computer pass an elementary school science exam as written, and our approach heavily leverages textual entailment technology. Frequently, exam questions can be transformed into entailment problems in which the entailment is from texts (e.g., school textbooks) presenting the relevant general and scientific knowledge, and the entailment transformations include rules, also derived from texts, that encode appropriate scientific and general inferences. In this talk I will overview the project and describe the textual question-answering component in detail. I will also discuss how the semi-formal representations of text, generate on the fly for textual entailment decisions, might also be aggregated together into a persistent knowledge base – a small step from entailment technology towards the ultimate goal of knowledgeable machines.

Entailment graphs for text exploration

Ido Dagan [†] **Bernardo Magnini** [‡]
[†] Bar-Ilan University, Israel
[‡] Fondazione Bruno Kessler (FBK-irst), Italy

Taxonomy-based representations are widely used to model compactly large amounts of textual data. While current methods allow organizing knowledge at the lexical level (keywords/concepts/topics), there is an increasing demand to move towards more informative representations, which express properties of concepts and relations among them. This demand triggered our research on statement entailment graphs. In these graphs, nodes are natural language statements (propositions), comprising of predicates with their arguments and modifiers, while edges represent entailment relations between nodes. In this talk we report initial research that defines the properties of entailment graphs and their potential applications. Particularly, we show how entailment graphs can be profitably used for both knowledge acquisition and text exploration.

Beyond providing a rich and informative representation, statement entailment graphs allow integrating multiple semantic inferences. So far, textual inference research focused on single, mutually independent, entailment judgments. However, in many scenarios there are dependencies among Text/Hypothesis pairs, which need to be captured consistently. This calls for global optimization algorithms for inter-dependent entailment judgments, taking advantage of the overall entailment graph structure (e.g. ensuring entailment graph transitivity).

From the applied perspective, we are experimenting with entailment graphs in the context of the EXCITEMENT project industrial scenarios. We focus on the text analytics domain, and particularly on the analysis of customer interactions across multiple channels, including speech, email, chat and social media, and multiple languages (English, German, Italian). For example, we would like to recognize that the complaint they charge too much for sandwiches entails food is too expensive, and allow an analyst to compactly navigate through an entailment graph that consolidates the information structure of a large number of customer statements. Our eventual applied goal is to develop a new generation of inference-based text exploration applications, which will enable businesses to better analyze their diverse and often unpredicted client content. This task will be exemplified with data collected from real customer interactions, while referring to the EXCITEMENT Open Platform that we developed as a generic open source framework for textual inferences.

Semantic Textual Similarity: past present and future

Mona Diab
George Washington University, USA

Similarity is at the core of scientific inquiry in general and is one of the basic functionalities in Natural Language Processing (NLP) in particular. To arrive at generalizations across different phenomena, we need to recognize patterns of similarity, or divergence, to make scientific claims. Semantic textual similarity plays a significant role in NLP research both directly and indirectly. For example, for document summarization, we need to compress redundant information which requires identifying where the text is similar; for question answering, we need to recognize the similarity between the questions and the answers; textual similarity is an important component of an entailment system; evaluating machine translation (MT) output relies on calculating the similarity between the system's output and some reference gold translations; textual generation technology benefits from sentence similarity by generating different expressions. In this talk, I will address the problem of textual semantic similarity. We have run 2 major tasks of STS over the span of two years within the context of Semeval in 2012 and *SEM shared task in 2013. The task to date is one of the most successful to be carried out within our community by virtue of being quite popular. I will share with you the details of the task, some interesting insights into the scientific merits of this enterprise and lessons learned. Finally I will share some thoughts on the future.

(Joint work with Eneko Agirre, Daniel Cer, Aitor Gonzalez, and Weiwei Guo)

Corpus-driven Lexical Analysis: Norms and Exploitations in Word Use

Patrick Hanks
Research Institute of Information and Language Processing,
University of Wolverhampton, UK
and
Bristol Centre for Linguistics,
University of the West of England, UK

It is a truism that meaning depends on context. Corpus evidence now shows us that normal contexts can be summarised and indeed quantified, while the creative exploitations of normal contexts by ordinary language users far exceed anything dreamed up in speculative linguistic theory. Human linguistic behaviour is indeed rule-governed, but in recent years, corpus analysis (e.g. Hanks 2013) has shown that there is not just a single monolithic system of rules: instead, language use is governed by two interlinked systems: one set of rules governing normal, idiomatic uses of words and another set of rules governing how we exploit those norms creatively. Types of creative exploitation include (among others):

- using anomalous arguments to make novel meanings
- ellipsis for verbal economy in discourse
- metaphors, metonymy, and other figurative uses for stylistic effect and other purposes

Traditional dictionaries do a good job of listing the many possible meanings of words. But they do a poor job of reporting phraseology and an even worse job of associating different meanings with phraseological patterns. Moreover, all too often, they list a creative use that happens to have been noticed by a lexicographer as if it were a conventional norm, with resultant confusion, for example:

- A riddle does not mean a hole made by a bullet (but OED says it does).
- To newspaper does not mean to work as a journalist (but Merriam Webster says it does).

The idiom principle formulated by the late John Sinclair (1991, 1998) argues that many meanings depend for their realization on the presence of more than one word. The Pattern Dictionary of English Verbs (PDEV; `http://deb.fi.muni.cz/pdev/`; publicly available, but note that it is work in progress) implements this principle by associating meanings with patterns rather than with words in isolation. A pattern consists of a verb and its valencies (otherwise known as clause roles or arguments). Each argument is populated by an open-ended set of lexical items and phrases, which share a semantic value. This means that different senses of a verb can be distinguished according to the semantic values of its arguments. Thus, executing an order and executing a plan go together and are distinguished from executing a dictatorthese are two different meanings of the same verb, activated by different collocates, even though all three examples have identical syntax. Sinclairs idiom principle can be usefully compared with the theory of construction grammar (Goldberg 1995). An important different is that the Sinclairian approach is empirically well founded: it is corpus-driven. It does not rely on the speculative invention of evidence, which has been shown to be methodologically unreliable. PDEV is likewise rigorously corpus-driven. Every verb (and in due course, every predicatorincluding predicative adjectives) has been or will be analysed on the basis of corpus evidence. Each entry in PDEV has the following components:

- A set of syntagmatically distinct patterns (the phraseological norms)
- An implicature (i.e. the meaning and context) for each pattern
- A set of corpus lines illustrating normal uses of each pattern
- Comparative frequencies of each pattern of use of each verb, showing which patterns are most frequent
- A smaller set of corpus lines illustrating creative exploitations
- A shallow ontology of nouns and noun phrases

The CPA shallow ontology serves as a device for grouping together noun phrases that distinguish one meaning of a verb from another.

References

Goldberg, Adele E. 1995. *Constructions: A Construction Grammar Approach to Argument Structure*. University of Chicago Press.

Hanks, Patrick. 2013. *Lexical Analysis: Norms and Exploitations*. MIT Press.

Sinclair, John. 1991. *Corpus, Concordance, Collocation*. Oxford University Press.

Sinclair, John. 1998. The lexical item. In Edda Weigand (ed.), *Contrastive Lexical Semantics*. John Benjamins.

Sweetening Ontologies cont'd

Elisabetta Jezek
Università di Pavia, Italy

By applying the Corpus Pattern Analysis procedure (CPA, Hanks 2004) to the analysis of concordances for ca 1000 English, Italian and Spanish verbs conducted with the aim of acquiring their most recurrent patterns, intended as corpus-derived argument structures with specification of the expected semantic type for each argument position (i.e. [[Human]] attends [[Event]]), we compiled a list of about 220 semantic types obtained from manual clustering and generalization over sets of lexical items found in the argument positions in the corpus (details of the Italian project in Jezek 2012).

These types look very much like conceptual / ontological categories for nouns but should instead be conceived as semantic classes, as they are induced by the analysis of selectional properties of verbs. They are language-driven, and reflect how we talk about entities in the world. As such, despite the obvious correlations, they differ from categories of entities defined on the basis of ontological axioms, such as those of DOLCE (Descriptive Ontology for Linguistic and Cognitive Engineering), which, despite "aiming at capturing the ontological categories underlying natural language and human common sense" (Gangemi et al. 2002) does not base category distinctions on systematic observation and clustering of language data.

In my presentation, I will report the preliminary results of the experiment of aligning the type inventory to the categories of DOLCE, with the aim of verifying how semantic classes obtained through pattern-based corpus analysis differ from categories which are defined on the basis of axiomatization. Also, I will discuss the opportunity to enhance the taxonomic structuring of our list using the OntoClean methodology (Guarino and Welty, 2009), which was also exploited for the development of DOLCE. Finally, I will highlight the mutual benefit of the experiment, and confirm the advantages of keeping the lexical level separated from the ontological level in language resource building (Oltramari et al. 2013).

References

Gangemi, A. Guarino, N., Masolo, C. Oltramari A., Schneider L. et al. (2002). Sweetening Ontologies with DOLCE. In Gómez-Pérez A. and V.R. Benjamins (eds.) Proceedings of the 13th International Conference on Knowledge Engineering and Knowledge Management (EKAW02), Ontologies and the Semantic Web, Berlin, Springer-Verlag, 166-181.

Guarino, N. and C. Welty. 2009. An overview of OntoClean. In Staab, S. and R. Studer (eds.) Handbook on Ontologies (second edition), Berlin, Springer-Verlag, 201-220.

Hanks, P. (2004) Corpus Pattern Analysis. In Williams, G. and S. Vessier (eds.) Proceedings of the Eleventh EURALEX International Congress, Lorient, France, 87-98.

Jezek, E. (2012) Acquiring typed predicate-argument structures from corpora, in Bunt H. (ed.) Proceedings of the Eighth Joint ISO - ACL SIGSEM Workshop on Interoperable Semantic Annotation ISA-8, Pisa, October 35, 2012, 28-33.

Oltramari, A. Vetere, G. Chiari, I. Jezek, E. Zanzotto, F.M. Nissim, M. Gangemi, A. (2013) "Senso Comune: A collaborative Knowledge Resource for Italian". In: Iryna Gurevych and Jungi Kim (eds.). The People's Web Meets NLP: Collaboratively Constructed Language Resources, Berlin-Heidelberg, Springer, 45-68.

Unsupervised Relation Extraction with General Domain Knowledge

Mirella Lapata
University of Edinburgh

Information extraction (IE) is becoming increasingly useful as a form of shallow semantic analysis. Learning relational facts from text is one of the core tasks of IE and has applications in a variety of fields including summarization, question answering, and information retrieval. Previous work has traditionally relied on extensive human involvement (e.g., hand-annotated training instances, manual pattern extraction rules, hand-picked seeds). Standard supervised techniques can yield high performance when large amounts of hand-labeled data are available for a fixed inventory of relation types, however, extraction systems do not easily generalize beyond their training domains and often must be re-engineered for each application.

In this talk I will present an unsupervised approach to relational information extraction which could lead to significant resource savings and more portable extraction systems that require less engineering effort. The proposed model partitions tuples representing an observed syntactic relationship between two named entities (e.g., "X was born in Y" and "X is from Y") into clusters corresponding to underlying semantic relation types (e.g., BornIn, Located). Our approach incorporates general domain knowledge which we encode as First Order Logic rules. Specifically and automatically combine with we combine a topic model developed for the relation extraction task with automatically extracted domain relevant rules, and present an algorithm that estimates the parameters of this model. Evaluation results on the ACE 2007 English Relation Detection and Categorization (RDC) task show that our model outperforms competitive unsupervised approaches by a wide margin and is able to produce clusters shaped by both the data and the rules.

(Joint work with Oier Lopez de Lacalle)

Design and Realization of the EXCITEMENT Open Platform for Textual Entailment

Günter Neumann † and Sebastian Padó ‡
† DFKI GmbH, Saarbrücken, Germany
‡ IMS, Universität Stuttgart, Germany

Textual Entailment (TE) is a binary relation between two natural language text which holds if the truth of a first text implies the truth of the second one, or at least makes it very likely. Good methods to recognize TE have the potential to impact many NLP tasks, where the ability to draw conclusions from textual expressed facts is a key challenge. The area of TE has seen the development of a range of algorithms, methods, and technologies over the last decade.

Unfortunately, research on TE (like semantics research more generally), is fragmented into studies focussing on various aspects of semantics such as world knowledge, lexical and syntactic relations, and so on. This fragmentation has problematic practical consequences. Notably, interoperability among existing RTE systems is poor, and reuse of resources and algorithms is mostly infeasible. This also makes systematic evaluations very difficult to carry out. Finally, TE presents a wide array of approaches to potential end users with little guidance on which to pick.

Our contribution to this situation is a novel architecture and platform, the EXCITEMENT Open Platform (EOP), which was developed to enable and encourage the consolidation of methods and resources in the TE area. Starting out from and generalizing over three existing systems (BIUTEE, EDITS, and TIE), our architecture decomposes RTE into components with strongly typed interfaces. The specifications cover (a) a modular linguistic analysis pipeline and (b) a decomposition of the "core" RTE methods into top-level algorithms and subcomponents. We identify four major subcomponent types, including different kinds of knowledge bases. The architecture was developed with a focus on generality, supporting all major approaches to RTE, as well as encouraging language independence.

The practical implementation of this architecture forms the EXCITEMENT open platform (EOP). It is a suite of textual entailment algorithms and components which contains the three systems named above, including linguistic-analysis pipelines for three languages (English, German, and Italian), and comprises a number of linguistic resources. By addressing the problems outlined above, the platform provides a comprehensive and flexible basis for research and experimentation in Textual Entailment. We discuss the current scope and functionality of the platform, which is available as free open source software, and outline existing and future use cases.

Regular Patterns - Probably Approximately Correct Language Model

Octavian Popescu
Fondazione Bruno Kessler (FBK-irst), Italy

Almost any word in natural language has a great potential of expressing different meanings. However, in certain contexts, this potential is limited up to the point that one and only one sense is possible. When this happens, we are not dealing with an individual phenomenon, but, rather, all the words in that context have their own meaning potential limited.

In this talk, we properly define such meaning restricting contexts, analyze their properties and propose an automatic procedure for their identification in large corpora. We show that these contexts are patternable and that the words are completely disambiguated. We therefore call such contexts sense discriminative patterns (SDP). By comparing minimally different SDPs, we discover a set of lexical semantic features that are used in devising a learning algorithm.

The form of patterns is regular, they are generated by a finite state automaton. Inducing the form of the grammar from annotated examples and finding the right generalization level is done using Angluin Algorithm. The patterns contain the syntactic and lexical information which is relevant for sense disambiguation, so they are SDPs. The patterns are minimally self-sufficient, thus the senses of the words matched by a pattern are in mutual disambiguation relationship. The disambiguation process of the meanings of all slots is sequential, identifying the meaning of one slots leads to the identification of the meaning of all slots. We call this relationship between the senses of the words which are caught in a pattern, chain clarifying relationship, CCR.

The main problem that needs to be addressed is the fact that pattern acquisition is very sensitive to errors. On the basis of the PAC-learning technique, we have developed a technique that produces an approximately correct grammar, having a high probability to be correct in spite of the noisy examples. We restrict the type of patterns that could be learned and we construct hypotheses which are statistically tested against large sample using the statistical query model for learning new patterns.

We will also present the applications of SDPs to various meaning related natural language processing tasks, like word sense disambiguation, textual entailment and meaning preserving translation.

Computational Frameworks for Supporting Textual Inference

Dan Roth
Computer Science and the Beckman Institute
University of Illinois at Urbana/Champaign, USA

Textual Inference requires the analyzing text at multiple levels as well as to disambiguating it and grounding it in knowledge resources to facilitate knowledge driven reasoning.

Computational approaches to these problems in Natural Language Understanding and Information Extraction are often modeled as structured predictions predictions that involve assigning values to sets of interdependent variables. Over the last few years, one of the most successful approaches to studying these problems involves Constrained Conditional Models (CCMs), an Integer Learning Programming formulation that augments probabilistic models with declarative constraints as a way to support such decisions.

I will focus on exemplifying this framework in the context of developing better semantic analysis of sentences Extended Semantic Role Labeling and the task of Wikification identifying concepts and entities in text and disambiguating them into Wikipedia or other knowledge bases.

Potential and limits of distributional approaches for semantic relatedness

Sabine Schulte in Walde
University of Stuttgart, Germany

Distributional models assume that the contexts of a linguistic unit (such as a word, a multi-word expression, a phrase, a sentence, etc.) provide information about the meaning of the linguistic unit (Firth, 1957; Harris, 1968). They have been widely applied in data-intensive lexical semantics (among other areas), and proven successful in diverse research issues, such as the representation and disambiguation of word senses (Schütze, 1998; McCarthy et al., 2004; Springorum et al., 2013), selectional preference modelling (Herdagdelen and Baroni, 2009; Erk et al., 2010; Schulte im Walde, 2010), the compositionality of compounds and phrases (McCarthy et al., 2003; Reddy et al., 2011; Boleda et al., 2013), or as a general framework across semantic tasks ('distributional memory', cf. Baroni and Lenci, 2010; Pado and Utt, 2012), to name just a few examples.

While it is clear that distributional knowledge does not cover all the cognitive knowledge humans possess with respect to word meaning (Marconi, 1997; Lenci, 2008), distributional models are very attractive, as the underlying parameters are accessible from even low-level annotated corpus data. We are thus interested in maximising the benefit of distributional information for lexical semantics, by exploring the meaning and the potential of comparatively simple distributional models.

In this respect, this talk will present four case studies on semantic relatedness tasks that demonstrate the potential and the limits of distributional models.

1. Motivation: Assuming that associations reflect semantic knowledge that can be captured by distributional information, I will present a study that explores the availability of various German association norms in window co-occurrence of standard web and newspaper corpora (Schulte im Walde and Müller, 2013).

2. Compositionality: I will compare two studies on predicting the compositionality for a set of German noun-noun compounds, i.e., the degree of semantic relatedness between a compound and its constituents. One model relies on simple corpus co-occurrence features to instantiate a distributional model of the compound nouns and their nominal constituents (Schulte im Walde et al., 2013); the other model integrates the lexical information into a multimodal LDA model, accomplished by cognitive and visual modalities (Roller and Schulte im Walde, 2013).

3. Paradigmatic relations: I will present two case studies relying on word co-occurrences to distinguish between the paradigmatic relations synonymy, antonymy and hypernymy with regard to German nouns, verbs and adjectives. The first study combines a word space model with a simple co-disambiguation approach, and uses decision trees to distinguish between the relations (Scheible et al., 2013); the second study is a pattern-based approach, and uses nearest-centroid classification (Schulte im Walde and Kper, 2013).

4. Application to Statistical Machine Translation (SMT): I will describe the integration and evaluation of source-side and target-side subcategorisation information into a hierarchical English-to-German SMT system (Weller et al., 2013).

Towards Compositional Tree Kernels

Paolo Annesi, Danilo Croce, Roberto Basili
Department of Enterprise Engineering
University of Roma, Tor Vergata
00133 Roma, Italy
{annesi,croce,basili}@info.uniroma2.it

Abstract

Distributional Compositional Semantics (DCS) methods combine lexical vectors according to algebraic operators or functions to model the meaning of complex linguistic phrases. On the other hand, several textual inference tasks rely on supervised kernel-based learning, whereas Tree Kernels (TK) have been shown suitable to the modeling of syntactic and semantic similarity between linguistic instances. While the modeling of DCS for complex phrases is still an open research issue, TKs do not account for compositionality. In this paper, a novel kernel called Compositionally Smoothed Partial Tree Kernel is proposed integrating DCS operators into the TK estimation. Empirical results over Semantic Text Similarity and Question Classification tasks show the contribution of semantic compositions with respect to traditional TKs.

1 Introduction

Since the introduction of Landauer and Dumais in (Landauer and Dumais, 1997) and Schutze in (Schütze, 1998), Distributional Semantic Models (DMSs) have been an active area of research in computational linguistics and a promising technique for solving the lexical acquisition bottleneck by unsupervised learning. However, it is very difficult to reconcile these techniques with existing theories of meaning in language, which revolve around logical and ontological representations. According to logical theories (Kamp and Reyle, 1993; Blackburn and Bos, 2005), sentences should be translated to a logical form that can be interpreted as a description of the state of the world. On the contrary, vector-based techniques are closer to the philosophy of "meaning as context", relying on the Wittgenstein's (1953) "*meaning just is use*" and Firth's "*you shall know a word by the company it keeps*" and the distributional hypothesis of Harris (1968), that *words will occur in similar contexts if and only if they have similar meanings*. In these years attention has been focused on the question of how to combine word representations in order to characterize a model for sentence semantics. Since these models are typically directed at the representation of isolated words, a well formed theory on how to combine vectors and to represent complex phrases still represents a research topic. Distributional Compositional Semantic (DCS) models capture bi-gram semantics, but they are not sensitive to the syntactic structure yet. On the other hand, Convolution Kernels (Haussler, 1999) are well-known similarity functions among such complex structures. In particular, Tree Kernels (TKs) introduced in (Collins and Duffy, 2001), are largely used in NLP for their ability in capturing text grammatical information, directly from syntactic parse trees.

In this paper, we investigate the combination of DCS and Convolution Kernels. We extend a kernel function recently proposed in (Croce et al., 2011), called Smoothed Partial Tree Kernel (SPTK), that enriches the similarity between tree structures with a function of node similarity. As words are leaves in constituency syntactic trees, the lexical semantic similarity can be easily evaluated in term of similarity between their vector counterparts. In our DCS perspective, this lexical semantic information will be distributed across all the parse tree, as a carrier of the lexical composition, e.g. head/modifier relations, already explicit in dependency formalisms. The idea here is to propagate lexical semantic information over the entire parse tree, by building a Compositionally enriched Constituency Tree (CCT). By making non-terminal nodes dependent on both syntactic (e.g. the `VP` grammatical category) and lexical semantic information, it is possible to formulate a new kernel function based on this tree representation, that takes into account for each node a distributional compositional metrics. Thus, the idea is to i) use the SPTK formulation in order to exploit the lexical information of the leaves, ii) define a procedure to mark nodes of a constituency parse tree that allow to spread lexical bigrams across the non-terminal nodes, iii) apply smoothing metrics sensible to the compositionality between the non-terminal labels. The resulting model has been called Compositionally Smoothed Partial Tree Kernel (CSPTK).

In Section 2, a summary of approaches for DCS and TKs is presented. The entire process of marking parse trees is described in Section 3. Therefore in Section 4 the CSPTK similarity function is presented. Finally, in Section 5, the CSPTK model is investigated in Semantic Text Similarity (STS) and Question Classification tasks.

2 Related Work

Distributional Compositional Semantics. Vector-based models typically represent isolated words and ignore grammatical structure (Turney and Pantel, 2010). They have thus a limited capability to model compositional operations over phrases and sentences. In order to overcome these limitations, Distributional Compositional Semantics (DCS) models have been investigated. In (Smolensky, 1990) compositionality of two vector $\vec{u}$ and $\vec{v}$ is accounted by the tensor product $\vec{u} \otimes \vec{v}$, while in (Foltz et al., 1998) lexical vectors are summed, keeping the resulting vector with the same dimension of the input ones. In (Mitchell and Lapata, 2008) two general classes of compositional models have been defined: a linear additive model $\vec{p} = \mathbf{A}\vec{u} + \mathbf{B}\vec{v}$ and a multiplicative model $\vec{p} = \mathbf{C}\vec{u}\vec{v}$. $\mathbf{A}$ and $\mathbf{B}$ are weight matrices and $\mathbf{C}$ is a weight tensor that project lexical vectors $\vec{u}$ and $\vec{v}$ onto the space of $\vec{p}$, i.e. the vector resulting from the composition.

These models usually assume that composition is a symmetric function of the constituents. While this might be reasonable for certain structures, such as lists, a model of composition based on syntactic structure requires some way of differentiating the contributions of each constituent. In (Erk and Pado, 2008), the concept of a *structured vector space* is introduced, where each word is associated to a set of vectors corresponding to different syntactic dependencies. Noun component of a composition between verb and noun is here given by an average of verbs that the noun is typically object of. In (Guevara, 2010) a regressor is trained for adjective-noun (AN) compositionality: pairs of adjective-noun vector concatenations are used as input in training data, whilst corpus-derived AN vectors as output. A similar approach was previously undertaken by (Zanzotto et al., 2010).

A specific linear model of semantic composition based on the idea of space projection is proposed in (Annesi et al., 2012) for simple grammatical structures, i.e. syntactically typed bi-grams. Given a phrase such as "*buy car*" they project the source vectors $\vec{buy}$ and $\vec{car}$, into a so-called Support Subspace, that is a subset of the original feature space. Space Projection depends on both the two involved lexicals and selects only their "common" features: these *concurrently* constraint the suitable lexical interpretation *local* to the phrase.

Given two phases p_1 and p_2, semantic similarity can be computed by first projecting the two pairs in the suitable Support Subspace and then applying the traditional cosine metrics. Projection is expressed by a (filter) diagonal matrix $\mathbf{M}$ that projects each word into a subset of the original features. Different projections are discussed in (Annesi et al., 2012) aimed at identifying suitable semantic aspects of the underlying head/modifier relationships. The compositional similarity judgment between phrases $p_1 = (u, v)$ and $p_2 = (u', v')$ over the support subspace of p_1 is thus expressed as:

$$\Phi^{(\circ)}(p_1, p_2) = (\mathbf{M}\vec{u} \cdot \mathbf{M}\vec{u}') \circ (\mathbf{M}\vec{v} \cdot \mathbf{M}\vec{v}') \quad (1)$$

where first cosine similarity $(\cdot)$ between the vectors projected in the selected support subspaces is computed and then a composition function $\circ$, such as the sum or the product, is applied. Notice how projection $\mathbf{M}$ may depend on the involved pairs in complex ways. A Support Subspace can be derived from just one pair p_i and then being imposed to the other with a corresponding asymmetric behavior of the Φ metrics, denoted by Φ_i. Alternatively, $\mathbf{M}$ can be derived from projecting in two Support Subspaces, as derived for the two pairs, and then combining them by making again Φ symmetric. The symmetric composition function is thus obtained as the combination:

$$\Phi_{12}^{(\diamond)}(p_1, p_2) = \Phi_1^{(\circ)}(p_1, p_2) \diamond \Phi_2^{(\circ)}(p_1, p_2) \quad (2)$$

where Φ_1, as well as Φ_2, projects both p_1 and p_2

into the Support Subspace of p_1 (and p_2, respectively), and Φ_i are then combined via the $\diamond$ operator (e.g. sum). Although Support Subspaces cannot be applied to estimate similarity between complex linguistic structures, they seem very effective for simple syntactic structures. In (Annesi et al., 2012) experiments over different variants of Eq. 1 and 2, i.e. different choices for projections $\mathbf{M}$ and compositions $\circ$ and $\diamond$, are there discussed. Best results are obtained within the dataset introduced in (Mitchell and Lapata, 2010) when a multiplicative operator $\circ$ is used in Eq. 1.

Recently, Compositional Semantics has been used in syntactic parsing, as shown in (Socher et al., 2013) where Compositional Vector Grammars (CVGs) have been defined to extend small-state Probabilistic Context-Free Grammars, introducing distributional semantic constraints in constituency parsing: interestingly, CVGs allows to estimate the plausibility of the corresponding syntactic constituent within a Recursive Neural Network, by assigning scores to nodes in the parse tree. A similar integrated contribution of lexical information (i.e. word vectors) and syntactic constituency is proposed in semantic extensions of TKs, as introduced in (Croce et al., 2011). As they offer a framework to define similarity metrics strongly tied to the syntactic structure of entire sentences, they will be hereafter discussed.

Tree Kernels. Kernels are representationally efficient ways to encode similarity metrics able to support complex textual inferences (e.g. semantic role classification) in supervised learning models. Tree Kernels (TK) as they have been early introduced by (Collins and Duffy, 2001) correspond to Convolution Kernel (Haussler, 1999) over syntactic parse trees of sentence pairs. A TK computes the number of substructures (as well as their partial fragments) shared by two parse trees T_1 and T_2. For this purpose, let the set $\mathcal{F} = \{f_1, f_2, \ldots, f_{|\mathcal{F}|}\}$ be a space of tree fragments and $\chi_i(n)$ be an indicator function: it is 1 if the target f_i is rooted at node n and 0 otherwise. A tree-kernel function is a function $TK(T_1, T_2) = \sum_{n_1 \in N_{T_1}} \sum_{n_2 \in N_{T_2}} \Delta(n_1, n_2)$, where N_{T_1} and N_{T_2} are the sets of the T_1's and T_2's nodes, respectively and $\Delta(n_1, n_2) = \sum_{i=1}^{|\mathcal{F}|} \chi_i(n_1)\chi_i(n_2)$. The Δ function recursively compute the amount of similarity due to the similarity among substructures. The type of fragments allowed determine the expressiveness of the kernel space and different tree kernels are characterized by different choices. Lexical information has been early neglected in recursive matching, so that only exact matching between node labels were given a weight higher than 0, (Collins and Duffy, 2001): even when leaves are involved they must be equal, so that no lexical generalization was considered. An effective modeling of lexical information is proposed by (Croce et al., 2011), in the so called Smoothed Partial Tree Kernel (SPTK). In SPTK, the TK extends the similarity between tree structures allowing a smoothed function of node similarity. The aim of SPTK is to measure the similarity between syntactic tree structures, which are semantically related, i.e. partially similar, even when nodes, e.g. words at the leaves, differ. This is achieved with the following formulation of the function Δ over nodes $n_i \in T_i$:

$$\Delta_\sigma(n_1, n_2) = \mu\lambda\sigma(n_1, n_2), \text{ where } n_1 \text{ and } n_2 \text{ are leaves, else}$$
$$\Delta_\sigma(n_1, n_2) = \mu\sigma(n_1, n_2)\Big(\lambda^2 + \sum_{\vec{I}_1, \vec{I}_2, l(\vec{I}_1) = l(\vec{I}_2)} \lambda^{d(\vec{I}_1) + d(\vec{I}_2)} \prod_{j=1}^{l(\vec{I}_1)} \Delta_\sigma(c_{n_1}(\vec{I}_{1j}), c_{n_2}(\vec{I}_{2j}))\Big) \quad (3)$$

In Eq. 4, $\vec{I}_{1j}$ represents the sequence of subtrees, dominated by node n_1, that are shared with the children of n_2 (i.e. $\vec{I}_{2j}$): as all other non-matching substructures are neglected. Parameter λ accounts for the decay factor penalizing embedded trees, whose contribution affects too many dominating structures towards the root. Moreover, σ is a similarity between two nodes: for non terminals it can be strict, such as the dot-product imposed to word vectors at the leaves. More details about SPTK as well as its efficient computation are discussed in (Croce et al., 2011). In constituency parse trees, the lexical similarity is only applied between leaves, which reflect words. One main limitation of SPTK is that lexical similarity does not consider compositional interaction between words. Given the following phrase pairs (*np* (*nn river*)(*nn bank*)) and (*np* (*nn savings*) (*nn bank*)), the SPTK estimates the similarity between *bank* without considering that they are compositionally modified with respect different meanings. Hereafter, the DCS operator of Eq. 1 and 2 will be adopted to model semantic similarity at the nodes in a parse tree, in general seen as head/modifier syntactic pairs. Notice that this is the role of the

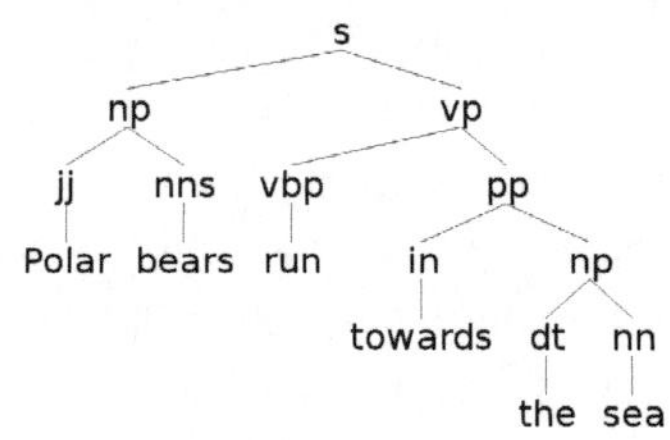

Figure 1: Constituency tree of the sentence "*Polar bears run towards the sea*"

function σ in Eq. 4.

3 Explicit compositions in Parse Tree

In order to consider compositional semantic constraints during a Tree Kernel computation, parse trees are here enriched to enable the definition of a Compositionally Smoothed Partial Tree Kernel, i.e. CSPTK. The input structures are thus tree pairs whose nodes are enriched with lexical information needed for the recursive compositional matching foreseen by the adopted convolution model. The syntactic structure of an individual sentence s is the constituency-based parse tree, as shown in Figure 1. Nodes can be partitioned into: *terminal nodes* n ($\mathcal{T}$), i.e. leaves representing lexical information, in terms of $\langle l_n$::$pos_n\rangle$, such as *polar::j* or *bear::n*, where l is the lemma of the token and pos its part-of-speech[1]; *Pre-terminal nodes* ($\mathcal{PT}$) are the direct ancestors of terminals and they are marked through the pos of their unique corresponding leaf; Non Pre-terminal nodes ($\mathcal{NPT}$), i.e. nodes that are neither terminal nor pre-terminal and reflect the phrase type, e.g. nominal phrase (np) or verb phrase (vp). Notice that all nodes in a tree express either lexical information (e.g. terminal $n \in \mathcal{T}$) or the compositional information between one head and a modifier corresponding to subtrees, such as the non pre-terminal in $\mathcal{NPT}$. In order to model this information, we need to associate each node with different types of information able to express every aspect of compositionality, i.e. lexical as well as grammatical properties. We model this information in a form of a complex mark-up of generic non pre-terminal nodes $n \in \mathcal{NPT}$, in order to exploit them in a compositional extension of a tree kernel (such as in Eq. 4). Compositionality operators acting on the subtrees depend on at least the following types of syntactic as well as lexical information:

Grammatical Types, denoted by $\mathcal{GT}$, that express the grammatical category of the constituent corresponding to the root of a subtree. Example of these types are the np or vp traditional categories of context-free grammars.

Lexical Information. Non pre-terminal nodes in general express binary grammatical relations between a varying number of dominated subtrees (i.e. direct descendants). Each node can be expressed in terms of an head/modifier pair, denoted by (h, m). In order to emphasize the semantic contribution that a subtree (compositionally) expresses, the lexical information about the involved head (l_h) and modifier (l_m) lexicals must be expressed: we denote this information through the 4-tuple $\langle$l$_h$::pos$_h$,l$_m$::pos$_m\rangle$. Notice that this information can be used as an index to a distributional semantic model where lexical entries are expressed by unique vectors for individual lemma and POS tag pairs.

Syntactic Relations. Usually each node expresses a specific syntactical relation between the head and its modifier. Depending on linguistic theories several system of types have been proposed. As in this work, syntactic relations are only used to constrain structural analogies between two trees, the reference relationship system adopted is not here discussed. We denote the set of syntactic relations $\mathcal{SR}$, and they are usually derived by simply juxtaposing grammatical labels of the involved head and modifier, h and m, subtrees. Every relation is denoted by $rel_{h,m} \in \mathcal{SR}$. Examples of the adopted syntactic relations are: vp/np for verb object relation or nn/nn for noun compounds.

Therefore, according to the definitions above, every non pre-terminal $n \in \mathcal{NPT}$ is marked with the following triple

$$\langle gT, rel_{h,m}, \langle l_h :: pos_h, l_m :: pos_m \rangle\rangle$$

where $gT \in \mathcal{GT}, rel_{h,m} \in \mathcal{SR}$, and l_i and pos_i are lexical entries, and POS tags. This triple enables the definition of a similarity function between sentence pairs through the recursive comparison of the marked subtrees. Given the recursive nature of a Convolution Kernel, we will show how the similarity estimation of two (sub)trees is made dependent on the semantic equivalence between the triples assigned to their roots.

A shallow compositional function, that ignores any syntactic information of gT and $rel_{h,m}$ for the head/modifier structure (h, m), can be straightfor-

[1]General POS tags are obtained from the PennTreebank standard by truncating at their first char (as in $bear :: n$).

wardly defined by adopting the DCS model discussed in Section 2, and in particular Eq. 2. Given two subtrees in T_1, T_2, rooted at n_1, n_2, the corresponding head-modifier pairs $(h_1, m_1), (h_2, m_2)$ are defined. This similarity metrics, based on the geometric projection into Support Subspace (Eq. 2), can be applied as follows:

$$\sigma_{Comp}\big((h_1, m_1), (h_2, m_2)\big) = \Phi_{12}^{(\diamond)}((h_1, m_1), (h_2, m_2)) \tag{4}$$

In particular, σ_{Comp} is evaluated through the *Symmetric model* introduced in (Annesi et al., 2012). This model is characterized by a projection **M** that selects the 50 dimensions of the space that maximize the component-wise product between compounds, and by the operator *diamond* that combines the similarity scores with the product function (Eq. 2). Moreover, similarity scores in each subspace are obtained by defining $\circ$ as the sum of cosine similarities in Eq. 1.

3.1 Mark-Up Rules for Constituency Trees

While marking terminal $\mathcal{T}$ nodes and pre-terminal $\mathcal{PT}$ nodes is quite simple, the labeling of non pre-terminal $\mathcal{NPT}$ nodes is complex. Grammar specific notations and rules are needed and mainly differ with respect to (1) the type of the children nodes, i.e. if they are all pre-terminal or not, and (2) the arity of the branching at the root of a subtree: n-ary , with $n > 2$, can be found indeed.

$\mathcal{NPT}$ nodes with binary branches correspond to simple labeling, since exactly two subtrees are always involved. On the basis of the underlying CFG rule, the head and the modifier are determined and labeled. In particular, the treatment of binary trees whose binary branches only involve pre-terminal nodes depends exclusively on lexical nodes $n \in \mathcal{T}$. Given two terminal nodes (n_1, n_2), described by $\langle l_1::pos_1, l_2::pos_2\rangle$, the mark-up rule for their direct (non pre-terminal) ancestor is

$$pos_2/pos_1[h = n_2, m = n_1] \leftarrow (n_1, n_2) \tag{5}$$

where $[h = p_2, m = p_1]$ denotes that the second leaf node has been selected as the *head*, and the first as the *modifier*, while the relation is rel_{pos_2,pos_1}. Figure 2 shows a fully labeled tree for the sentence whose unlabeled version has been shown in Figure 1. The np node spanning the *polar bear* phrase is labeled s $\langle np, nns/jj, (bear :: n, polar :: j)\rangle$.

Notice how usually the grammatical type assigned to a node does not change the assignment

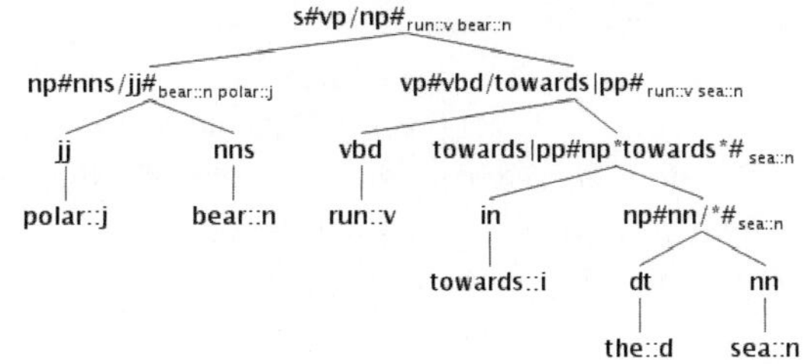

Figure 2: Marking of a Compositional constituency tree of the example in Figure 1

already provided by the tree. In some particular cases, the pair head h and modifier m and the syntactic relation $rel_{h,m}$ implied by a node in the tree are not fully defined either because some null semantic content is encountered (e.g. a missing modifier) or because it is not possible to model some lexical as it is not present in distributional semantic representation. Some relations exist where the modifier seems not to carry relevant lexical information, as the case of the relation between a determiner and a noun. In these cases, the modifier of a non pre-terminal node as well as the syntactic relation are neglected and null slots, i.e. $*$, are used. An example in Figure 2 is the labeling of the bi-gram *the sea*.

The labeling of prepositional phrases constitute a somehow special case of the marking of non pre-terminal nodes $\mathcal{NPT}$. The lexical information carried out by prepositions is not directly expressed lexically but it is integrated both in the grammatical type gT and in the $rel_{h,m}$. This is the case of the triple $\langle towards|pp, np/towards, (sea :: n, *)\rangle$ in Figure 2. The treatment of binary trees whose binary branches involves pre-terminal nodes or non pre-terminal nodes is also straightforward. Where $\mathcal{PT}$ nodes depend strictly from the lexical leaves, $\mathcal{NPT}$ node dominate complex subtrees. The main difference with respect the Equation 5 is that n_1, n_2 or both subtrees may correspond to $\mathcal{NPT}$ node n_i. In a bottom up fashion, the head modifier pair (h_i, m_i) already assigned to n_i is propagated upward. The dominating node is marked-up according to the head h_i of its corresponding dominated branches. For $\mathcal{NPT}$ nodes, the head and the modifier are still assigned by Equation 5, whereas only the heads of the involved subtrees are used. For example, in Figure 2, the root is marked as $\langle s, np/vp, (run :: v, bear :: n)\rangle$ according to the heads, i.e. *run::v* and *bear::n*, of the corresponding branches (i.e. the right *vp* and the left *np*). When $\mathcal{NPT}$ nodes have more than 2 branches (e.g. all pre-terminal nodes or other $\mathcal{NPT}$ nodes), criteria depending on the specific context free rules of the underlying grammar are adopted to select the proper head and modifier.

4 The Compositionally Smoothed Partial Tree Kernel

When the compositionally enriched parse tree is available, it is possible to measure the similarity between this constituency structures through a Tree Kernel. We define here the Compositionally Smoothed Partial Tree Kernel (CSPTK) as a similarity function for such that structures, by extending the SPTK formulation. Let us consider the application of the SPTK on the tree shown in Figure 2. When estimating the similarity with a tree derived from sentences such as "*Bear market runs towards the end*" or "*The commander runs the offense*", the kernel will estimate the similarity among all nodes. Then, the σ function in Equation 4 would not be able to exploit the different senses of the verb *run*, as a traditional distributional model would provide a unique representation. The aim of the CSPTK is to exploit the observable compositional relationships in order to emphasize the contributions of the compounds to the overall meaning, even where the syntactic structure does not change, such as in "*run the offense*", i.e. attacking someone, vs. "*run towards the end*".

The core novelty of the CSPTK is the new estimation of σ as described in Algorithm 1. For the terminal nodes (i.e. LEX type) a lexical kernel σ_{LEX}, i.e. the cosine similarity between words sharing the same POS-Tag, is applied. Otherwise between pre-terminal nodes, a strong matching is required, assigning 0/1 similarity only if pre-terminal nodes share the same POS. The novel part of Algorithm 1 is introduced with the similarity computation over non pre-terminal nodes. In order to activate the similarity function between $\mathcal{NPT}$ nodes, they must have the same gT and $rel_{h,m}$. In this case, the Subspace operator in Equation 2 is applied between the involved (h, m) compounds: lexical information pairs are checked and if their respective heads and modifiers share the corresponding POS, the compositional similarity function is applied.

As discussed in Section 3.1, modifier could be missing in lexical information pair. The DCS model is applied according to three strategies:

General case. If nodes have both heads and modifiers, the similarity function of Equation 4 is applied as usual. Notice that the *pos-tags* of heads and modifiers must be the same.

A modifier is missing. An "optimistic" similarity estimator can be defined in this case. Let be $(h_x, *)$ and (h_y, m_y) the lexical information of two nodes x (that lacks of the modifier) and y. The forced pair (h_x, m_y) and the pair (h_y, m_y) projected and compared into their own subspaces, provide a measure of how the head h_x is similar to h_y, with respect to the meaning that they evoke together with m_y. The more h_x and h_y could be both modified by m_y to specify the same meaning, the higher is the received score.

Both modifiers are missing. This case is reduced to the treatment of lexical nodes (i.e. LEX type), and no composition is observed: the lexical kernel σ_{LEX}, i.e. the cosine similarity between word vectors, is adopted as no subspace is needed.

Algorithm 1 $\sigma_\tau(n_x, n_y, lw)$ Compositional estimation of the lexical contribution to semantic tree kernel

$\sigma_\tau \leftarrow 0,$
if $n_x = \langle lex_x{::}pos\rangle$ **and** $n_y = \langle lex_y{::}pos\rangle$ **then**
$\sigma_\tau \leftarrow lw \cdot \sigma_{LEX}(n_1, n_2)$
end if
if $n_x = pos$ **and** $n_x = n_y$ **then**
$\sigma_\tau \leftarrow 1$
end if
if $n_x = \langle gT, syntRel, \langle li_x\rangle\rangle$ **and** $n_y = \langle gT, syntRel, \langle li_y\rangle\rangle$ **then**
*/*Both modifiers are missing*/*
if $li_x = \langle h_x{::}pos\rangle$ **and** $li_y = \langle h_y{::}pos\rangle$ **then**
$\sigma_\tau \leftarrow \sigma_{COMP}((h_x), (h_y)) = \sigma_{LEX}(n_x, n_y)$
end if
*/*One modifier is missing*/*
if $li_x = \langle h_x{::}pos_h\rangle$ **and** $li_y = \langle h_y{::}pos_h, m_y{::}pos_m\rangle$ **then**
$\sigma_\tau \leftarrow \sigma_{COMP}((h_x, m_y), (h_y, m_y))$
end if
*/*General Case*/*
if $li_x = \langle h_x{::}pos_h, m_x{::}pos_m\rangle$ **and** $li_y = \langle h_y{::}pos_h, m_y{::}pos_m\rangle$ **then**
$\sigma_\tau \leftarrow \sigma_{COMP}((h_x, m_x), (h_y, m_y))$
end if
end if
return σ_τ

Notice that Algorithm 1 could be be still modified further depending on how the non terminal similarity has to be strict on gT and $rel_{h,m}$ and on how much is the weight of terminal and pre-terminal nodes.

5 Experimental Evaluations

In this section the CSPTK model is used in Semantic Textual Similarity (STS) and Question Classification (QC) tasks. The aim of this section is to measure the CSPTK capability to account for the similarity between sentences and as a feature to train machine learning classifiers.

5.1 Experimental Setup

In all experiments, sentences are processed with the Stanford CoreNLP[2], for Part-of-speech tagging, lemmatization, and dependency and compositionally enriched parsing. In order to reduce data sparseness introduce by fined grained Part-of-Speech classes, node are marked by coarse grained classes, e.g. *looking*:`VBG` or *looked*:`VBD` are simplified in *look*:`V`. In order to estimate the basic lexical similarity function employed in the Tree Kernels operators, a co-occurrence Word Space is acquired through the distributional analysis of the UkWaC corpus (Baroni et al., 2009). First, all words occurring more than 100 times (i.e. the *targets*) are represented through vectors. The original space dimensions are generated from the set of the 20,000 most frequent words (i.e. *features*) in the UkWaC corpus. A co-occurrence Word-Space with a window of size 3 is acquired. Co-occurrencies are weighted by estimating the Point-wise Mutual Information between the 20k most frequent words. The SVD reduction is then applied with a dimensionality cut of $d = 250$. Left contexts are treated differently from the right ones, in order to capture asymmetric syntactic behaviors (e.g., useful for verbs): 40,000 dimensional vectors are thus derived for each target. Similarity between lexical nodes is estimated as the cosine similarity in the co-occurrence Word Space, as in (Croce et al., 2011).

5.2 The Semantic Text Similarity task

The first experiment aims to evaluate the contribution of the Kernel-based operators in a STS task. In the **Core STS task** given two sentences, s_1 and s_2, participants are asked to provide a score reflecting the corresponding text similarity (Agirre et al., 2013). PTK, SPTK and CSPTK similarity functions are employed over the dataset of the *SEM 2013 shared task. In Table 1 results of Pearson Correlations between the Kernels operators and the human scores are shown. We considered all datasets composing the challenge training set, i.e. MSRvid, MSRpar, SMTEuroparl, surprise.OnWn and surprise.SMTnews as well as the test set Headlines, FNWN and SMTnews. We did not report any comparison with the best results of the SemEval STS competition as those approaches are mostly supervised. On the contrary the presented approach for the STS estimation is fully unsupervised. The purpose of the experiments is to i) investigate the differences between Kernels operators when lexical semantics (i.e. SPTK and CSPTK) is added to the syntactic information (i.e. PTK), ii) analyze the role of the the compositional compounds made explicit in parse trees and iii) measure the contribution of the DCS model adopted in the recursive CSPTK computation.

PTK and SPTK functions are both applied to the Constituency Tree representations, labeled with ct, while the CSPTK model consists in: i) lexical mark-up as a form of lexical compositional caching that generates the input Compositionally labeled Constituency Tree representation (denoted by cct) as introduced and discussed in Section 3 and ii) the matching function among the subtrees [3]

Dataset	PTK_{ct}	$SPTK_{ct}$	$CSPTK_{cct}$
MSRVid	.12	.18	**.65**
MSRPar	.26	.28	**.32**
SMTEuroparl	.45	.45	**.50**
surprise.OnWN	.49	.55	**.59**
surprise.SMTNews	.46	.46	**.46**
FNWN	.15	.19	**.21**
Headlines	.40	.49	**.52**
OnWN	.04	.24	**.37**
SMTNews	.28	.31	**.33**

Table 1: Unsupervised results of Pearson correlation for Kernel-based features adopted in *SEM - Task 6 datasets

First and second columns in Table 1 show Pearson results of PTK_{ct} and $SPTK_{ct}$ functions applied over a constituency tree, while the last column shows the $CSPTK_{cct}$ results over the compositionally labeled tree. Notice how the introduction of the compositionality enrichment in a constituency tree structure, together with the CSPTK function led to a performance boost over all the training and test datasets. In some cases, the boost between $SPTK_{ct}$ and $CSPTK_{cct}$ is remarkable, switching from .18 to .65 in MSRvid and from .24 to .37 in OnWN.

The above difference is mainly due to the increasing sensitivity of PTK, SPTK and CSPTK to the incrementally rich lexical information. This is especially evident in sentence pairs with very

[2] http://nlp.stanford.edu/software/corenlp.shtml

[3] For the SPTK, we selected the parameters $\lambda = 0.1$, $\mu = 0.1$ and $lexical\_weight = 100$ that provided best results in (Croce et al., 2012). Otherwise for CSPTK we selected $\lambda = 0.4$, $\mu = 0.4$ and $lexical\_weight = 10$.

similar syntactic structure. For example in the MSRvid dataset, a sentence pair is given by *The man are playing soccer* and *A man is riding a motorcycle*, that are strictly syntactically correlated. As a side effect, PTK provides a similarity score of .647 between the two sentences. It is a higher score with respect to the SPTK and CSPTK: differences between tree structures are confined only to the leaves. By scoring .461, SPTK introduces an improvement as the distributional similarity (function σ in Eq. 4) that acts as a smoothing factor between leaves better discriminates uncorrelated words, like *motorcycle* and *soccer*. However, ambiguous words such verbs *ride* and *play* are still promoting a similarity that is locally misleading. Notice that both PTK and SPTK receive a strong contribution in the recursive computation of the kernels by the left branching of the tree, as the subject is the same, i.e. *man*. Compositional information about direct objects (*soccer* vs. *motorcycle*) is better propagated by the CSPTK operator. Its final scores for the pair is .36, as semantic differences between the sentences are emphasized. Even if grammatical types strongly contribute to the final score (as in PTK or SPTK), now the DCS computation over these nodes (the compounds traced from the leaves, i.e. (*ride::v, motorcycle::n*) and (*play::v, soccer::n*) is faced with less ambiguous verb phrases, that contribute with lower scores.

5.3 CSPTK for Question Classification

Thanks to structural kernel similarity, a question classification (QC) task can be easily modeled by representing questions, i.e., the classification targets, with their parse trees. The aim of the experiments is to analyze the role of lexical similarity embedded in the compositionally enriched constituency trees by the CSPTK operator. Thus, questions have been represented by the classic constituency tree, i.e. *ct*, and by the compositionally enriched variant, i.e. *cct*. The first representation is used over PTK and SPTK functions, while the latter over the CSPTK function. Our referring corpus is the UIUC dataset (Li and Roth, 2002). It is composed by a training set of 5,452 questions and a test set of 500 questions[4]. The latter are organized in six coarse-grained classes, i.e. ABBREVIATION, ENTITY, DESCRIPTION, HUMAN, LOCATION and NUMBER. For learning our models we employed LIBSVM[5] after computing the entire Gram Matrix. The F1 of SVMs using (i) PTK and SPTK applied to *ct* and (ii) CSPTK applied to *cct* for QC, is reported in Table 2. Notice that we want to carry out a comparative evaluation of different syntactic kernels and not to optimize the QC accuracy as this requires a combination of lexical and syntagmatic kernels as discussed in (Croce et al., 2011). The results are in general outperforming the alternative kernel formulations, even if the improvement is modest. First, we outline that a more stable behavior *wrt* parameters is observed, with a corresponding lower risk of over-fitting the training data. Second, it is to be noticed that a large number of questions have a really simple syntactic structure: as a consequence the interrogative form of the sentence is very simple and very few compositional phenomena are observed that are captured by the distributional information about word vectors.

SVM par	PTK_{ct}	SPTK_{ct}	CSPTK_{cct}
c=1	.78	.89	**.91**
c=2	.83	.90	**.90**
c=5	.88	.92	**.92**

Table 2: Results in the Question Classification task

6 Conclusions

In this paper, a novel kernel function has been proposed in order to exploit Distributional Compositional operators within Tree Kernels. The proposed approach propagates lexical semantic information over an entire constituency parse tree, by building a Compositionally labeled Constituency Tree. It enables the definition of the Compositional Smoothed Partial Tree Kernel as a Convolution Kernel that measures the semantic similarity between complex linguistic structures by applying metrics sensible to the compositionality. First empirical results of the CSPTK in STS and QC tasks demonstrate the robustness and the generalization capability of the proposed kernel. Future investigation is needed in the adoption of the same compositionality perspective on dependency graphs, were the compositional representations of the head/modifier compound are even more explicit. Further experiments for assessing the methodology are also foreseen against other NLP-tasks, e.g. verb classification.

[4] http://cogcomp.cs.illinois.edu/Data/QA/QC/

[5] http://www.csie.ntu.edu.tw/cjlin/libsvm/

References

Eneko Agirre, Daniel Cer, Mona Diab, Aitor Gonzalez-Agirre, and Weiwei Guo. 2013. *sem 2013 shared task: Semantic textual similarity. In *Second Joint Conference on Lexical and Computational Semantics (*SEM), Volume 1: Proceedings of the Main Conference and the Shared Task: Semantic Textual Similarity*, pages 32–43, Atlanta, Georgia, USA, June. Association for Computational Linguistics.

P. Annesi, V. Storch, and R. Basili. 2012. Space projections as distributional models for semantic composition. In *In Proceedings of CICLing 2012*, volume 7181 of *Lecture Notes in Computer Science*, pages 323–335. Springer.

M. Baroni, S. Bernardini, A. Ferraresi, and E. Zanchetta. 2009. The wacky wide web: a collection of very large linguistically processed web-crawled corpora. *Language Resources and Evaluation*, 43(3):209–226.

P. Blackburn and J. Bos. 2005. *Representation and Inference for Natural Language. A First Course in Computational Semantics*. CSLI Publications.

M. Collins and N. Duffy. 2001. Convolution kernels for natural language. In *Proceedings of Neural Information Processing Systems (NIPS)*, pages 625–632.

D. Croce, A. Moschitti, and R. Basili. 2011. Structured lexical similarity via convolution kernels on dependency trees. In *Proceedings of EMNLP*, Edinburgh, Scotland, UK.

D. Croce, P. Annesi, V. Storch, and R. Basili. 2012. Unitor: Combining semantic text similarity functions through sv regression. In **SEM 2012*, pages 597–602, Montréal, Canada, 7-8 June.

K. Erk and S. Pado. 2008. A structured vector space model for word meaning in context. In *EMNLP '08: Proceedings of the Conference on Empirical Methods in Natural Language Processing*, pages 897–906. ACL.

P. Foltz, W. Kintsch, and T. Landauer. 1998. The measurement of textual coherence with latent semantic analysis. *Discourse Processes*, 25:285–307.

E. Guevara. 2010. A regression model of adjective-noun compositionality in distributional semantics. In *Proceedings of the GEMS '10*, pages 33–37, Stroudsburg, PA, USA. Association for Computational Linguistics.

D. Haussler. 1999. Convolution kernels on discrete structures. Technical report, Dept. of Computer Science, University of California at Santa Cruz.

H. Kamp and U. Reyle. 1993. *From discourse to logic: introduction to modeltheoretic semantics of natural language, formal logic and discourse representation theory. Part 1.* Kluwer Academic.

T. Landauer and S. Dumais. 1997. A solution to platos problem: The latent semantic analysis theory of acquisition, induction, and representation of knowledge. *Psychological review*, pages 211–240.

X. Li and D. Roth. 2002. Learning question classifiers. In *Proceedings of ACL '02*, COLING '02, pages 1–7, Stroudsburg, PA, USA. Association for Computational Linguistics.

J. Mitchell and M. Lapata. 2008. Vector-based models of semantic composition. In *In Proceedings of ACL/HLT 2008*, pages 236–244.

J. Mitchell and M Lapata. 2010. Composition in distributional models of semantics. *Cognitive Science*, 34(8):1388–1429.

H. Schütze. 1998. Automatic word sense discrimination. *Comput. Linguist.*, 24(1):97–123, March.

P. Smolensky. 1990. Tensor product variable binding and the representation of symbolic structures in connectionist systems. *Artif. Intell.*, 46:159–216, November.

Richard Socher, John Bauer, Christopher D. Manning, and Ng Andrew Y. 2013. Parsing with compositional vector grammars. In *Proceedings of the 51st Annual Meeting of the Association for Computational Linguistics (Volume 1: Long Papers)*, pages 455–465, Sofia, Bulgaria, August. Association for Computational Linguistics.

Peter D. Turney and Patrick Pantel. 2010. From frequency to meaning: Vector space models of semantics. *Journal of artificial intelligence research*, 37:141.

Fabio Massimo Zanzotto, Ioannis Korkontzelos, Francesca Fallucchi, and Suresh Manandhar. 2010. Estimating linear models for compositional distributional semantics. In *Proceedings of the 23rd International Conference on Computational Linguistics (COLING)*.

Detecting Bipolar Semantic Relations among Natural Language Arguments with Textual Entailment: a Study.

Elena Cabrio and **Serena Villata**
INRIA
2004 Route des Lucioles BP93
06902 Sophia-Antipolis cedex, France.
{elena.cabrio, serena.villata}@inria.fr

Abstract

In the knowledge representation and reasoning research area, argumentation theory aims at representing and reasoning over information items called *arguments*. In everyday life, arguments are reasons to believe and reasons to act, and they are usually expressed in natural language. Even if *ad-hoc* natural language examples are often provided in argumentation theory works, no automated processing of such natural language arguments is carried out, making it impossible to exploit the results of this research area in real world scenarios. In this paper, we propose to adopt textual entailment to address this issue. In particular, we discuss and evaluate, on a sample of natural language arguments extracted from Debatepedia, the support and attack relations among arguments in bipolar abstract argumentation with respect to the more specific notions of textual entailment and contradiction.

1 Introduction

Until recent years, the idea of "argumentation" as the process of creating arguments for and against competing claims was a subject of interest to philosophers and lawyers. In recent years, however, there has been a growth of interest in the subject from formal and technical perspectives in Artificial Intelligence, and a wide use of argumentation technologies in practical applications. However, such applications are always constrained by the fact that natural language arguments cannot be automatically processed by such argumentation technologies. Arguments are usually presented either as the abstract nodes of a directed graph where the edges represent the relations of attack and support (e.g., in abstract argumentation theory (Dung, 1995) and in bipolar argumentation (Cayrol and Lagasquie-Schiex, 2005)) or as a set of premises which lead to a certain conclusion thanks to the application of a number of inference rules (e.g., in structured approaches to argumentation as ASPIC (Prakken, 2010)). Natural language arguments are usually used in such works to provide *ad-hoc* examples to help the reader in the understanding of the rationale behind the formal approach which is then introduced, but the need to find automatic ways to process natural language arguments to detect the semantic relations among them is becoming more and more important.

To fill this gap, we propose to investigate semantic inference approaches in Natural Language Processing (NLP) in search of a suitable computational framework to account for bipolar argumentation models. In particular, in this paper, we study *how bipolar semantic relations among natural language arguments can be discovered in an automated way using textual entailment.* This issue breaks down into the following research questions: (1) what is the relation between the notion of support in bipolar argumentation and the notion of Textual Entailment (TE) in NLP?, and given that additional attacks have been proposed in the literature to highlight possible inconsistencies arising among sets of arguments connected by supports and attacks (2) what is the distribution and thus the inner semantics of such additional attacks in real data?

First, we study the relation among the notion of support in bipolar argumentation (Cayrol and Lagasquie-Schiex, 2005), and the notion of TE in NLP (Dagan et al., 2009). In a recent proposal, (Cabrio and Villata, 2012) represent the TE relation extracted from NL texts as a support relation in bipolar argumentation. This is a strong assumption, and we aim at verifying on a sample of real data from Debatepedia whether it is always the case that support is equivalent to TE. In particular, for addressing this issue, we focus both on the relations between support and entailment, and on the relations between attack and contradiction. We show that TE and contradiction are more specific concepts than support and attack, but still hold in most of the argument pairs.

Second, starting from the comparative study addressed by (Cayrol and Lagasquie-Schiex, 2011), we consider four additional attacks proposed in the literature: *supported* (if argument a supports argument b and b attacks argument c, then a attacks c) and *secondary* (if a supports b and c attacks a, then c attacks b) attacks (Cayrol and Lagasquie-Schiex, 2010), *mediated* attacks (Boella et al., 2010) (if a supports b and c attacks b, then c attacks a), and *extended* attacks (Nouioua and Risch, 2010; Nouioua and Risch, 2011) (if a supports b and a attacks c, then b attacks c). We investigate the distribution of these attacks in NL debates basing on a data set extracted from Debatepedia, and we show that all these models are verified in human debates, even if with a different frequency.

The benefit of the proposed analysis is twofold. First, it is used to verify, through a data driven evaluation, the "goodness" of the proposed models of bipolar argumentation to be used in real settings, going beyond *ad hoc* NL examples. Second, it can be used to guide the construction of cognitive agents whose major need is to achieve a behavior as close as possible to the human one. Thanks to such a kind of analysis, we highlight that the mutual influence of these two related research areas can actually bring to textual entailment more than just an application scenario, but it opens further challenges to be addressed with a joint effort by the two research communities.

The paper is organized as follows. Section 2 summarizes the basic notions of bipolar argumentation, and describes the four kinds of additional attacks we consider in this paper. Section 3 describes the experimental setting, and addresses the analysis of the meaning of support and attack in natural language dialogues, as well as the comparative study on the existing additional attacks.

2 Bipolar argumentation

We provide the basic concepts of Dung's (1995) abstract argumentation.

Definition 1 *(Abstract argumentation framework) An abstract argumentation framework (AF) is a pair $\langle A, \rightarrow \rangle$ where A is a set of elements called arguments and $\rightarrow \subseteq A \times A$ is a binary relation called attack. We say that an argument a attacks an argument b if and only if $(a, b) \in \rightarrow$.*

Dung presents several acceptability semantics that produce zero, one, or several sets of accepted arguments called *extensions*. For more details, see (Dung, 1995).

Bipolar argumentation frameworks, firstly proposed by (Cayrol and Lagasquie-Schiex, 2005), extend Dung's framework taking into account both the attack relation and the support relation. In particular, an abstract bipolar argumentation framework is a labeled directed graph, with two labels indicating either attack or support. In this paper, we represent the attack relation by $a \rightarrow b$, and the support relation by $a \dashrightarrow b$.

Definition 2 (Bipolar argumentation framework) *A bipolar argumentation framework (BAF) is a tuple $\langle A, \rightarrow, \dashrightarrow \rangle$ where A is the set of elements called arguments, and two binary relations over A are called attack and support, respectively.*

(Cayrol and Lagasquie-Schiex, 2011) address a formal analysis of the models of support in bipolar argumentation to achieve a better understanding of this notion and its uses. In the rest of the paper, we will adopt their terminology to refer to additional attacks, i.e., *complex attacks*. (Cayrol and Lagasquie-Schiex, 2005; Cayrol and Lagasquie-Schiex, 2010) argue about the emergence of new kinds of attacks from the interaction between the attacks and supports in BAF. In particular, they specify two kinds of complex attacks called *secondary* and *supported* attacks, respectively.

Definition 3 (Secondary and supported attacks) *Let BAF = $\langle A, \rightarrow, \dashrightarrow \rangle$ where $a, b \in A$. A supported attack for b by a is a sequence $a_1 R_1 \ldots R_{n-1} a_n$, $n \geq 3$, with $a_1 = a, a_n = b$, such that $\forall i = 1 \ldots n-2, R_i = \dashrightarrow$ and $R_{n-1} = \rightarrow$. A secondary attack for b by a is a sequence $a_1 R_1 \ldots R_{n-1} a_n$, $n \geq 3$, with $a_1 = a, a_n = b$, such that $R_1 = \rightarrow$ and $\forall i = 2 \ldots n\text{-}1, R_i = \dashrightarrow$.*

According to the above definition, these attacks hold in the first two cases depicted in Figure 1, where there is a supported attack from a to c, and there is a secondary attack from c to b.

The support relation has been specialized in other approaches where new complex attacks emerging from the combination of existing attacks and supports are proposed. (Boella et al., 2010)

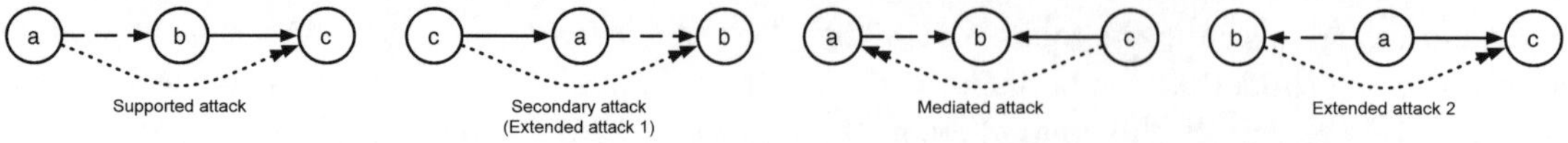

Figure 1: Additional attacks emerging from the interaction of supports and attacks.

propose a *deductive* view of support in abstract argumentation where, given the support $a \dashrightarrow b$ the acceptance of a implies the acceptance of b, and the rejection of b implies the rejection of a. They introduce a new kind of complex attack called *mediated* attacks (Figure 1).

Definition 4 (Mediated attacks) *Let* $BAF = \langle A, \rightarrow, \dashrightarrow \rangle$ *where* $a, b \in A$. *A mediated attack on* b *by* a *is a sequence* $a_1 R_1 \ldots R_{n-2} a_{n-1}$ *and* $a_n R_{n-1} a_{n-1}$, $n \geq 3$, *with* $a_1 = a, a_{n-1} = b, a_n = c$, *such that* $R_{n-1} = \rightarrow$ *and* $\forall i = 1 \ldots n\text{-}2, R_i = \dashrightarrow$.

(Nouioua and Risch, 2010; Nouioua and Risch, 2011) propose, instead, an account of support called *necessary* support. In this framework, given $a \dashrightarrow b$ then the acceptance of a is necessary to get the acceptance of b, i.e., the acceptance of b implies the acceptance of a. They introduce two new kinds of complex attacks called *extended attacks* (Figure 1). Note that the first kind of extended attacks is equivalent to the secondary attacks introduced by (Cayrol and Lagasquie-Schiex, 2005; Cayrol and Lagasquie-Schiex, 2010), and that the second case is the dual of supported attacks.

Definition 5 (Extended attacks) *Let* $BAF = \langle A, \rightarrow, \dashrightarrow \rangle$ *where* $a, b \in A$. *An extended attack on* b *by* a *is a sequence* $a_1 R_1 a_2 R_2 \ldots R_n a_n$, $n \geq 3$, *with* $a_1 = a, a_n = b$, *such that* $R_1 = \rightarrow$ *and* $\forall i = 2 \ldots n, R_i = \dashrightarrow$, *or a sequence* $a_1 R_1 \ldots R_n a_n$ *and* $a_1 R_p a_p$, $n \geq 2$, *with* $a_n = a, a_p = b$, *such that* $R_p = \rightarrow$ *and* $\forall i = 1 \ldots n, R_i = \dashrightarrow$.

All these models of support in bipolar argumentation address the problem of how computing the set of extensions from the extended framework providing different kinds of solutions, i.e., introducing the notion of *safety* in BAF (Cayrol and Lagasquie-Schiex, 2005), or computing the extensions in the meta-level (Boella et al., 2010; Cayrol and Lagasquie-Schiex, 2010). In this paper, we are not interested in discussing and evaluating these different solutions. Our aim is to evaluate how much these different models of support occur and are effectively "exploited" in NL dialogues, to provide a better understanding of the notion of support and attack in bipolar argumentation.

We are aware that the notion of support is a controversial one in the field of argumentation theory. In particular, another view of support sees this relation as a relation holding among the premises and the conclusion of a structured argument, and not as another relation among the arguments (Prakken, 2010). However, given the amount of attention bipolar argumentation is receiving in the literature (Rahwan and Simari, 2009), a better account of this kind of frameworks is required.

Another approach to support has been proposed by (Oren and Norman, 2008; Oren et al., 2010) where they distinguish among *prima-facie* arguments and standard ones. They show how a set of arguments described using Dung's argumentation framework can be mapped from and to an argumentation framework that includes both attack and support relations. The idea is that an argument can be accepted only if there is an evidence supporting it, i.e., evidence is represented by means of *prima-facie* arguments. In this paper, we concentrate our analysis on the abstract models of bipolar argumentation proposed in the literature (Cayrol and Lagasquie-Schiex, 2010; Boella et al., 2010; Nouioua and Risch, 2011), and we leave as future work the account of support in structured argumentation and the model proposed by (Oren and Norman, 2008; Oren et al., 2010).

3 Empirical studies on NL debates

Starting from (Cabrio and Villata, 2012), as a case study to carry out our analysis we select Debatepedia[1], the Wikipedia of debates. Specifically, Debatepedia is an encyclopedia of *pro* and *con* arguments where users can freely contribute to online discussions about critical issues. We collect a sample of the discussions extracting a set of arguments from Debatepedia topics, as described in Section 3.1. Even if our data set cannot be exhaustive, the methodology we apply for the arguments extraction aims at preserving the original structure

[1] http://idebate.org

of the debate, to make it as representative as possible of human daily natural language interactions.

Two different empirical studies are then presented in this section. The first one (Section 3.2) starts from (Cabrio and Villata, 2012), and explores the relation among the notion of *support* and *attack* in bipolar argumentation, and the *semantic inferences* as defined in the NLP research field. The second analysis (Section 3.3) starts instead from the comparative study of (Cayrol and Lagasquie-Schiex, 2011) of the four complex attacks proposed in the literature, and investigates their distribution in NL debates.

3.1 Data set

To have a stable version of the data to perform our studies, we build a reference data set extracting a sample of debates from Debatepedia[2]. Here, the users manually insert their arguments in the column PRO if they agree with the issue under discussion, or in the column CON if they disagree. To make our sample of NL debates comparable with current works in the literature, e.g. (Wyner and van Engers, 2010; Carenini and Moore, 2006; Cabrio and Villata, 2012), we select the same topics as (Cabrio and Villata, 2012), since this is the only freely available data set of natural language arguments (Table 1, column *Topics*). To create the Debatepedia data set, for each topic of our sample we apply the following procedure:

1. the main issue (i.e., the title of the debate in its affirmative form) is considered as the starting argument;
2. each user opinion is extracted and considered as an argument;
3. since *attack* and *support* are binary relations, the arguments are coupled with:
   (a) the starting argument, or
   (b) other arguments in the same discussion to which the most recent argument refers (e.g., when a user opinion supports or attacks an argument previously expressed by another user), following the chronological order (we maintain the dialogue structure);
4. the resulting pairs of arguments are then tagged with the appropriate relation, i.e., *attack* or *support*.

[2]http://bit.ly/VZIs6M

To show a step-by-step application of the procedure, let us consider the debated issue *Can coca be classified as a narcotic?*. At step 1, we transform its title into the affirmative form, and we consider it as the starting argument **(a)**:

(a) *Coca can be classified as a narcotic.*

At step 2, we extract all the users opinions on this issue (PRO and CON), e.g., **(b)**, **(c)** and **(d)**:

(b) *In 1992 the World Health Organization's Expert Committee on Drug Dependence (ECDD) undertook a 'prereview' of coca leaf at its 28th meeting. The 28th ECDD report concluded that, "the coca leaf is appropriately scheduled as a narcotic under the Single Convention on Narcotic Drugs, 1961, since cocaine is readily extractable from the leaf." This ease of extraction makes coca and cocaine inextricably linked. Therefore, because cocaine is defined as a narcotic, coca must also be defined in this way.*

(c) *Coca in its natural state is not a narcotic. What is absurd about the 1961 convention is that it considers the coca leaf in its natural, unaltered state to be a narcotic. The paste or the concentrate that is extracted from the coca leaf, commonly known as cocaine, is indeed a narcotic, but the plant itself is not.*

(d) *Coca is not cocaine. Coca is distinct from cocaine. Coca is a natural leaf with very mild effects when chewed. Cocaine is a highly processed and concentrated drug using derivatives from coca, and therefore should not be considered as a narcotic.*

At step 3a we couple the arguments **(b)** and **(d)** with the starting issue since they are directly linked with it, and at step 3b we couple argument **(c)** with argument **(b)**, and arguments **(d)** with argument **(c)** since they follow one another in the discussion. At step 4, the resulting pairs of arguments are then tagged with the appropriate relation: **(b)** *supports* **(a)**, **(d)** *attacks* **(a)**, **(c)** *attacks* **(b)** and **(d)** *supports* **(c)**.

Table 1 reports the number of arguments and pairs we extracted applying the extraction methodology described before to all the mentioned topics. In total, our data set contains 310 different arguments and 320 argument pairs (179 expressing the *support* relation among the involved arguments, and 141 expressing the *attack* relation). We consider the obtained data set as representative of human debates in a non-controlled setting (Debatepedia users position their arguments w.r.t. the others as PRO or CON, the data are not biased), and therefore we use it for our empirical studies.

DEBATEPEDIA data set		
Topic	**#argum**	**#pairs**
VIOLENT GAMES BOOST AGGRESSIVENESS	17	23
CHINA ONE-CHILD POLICY	11	14
CONSIDER COCA AS A NARCOTIC	17	22
CHILD BEAUTY CONTESTS	13	17
ARMING LIBYAN REBELS	13	15
RANDOM ALCOHOL BREATH TESTS	11	14
OSAMA DEATH PHOTO	22	24
PRIVATIZING SOCIAL SECURITY	12	13
INTERNET ACCESS AS A RIGHT	15	17
GROUND ZERO MOSQUE	11	12
MANDATORY MILITARY SERVICE	15	17
NO FLY ZONE OVER LIBYA	18	19
AIRPORT SECURITY PROFILING	12	13
SOLAR ENERGY	18	19
NATURAL GAS VEHICLES	16	17
USE OF CELL PHONES WHILE DRIVING	16	16
MARIJUANA LEGALIZATION	23	25
GAY MARRIAGE AS A RIGHT	10	10
VEGETARIANISM	14	13
TOTAL	310	**320**

Table 1: Debatepedia data set.

3.2 First study: support and TE

Our first empirical study aims at a better understanding of the relation among the notion of support in bipolar argumentation (Cayrol and Lagasquie-Schiex, 2011), and the definition of semantic inference in NLP (in particular, the more specific notion of TE) (Dagan et al., 2009). In a recent work, (Cabrio and Villata, 2012) propose to combine NLP and Dung-like abstract argumentation to generate the arguments from NL text, and compute the accepted ones. They represent the TE relation as a support relation in BAF. Even if they narrow their work by considering only favorable arguments implying another argument, explicitly stating that arguments supporting another argument but without inferring it are out of the scope of that work, the assumption that there exists an identity between support and TE is still a claim to verify.

3.2.1 Textual Entailment

The notion of TE has been defined as a directional relation between two textual fragments, termed *text (T)* and *hypothesis (H)*, respectively (Dagan et al., 2009). The relation holds (i.e. $T \Rightarrow H$) whenever the truth of one text fragment follows from the other, as interpreted by a typical language user. Let us consider for instance the two textual fragments **(a)** and **(b)** from Debatepedia. According to the TE framework we set **(b)** as T and **(a)** as H:

(b) $\mapsto$ **T:** *In 1992 the World Health Organization's Expert Committee on Drug Dependence (ECDD) undertook a 'prereview' of coca leaf at its 28th meeting. [...] This ease of extraction makes coca and cocaine inextricably linked. Therefore, because cocaine is defined as a narcotic, coca must also be defined in this way.*
(a)$\mapsto$ **H:** *Coca can be classified as a narcotic.*

A human reading T would infer that H is most likely true (i.e. the meaning of H can be derived from the meaning of T, so the entailment holds). On the contrary, if we consider Debatepedia examples **(a)** and **(d)**, and we set **(d)** as T and **(a)** as H, there is a contradiction between T and H:

(d) $\mapsto$ **T:** *Coca is not cocaine. Coca is distinct from cocaine. Coca is a natural leaf with very mild effects when chewed. Cocaine is a highly processed and concentrated drug using derivatives from coca, and therefore should not be considered as a narcotic.*
(a)$\mapsto$ **H:** *Coca can be classified as a narcotic.*

(de Marneffe et al., 2008) provide a definition of contradiction for the TE task, claiming that it occurs when two sentences *i)* are extremely unlikely to be true simultaneously, and *ii)* involve the same event. As an applied framework, TE has been proposed to capture major semantic inference needs across NLP applications (e.g., question answering, information extraction).

3.2.2 Analysis on the Debatepedia data set

Based on the TE definition, an annotator with skills in linguistics has carried out a first phase of annotation of the Debatepedia data set (Section 3.1). The goal of such annotation is to individually consider each pair of *support* and *attack* among arguments, and to additionally tag them as *entailment*, *contradiction* or *null*. The *null* judgment can be assigned in case an argument is supporting another argument without inferring it, or the argument is attacking another argument without contradicting it. As exemplified above, a correct entailment pair is **(b) entails (a)**, while a contradiction is **(d) contradicts (a)**. A *null* judgment is assigned to **(d) - (c)**, since the former argument supports the latter without inferring it. Our data set is an extended version of (Cabrio and Villata, 2012)'s one allowing for a deeper investigation.

To assess the validity of the annotation task, we

calculated the inter-annotator agreement. Another annotator with skills in linguistics has therefore independently annotated a sample of 100 pairs of the data set. To calculate the inter-rater agreement we used Cohen's kappa coefficient (Carletta, 1996). For NLP tasks, the agreement is considered as significant when $\kappa > 0.6$. We calculated the inter-annotator agreement on the argument pairs tagged as *support* and *attacks* by both annotators. For supports, we calculated the agreement between the pairs tagged as *entailment* and as *null* (i.e. no entailment); for the contradictions, the agreement between the pairs tagged as *contradiction* and as *null* (i.e. no contradiction). Applying κ to our data, the agreement for our task is $\kappa = 0.74$, that is a satisfactory agreement.

Table 2 reports the results of the annotation on our Debatepedia data set, as resulting after a reconciliation phase carried out by the annotators.

Relations		%arguments (#arg)
support	+ *entailment*	61.6 (111)
	- *entailment (null)*	38.4 (69)
attack	+ *contradiction*	71.4 (100)
	- *contradiction (null)*	28.6 (40)

Table 2: Support and TE on Debatepedia data set.

On the 320 pairs of the data set, 180 represent a *support* relation, while 140 are *attacks*. Considering only the *supports*, we can see that 111 argument pairs (i.e., 61.6%) are an actual entailment, while in 38.4% of the cases the first argument of the pair supports the second one without inferring it (as for example **(d)** - **(c)**). With respect to the *attacks*, we can notice that 100 argument pairs (i.e., 71.4%) are both attack and contradiction, while only the 28.6% of the argument pairs does not contradict the arguments they are attacking, as in the following example:

(e) *Coca chewing is bad for human health. The decision to ban coca chewing fifty years ago was based on a 1950 report elaborated by the UN Commission of Inquiry on the Coca Leaf with a mandate from ECOSOC: "We believe that the daily, inveterate use of coca leaves by chewing is thoroughly noxious and therefore detrimental".*

(f) *Chewing coca offers an energy boost. Coca provides an energy boost for working or for combating fatigue and cold.*

Differently from the relationship between support-entailment, the difference between attack and contradiction is more subtle, and it is not always straightforward to say when an argument attacks another argument without contradicting it. In the example, we consider that **(e)** does not explicitly contradict **(f)** even if it attacks **(f)**, since chewing coca can offer an energy boost, and still be bad for human health. As we can notice from the results in Table 2, this kind of attacks is less frequent than the attacks-contradictions.

Considering the TE three way scenario (*entailment, contradiction, unknown*) to map TE relation with bipolar argumentation, argument pairs connected by a relation of support (but where the first argument does not entail the second one), and argument pairs connected by a relation of attack (but where the first argument does not contradict the second one) have to be mapped as *unknown* pairs in the TE framework. The *unknown* relation in TE refers to the T-H pairs where the entailment cannot be determined because the truth of H cannot be verified on the basis of the content of T. This is a broad definition, that can apply also to pairs of non related sentences (that are considered as unrelated arguments in bipolar argumentation).

From an application viewpoint, as highlighted in (Reed and Grasso, 2007; Heras et al., 2010), argumentation theory should be used as a tool in online discussions applications to identify the relations among the statements, and to provide a structure to the dialogue to easily evaluate the user's opinions. Starting from the methodology proposed by (Cabrio and Villata, 2012) for passing from NL arguments to a Dung's system towards a fully automated system to identify the accepted arguments, our study demonstrates that applying the TE approach would be productive in the 66% of the Debatepedia data set. Other techniques should be investigated to cover the other cases, for instance measuring the semantic relatedness of the two propositions, e.g., Latent Semantics Analysis techniques (Landauer et al., 1997).

3.3 Second study: complex attacks

As a second step of our survey, we carry out a comparative evaluation of the four proposals of attacks suggested in the literature, and we investigate their distribution and meaning on the sample of NL arguments.

3.3.1 Analysis on the Debatepedia data set

Relying on the additional attacks (Section 2), and the original AF of each topic in our data set (Table 1), the following procedure is applied: the *supported* (secondary, mediated, and extended, respectively) attacks are added, and the argument pairs resulting from coupling the arguments linked by this relation are collected in the data set "supported (secondary, mediated, and extended, respectively) attack".

Collecting the arguments pairs generated from the different types of complex attacks in separate data sets allows us to independently analyze each type, and to perform a more accurate evaluation.[3] Figures 2a-d show the four AFs resulting from the addition of the complex attacks in the example *Can coca be classified as a narcotic?*. The reader may observe that the AF in Figure 2a, where the supported attack is introduced, is the same of Figure 2b where the mediated attack is introduced. Notice that, even if the attack which is introduced is the same, i.e., d attacks b, this is due to different interactions among supports and attacks (as highlighted in the figure), i.e., in the case of supported attacks this is due to the support from d to c and the attack from c to b, while in the case of mediated attacks this is due to the support from b to a and the attack from d to a.

A second annotation phase is then carried out on the data set, to verify if the generated arguments pairs of the four data sets are actually attacks (i.e., if the models of complex attacks proposed in the literature are represented in real data). More specifically, an arguments pair resulting from the application of a complex attack can be annotated as: *attack* (if it is a correct attack) or as *unrelated* (in case the meanings of the two arguments are not in conflict). For instance, the pair **(g)**-**(h)** resulting from the insertion of a *supported* attack, cannot be considered as an attack since the arguments are considering two different aspects of the issue.

(g) *Chewing coca offers an energy boost. Coca provides an energy boost for working or for combating fatigue and cold.*
(h) *Coca can be classified as a narcotic.*

In the annotation, *attacks* are then annotated also as *contradiction* (if the first argument contradicts the other) or *null* (in case the first argument does not contradict the argument it is attacking, as in the example **(e)**-**(f)** showed in Section 3.2.2). Due to the complexity of the annotation, the same annotation task has been independently carried out also by a second annotator, so as to compute inter-annotator agreement. It has been calculated on a sample of 80 argument pairs (20 pairs randomly extracted from each of the "complex attacks" data set), and it has the goal to assess the validity of the annotation task (counting when the judges agree on the same annotation). We calculated the inter-annotator agreement for our annotation task in two steps. We *(i)* verify the agreement of the two judges on the argument pairs classification *attacks/unrelated*, and *(ii)* consider only the argument pairs tagged as *attacks* by both annotators, and we verify the agreement between the pairs tagged as *contradiction* and as *null* (i.e. non contradiction). Applying κ to our data, the agreement for the first step is $\kappa = 0.77$, while for the second step $\kappa = 0.71$. Both agreements are satisfactory, although they reflect the higher complexity of the second annotation task (*contradiction/null*), as pointed out in Section 3.2.2.

The distribution of complex attacks in the Debatepedia data set, as resulting after a reconciliation phase carried out by the annotators, is shown in Table 3. As can be noticed, the *mediated* attack is the most frequent type of attack, generating 335 new arguments pairs in the NL sample we considered (i.e., the conditions that allow the application of this kind of complex attacks appear more frequently in real debates). Together with the *secondary* attacks, they appear in the AFs of all the debated topics. On the contrary, *extended* attacks are added in 11 out of 19 topics, and *supported* attacks in 17 out of 19 topics. Considering all the topics, on average only 6 pairs generated from the additional attacks were already present in the original data set, meaning that considering also these attacks is a way to hugely enrich our data set.

Proposed models	**# occ.**	**attacks**		**unrel.**
		+contr(null)	*-contr(null)*	
Supported attacks	47	23	17	7
Secondary attacks	53	29	18	6
Mediated attacks	335	84	148	103
Extended attacks	28	15	10	3

Table 3: Complex attacks distribution in our data.

Figure 3 graphically represents the complex attacks distribution. Considering the first step of the annotation (i.e. *attacks* vs *unrelated*), the figure shows that the latter case is very infrequent, and that (except for the *mediated* attack) on average only 10% of the argument pairs are tagged as *unrelated*. This observation can be considered as a proof of concept of the four theoretical models of complex attacks we analyzed. Due to the

[3]Freely available at `http://bit.ly/VZIs6M`

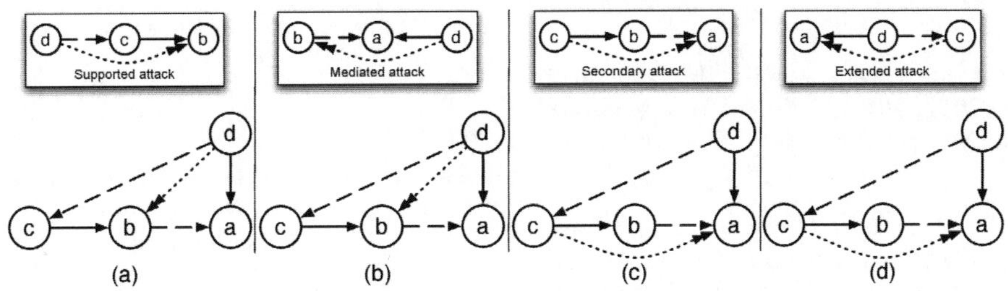

Figure 2: Example of bipolar argumentation framework with the introduction of supported attacks.

fact that the conditions for the application of the *mediated* attacks are verified more often in the data, it has the drawback of generating more unrelated pairs. Still, the number of successful cases is high enough to consider this kind of attack as representative of human interactions. Considering the second step of the annotation (i.e., *attacks* as *contradiction* or *null*), we can see that results are in line with those reported in our first study (Table 2), meaning that also among complex attacks the same distribution is maintained.

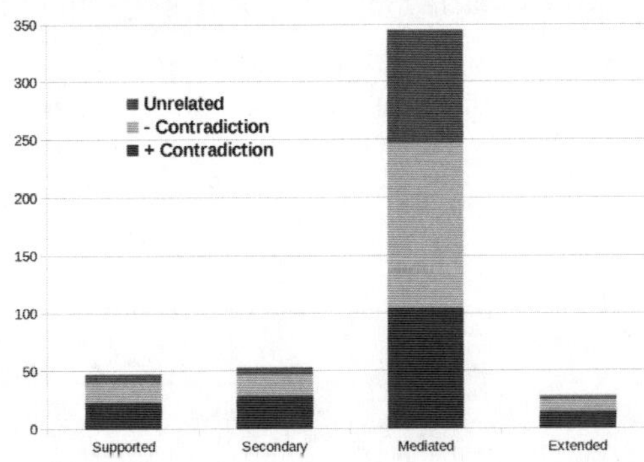

Figure 3: Complex attacks distribution in our data.

4 Concluding remarks

In this paper, we provide a further step towards a better comprehension of the support and attack notions in bipolar argumentation (invoked by the community, e.g. (Cayrol and Lagasquie-Schiex, 2011)) by evaluating them against *naturally occurring data* extracted from NL online debates. The results show that the support relation includes the TE relation, i.e. it is more general (in about 60% of the argument pairs in relation of support, also TE holds). Similarly, the study on the attack-contradiction relations shows that the attack relation is more general than the contradiction (as underlined by (de Marneffe et al., 2008)): in about 70% of the attacks also contradiction holds.

The proposed study shows that the research carried out on semantic inferences in NLP, and argumentation theory in knowledge representation could fruitfully influence each other, raising new open challenges with a significant potential impact on the future interactions among humans and machines. On the one side, NLP provides to the argumentation theory community *i)* textual inference paradigms like TE that make inference algorithms and tools available to automatically process NL arguments, and to detect the semantic relations linking them, and *ii)* annotated natural language corpora that can be investigated in depth to prove the proposed formal models on naturally occurring data. On the other side, argumentation theory can provide to TE, and in general to NLP approaches to semantic inference, a new framework where the semantic relations are not only identified between pairs of textual fragments, but such pairs are also part of an argumentation graph that provides an overall view of the arguments' interactions such that the influences of the arguments on the others emerge, even if they are not direct (see the additional attacks in Section 3.3, and (Berant et al., 2012)'s work on the structural constraints of TE in the context of entailment graphs). Formal models of argumentation are also proposed to check the consistency of a set of information items represented as the nodes of an argumentation graph, allowing for the detection of the precise portions of the graph where the inconsistency arises (e.g., argument a supports and attacks the same argument). This would open new challenges for TE, that in the original definition considers the T-H pairs as "self-contained" (i.e., the meaning of H has to be derived from the meaning of T). On the contrary, in arguments extracted from human linguistic interactions a lot is left implicit (following Grice's conversational Maxim of Quantity), and anaphoric expressions should be solved to correctly assign semantic relations among arguments.

References

Jonathan Berant, Ido Dagan, Meni Adler, and Jacob Goldberger. 2012. Efficient tree-based approximation for entailment graph learning. In *ACL (1)*, pages 117–125.

Guido Boella, Dov M. Gabbay, Leendert van der Torre, and Serena Villata. 2010. Support in abstract argumentation. In *Procs of COMMA, Frontiers in Artificial Intelligence and Applications 216*, pages 111–122.

Elena Cabrio and Serena Villata. 2012. Natural language arguments: A combined approach. In *Procs of ECAI, Frontiers in Artificial Intelligence and Applications 242*, pages 205–210.

Giuseppe Carenini and Johanna D. Moore. 2006. Generating and evaluating evaluative arguments. *Artif. Intell.*, 170(11):925–952.

Jean Carletta. 1996. Assessing agreement on classification tasks: the kappa statistic. *Comput. Linguist.*, 22(2):249–254.

Claudette Cayrol and Marie-Christine Lagasquie-Schiex. 2005. On the acceptability of arguments in bipolar argumentation frameworks. In *Procs of ECSQARU, LNCS 3571*, pages 378–389.

Claudette Cayrol and Marie-Christine Lagasquie-Schiex. 2010. Coalitions of arguments: A tool for handling bipolar argumentation frameworks. *Int. J. Intell. Syst.*, 25(1):83–109.

Claudette Cayrol and Marie-Christine Lagasquie-Schiex. 2011. Bipolarity in argumentation graphs: Towards a better understanding. In *Procs of SUM, LNCS 6929*, pages 137–148.

Ido Dagan, Bill Dolan, Bernardo Magnini, and Dan Roth. 2009. Recognizing textual entailment: Rational, evaluation and approaches. *Natural Language Engineering (JNLE)*, 15(04):i–xvii.

Marie-Catherine de Marneffe, Anna N. Rafferty, and Christopher D. Manning. 2008. Finding contradictions in text. In *Procs of ACL*.

Phan M. Dung. 1995. On the acceptability of arguments and its fundamental role in nonmonotonic reasoning, logic programming and n-person games. *Artif. Intell.*, 77(2):321–358.

Stella Heras, Katie Atkinson, Vicente J. Botti, Floriana Grasso, Vicente Julián, and Peter McBurney. 2010. How argumentation can enhance dialogues in social networks. In *Procs of COMMA, Frontiers in Artificial Intelligence and Applications 216*, pages 267–274.

Thomas K. Landauer, Darrell Laham, Bob Rehder, and M. E. Schreiner. 1997. How well can passage meaning be derived without using word order? a comparison of latent semantic analysis and humans. In *Procs of CSS*, pages 412–417.

Farid Nouioua and Vincent Risch. 2010. Bipolar argumentation frameworks with specialized supports. In *Procs of ICTAI*, pages 215–218. IEEE Computer Society.

Farid Nouioua and Vincent Risch. 2011. Argumentation frameworks with necessities. In *Procs of SUM, LNCS 6929*, pages 163–176.

Nir Oren and Timothy J. Norman. 2008. Semantics for evidence-based argumentation. In *Procs of COMMA, Frontiers in Artificial Intelligence and Applications 172*, pages 276–284.

Nir Oren, Chris Reed, and Michael Luck. 2010. Moving between argumentation frameworks. In *Procs of COMMA, Frontiers in Artificial Intelligence and Applications 216*, pages 379–390.

Henry Prakken. 2010. An abstract framework for argumentation with structured arguments. *Argument & Computation*, 1:93–124.

Iyad Rahwan and Guillermo Simari, editors. 2009. *Argumentation in Artificial Intelligence*. Springer.

Chris Reed and Floriana Grasso. 2007. Recent advances in computational models of natural argument. *Int. J. Intell. Syst.*, 22(1):1–15.

Adam Wyner and Tom van Engers. 2010. A framework for enriched, controlled on-line discussion forums for e-government policy-making. In *Procs of eGov 2010*.

Aligning Verb Senses in Two Italian Lexical Semantic Resources

Tommaso Caselli
Trento RISE
Via Sommarive, 18
Povo I-38123
t.caselli@trentorise.eu

Laure Vieu
IRIT - CNRS
118 route de Narbonne
Toulouse F-31062
vieu@irit.fr

Strapparava Carlo
HLT-FBK
Via Sommarive, 18
Povo I-38123
strappa@fbk.eu

Guido Vetere
IBM - CAS Trento
P.zza Manci, 17
Povo I-38123
gvetere@it.ibm.com

Abstract

This work describes the evaluations of three different approaches, Lexical Match, Sense Similarity based on Personalized Page Rank, and Semantic Match based on Shallow Frame Structures, for word sense alignment of verbs between two Italian lexical-semantic resources, MultiWordNet and the Senso Comune Lexicon. The results obtained are quite satisfying with a final F1 score of 0.47 when merging together Lexical Match and Sense Similarity.

1 Introduction

Lexical-semantic resources play a key role in many Natural Language Processing tasks, such as Word Sense Disambiguation, Information Extraction, and Question-Answering, among others. The creation of lexical-sematic resources is costly in terms of manual efforts and time, and often important information is scattered in different lexica and difficult to use. Semantic interoperability between resources could represent the viable solution to allow reusability and develop more robust and powerful resources. Word sense alignment (WSA), a research area which has seen an increasing interest in recent years, qualifies as the preliminary requirement for achieving this goal (Matuschek and Gurevych, 2013).

The purpose of this work is to merge two Italian lexical-semantic resources, namely MultiWordNet (Pianta et al., 2002) (MWN) and Senso Comune Lexicon (SCL) (Oltramari et al., 2013), by automatically linking their entries. The final result will be two-folded. On the MWN side, this will provide Italian with a more complete and robust version of this lexicon. On the SCL side, the linking with MWN entries will introduce lexical-semantic relations, thus facilitating its use for NLP tasks in Italian, and it will make SCL a structurally and semantically interoperable resource for Italian, allowing its connection to other lexical-semantic resources, sense annotated corpora (e.g. the MultiSemCor corpus (Bentivogli and Pianta, 2005)), and Web-based encyclopedia (e.g. Wikipedia).

This work will focus on our experience on the alignment of verb senses. The remaining of this paper is organized as follows. Section 2 will state the task and describe the characteristics of the two lexica. In Section 3 some related works and the perculiarities of our work are discussed. The approaches we have adopted are described in Section 4. The evaluation is carried out in Section 5. Finally, in Section 6 conclusions and future work are reported.

2 Task and Resources

Following (Matuschek and Gurevych, 2013), WSA can be defined as the identification of pairs of senses from two lexical-semantic resources which denote the same meaning. For instance, the two senses of the verb "*love*", "`feel love or affection for someone`" and "`have a great affection or liking for`" (taken from translated SCL and MWN, respectively), must be aligned as they are clearly equivalent in meaning.

2.1 MultiWordNet

MWN is a multilingual lexicon perfectly aligned to Princeton WN 1.6. As in WN, concepts are organized in synonym sets (*synsets*) which are hierarchically connected by means of hypernym relations (*is_a*). Additional semantic relations such as meronymy, troponymy, nearest synonym and others are encoded as well. The Italian section of MWN is composed of 38,653 synsets, with 4,985 synsets for verbs. Each synset is accompanied by a gloss describing its meaning and, when present, one or more examples of use. Overall 3,177 glosses (8,21%) are in Italian and, in particular, 402 for verbs.

2.2 Senso Comune Lexicon

SCL is part of a larger research initiative (Oltramari et al. (2013)) which aims at building an open knowledge base for the Italian language. The lexicon entries have been obtained from the De Mauro GRADIT dictionary and consist in the 2,071 most frequent Italian words, for a total of 11,939 fundamental senses. As for verbs we have 3,827 senses, corresponding to 643 lemmas, with an average polysemy of 5.9 senses per lemma. In SCL, word senses are encoded following lexicographic principles and are associated with lexicographic examples of usage.

SCL comprises three modules: i.) a module for basic ontological concepts; ii.) a lexical module for linguistic and lexicographic structures; and iii.) a frame module for modeling the predicative structure of verbs and nouns. The top level ontology is inspired by DOLCE (Descriptive Ontology for Linguistic and Cognitive Engineering) (Masolo et al., 2002). Ontological classification of verb entries will start in the near future. With respect to MWN, word senses are not hierarchically structured and no semantic relation has been encoded yet. Senses of polysemous entries have a flat representation, one following the other.

3 Related Works

Previous works in WSA can be divided into two main groups: a.) approaches and frameworks which aim at linking entries to WN from lexica based on different models (Rigau and Agirre (1995); Navigli (2006); Roventini et al. (2007)) or language resources, such as Wikipedia (Ruiz-Casado et al. (2005); Mihalcea (2007); Niemann and Gurevych (2011)), and b.) approaches towards the merging of different language resources (Navigli and Ponzetto (2012)). Our work clearly fits into the first group. While different methods are employed (similarity-based approaches *vs.* graph-based approaches), common elements of these works are: i.) the extensive use of the lexical knowledge of the sense descriptions; e.g. the WN glosses or an article first paragraph as in the case of Wikipedia; and ii.) the extension of the basic sense descriptions with additional information such as hypernyms for WN entries, domains labels or categories for dictionaries or Wikipedia entries to expand the set of available information, thus improving the quality of the alignments. The large of these works focuses on aligning noun senses. The only work which also tackles verb sense alignment is (Navigli, 2006) where entries from the Oxford English Dictionary (OED) are mapped to WN. The author explores two methods: a.) a pure lexical matching function based on the notion of lexical overlap (Lesk, 1986) of the lemmas in the sense descriptions; and b.) a semantic matching based on a knowledge-based WSD system, Structural Semantic Interconnections (SSI), built upon WN and enriched with collocation information representing semantic relatedness between sense pairs. Both approaches are evaluated with respect to a manually created gold standard. The author reports an overall F1 measure of 73.84% for lexical matching (accuracy 66.08%), and of 83.11% for semantic matching (accuracy 77.94%). Alignment performances on single parts of speech are not reported.

With respect to the SCL, the OED has some advantages, namely i.) the distinction between core senses and subsenses for polysemous entries; ii.) the presence of hypernyms explicitly signalled; and iii.) domain labels associated with word senses. Such kind of information is not present in the SCL where senses are presented as a flat list and no enrichment of the sense descriptions with additional information is available. Moreover, the low number of MWN glosses in Italian prevents a straightforward application of state-of-the-art methods for sense alignment. MWN sense descriptions must be built up in different ways. Summing up, the main issue we are facing is related to data sparseness, that is how to tackle sense alignment when we have few descriptions in Italian (MWN side) and few meta-data and no structuration over senses (SCL side).

4 Methodology

The automatic alignment of senses has been conducted by applying three approaches Lexical Match, Sense Similarity and Semantic Match.

4.1 Lexical Match

In the first approach, Lexical Match, for each word w and for each sense s in the given resources $R \in \{\text{MWN, SCL}\}$ we constructed a sense description

d_R(s) as a bag of words in Italian. Provided the different characteristics of the two resources, two different types of bag of words have been built. As for the SCL, the bag of words is represented by the lexical items in the textual definition of s_w, automatically lemmatized and part-of-speech analyzed with the TextPro tool suite (Pianta et al., 2008) with standard stopword removal. On the other hand, for each synset, *S*, the sense description of each MWN synset was built by optionally exploiting:

- the set of synset words in a synset excluding *w*;
- the set of direct hypernyms of *s* in the taxonomy hierarchy in MWN (if available);
- the set of synset words in MWN standing in the relation of *nearest synonyms* with *s* (if available);
- the set of synset words in MWN composing the manually disambiguated glosses of *s* from the "Princeton Annotated Gloss Corpus"[1]. To extract the corresponding Italian synset(s), we have ported MWN to WN 3.0;
- the set of synset words in MWN composing the gloss of *s* in Italian (when available);
- the set of synset words in MWN standing in the relations of *entailment/is_entailed*, *causes/is_caused* with *s*;

The alignment of senses is based on the notion of lexical overlap. We used the `Text::Similarity` v.0.09 module[2] to obtain the overlap value between two bags of words. Text similarity is based on counting the number of overlapping tokens between the two strings, normalized by the length of the strings.

4.2 Sense Similarity

In the second approach, Sense Similarity, the basis for sense alignment is the Personalized Page Rank (PPR) algorithm (Eneko and Soroa, 2009) relying on a lexical-semantic knowledge base model as a graph *G* = (V, E) as available in the UKB tool suite[3]. As knowledge base we have used WN 3.0 extended with the "Princeton Annotated Gloss Corpus". Each vertex *v* of the graph is a synset, and the edges represent semantic relations between synsets (e.g. hyperonymy, hyponymy, etc.). The PPR algorithm ranks the vertices in a graph according to their importance within the set and assigns stronger initial probabilities to certain kinds of vertices in the graph. The result of the PPR algorithm is a vector whose elements denote the probability for the corresponding vertex that a jumper ends on that vertex if randomly following the edges of the graph.

To obtain the PPR vector for a sense *s* of the SCL, we translated the Italian textual definitions in English by means of a state-of-the-art Machine Translation system[4], automatically lemmatized and part-of-speech analyzed with the TextPro tool suite, removed standard stopwords, and applied the UKB tool suite. The PPR vector is, thus, a semantic representation overall the entire WN synsets of the textual definition of *s* in SCL.

As for the MWN synsets, instead of building the PPR vector by means of the lexical items composing the sense description, we have passed to the UKB tool suite the WN synset id, thus assuming that the MWN synset is already disambiguated. Given two PPR vectors, namely ppr_{mwn} and ppr_{scdm} for the MWN synset w_{syn} and for the SCL sense w_{scdm}, we calculated their cosine similarity. On the basis of the similarity score, the sense pair is considered as aligned or not.

4.3 Semantic Match: Exploiting Shallow Frames Structures

On the basis of (Roland and Jurafsky, 2002) and current research activities in Senso Comune (Chiari et al., 2013), we assume as working hypothesis that different verb senses tend to correlate with different shallow frame patterns. Thus, we consider two verb senses to be aligned if the shallow frames structures (SFS) of their examples of use are the same. We assume as a SF structure the syntactic complements of the verb, with no distinction between arguments and adjuncts, and the semantic type of the complement filler(s). An example of an SFS is reported in example 1.

1. *Marco ha comprato un libro.*
   [Marco bought a book.]
   Verb: *comprare* [to buy]
   SFS: SUBJ[person] OBJ[artifact]

To obtain the SFSs, two different strategies have been used. For the SCL, we have extracted all

[1] http://wordnet.princeton.edu/glosstag.shtml

[2] http://www.d.umn.edu/~tpederse/text-similarity.html

[3] http://ixa2.si.ehu.es/ukb/

[4] We use Google Translate API.

the lexicographic examples of use associated to each verb sense. For MWN, to recover a larger number of examples of use in Italian, we have exploited the data in the MultiSemCor corpus v1.0, a parallel corpus of English and Italian annotated with WN senses. For each sense annotated verb in the Italian section of MultiSemCor, we extracted all available corpus-based examples and obtain the SFS to be compared with the SCL instances. The acquisition of the SFSs has been obtained as follows:

- the SCL examples and the MultiSemCor data have been parsed with a state-of-the-art dependency parser (Attardi and Dell'Orletta, 2009);
- for each verb, we have automatically extracted all syntactic complements standing in a dependency relation of argument or complement, together with the lemma of the slot filler;
- nominal lemmas of syntactic complements have been automatically assigned with one of the 26 semantic types composing the WN supersenses (i.e. *noun.artifact*; *noun.object* etc. (Ciaramita and Johnson, 2003)) on the line of (Lenci et al., 2012). For each nominal filler, we selected the most frequent WN supersense. Sense frequency had been computed on the basis of MultiSemCor. In case a polysemous noun lemma was not present in the MultiSemCor data or its senses have the same frequency, all associated WN supersenses were assigned. As for verbal fillers, we assigned the generic semantic type of "*verb.eventuality*". Finally, in case a lemma filler of a syntactic complement is not attested in MWN such as a pronoun or a missing synset word, no values is assigned and the SFS is excluded from the possible matches. Optionally, when the noun filler was annotated with a synset in MultiSemCor, we have associated it to its corresponding WN supersense.

To clarify how this type of sense alignment works, consider the data in example 2. In 2a., we report the SFSs for the examples of use associated with the sense "`vivere abitualmente in un luogo`" [to live habitually in a place] of the verb "*abitare*' [to live] in the SCL. In 2b., we report the SFSs extracted from the MultiSemCor corpus for the MWN synset v#01809405, with gloss "`make one's home or live in`"[5].

2a. COMP-PREP$_{IN}$ [noun.location].
COMP-PREP$_{CON}$ [noun.group]
COMP-PREP$_{A}$ [noun.location]

2b. COMP-PREP$_{DA}$ [noun.person]
SUBJ[noun.person] COMP-PREP$_{DA}$[noun.group]
COMP-PREP$_{IN}$ [noun.location]

By comparing the SFSs, the COMP-PREP$_{IN}$ [noun.location] structure is the same in both senses, thus pointing to the alignment of the two entries.

5 Experiments and Evaluation

5.1 Gold Standard

To evaluate the reliability of the approaches with respect to our data, we developed a gold standard. The gold standard is composed by 44 lemmas selected according to frequency and patterns in terms of semantic and syntactic features[6]. It is composed by 350 sense pairs obtained by manually mapping the MWN synsets to their corresponding senses in the SC lexicon. These verbs correspond to 279 synsets and 424 senses in the SCL. Overall, 211 of the 279 MWN synsets have a corresponding sense in the SCL (i.e. SCL covers 84.22% of the MWN senses in the data set), while 235 out of 424 SCL senses have a correspondence in MWN (i.e MWN covers 49.76% of the SCL senses). Average degree of polysemy for MWN entries is 6.34, while for the SCL is 9.63.

5.2 Results

The evaluation is based on Precision (the ratio of the correct alignment with respect to all proposed alignments), Recall (the ratio of extracted correct alignment with respect to the alignments in the gold standard), and F-measure (the harmonic mean of Precision and Recall calculated as $2PR/P+R$). As baseline, we implemented a random match algorithm, *rand*, which for the same word *w* in SCL and in MWN assigns a random

[5]No Italian gloss available for this synset.

[6]A subset of these verbs have been taken from (Jezek and Quochi, 2010)

SCL sense to each synset with w as synset word, returning a one-to-one alignment. For the Lexical Match and Sense Similarity approaches, the selection of the correct alignments has been obtained by applying two types of thresholds with respect to all proposed alignments (the "no_threshold" row in the tables): i.) a simple cut-off at specified values (0.1; 0.2); ii.) the selection of the maximum score (either overlap measure or cosine; row "max_score" in the tables) between each synset S and the proposed aligned senses of the SCL. For the maximum score threshold, we retained as good alignments also instances of a tie, allowing the possibility of having one MWN synset aligned to more than one SCL sense.

5.2.1 Lexical Match Results

We have analyzed different combinations of the sense representation of a synset. We developed two basic representations: SYN, which is composed by the set of synset words excluding the target word w to be aligned, all of its direct hypernyms, the set of synset words in MWN standing in the relation of *nearest synonyms* and the synset words obtained from the "Princeton Annotated Gloss Corpus"; and SREL, which contains all the items of SYN plus the synset words included in the selected set of semantic relations. The results are reported in Table 1.

Lexical Match	P	R	F1
SYN - no_threshold	0.41	0.29	0.34
SYN - $\geq$ 0.1	0.42	0.26	0.32
SYN - $\geq$ 0.2	0.54	0.11	0.18
SYN - max_score	0.59	0.19	**0.29**
SREL - no_threshold	0.38	0.32	**0.35**
SREL - $\geq$ 0.1	0.40	0.27	0.32
SREL - $\geq$ 0.2	0.53	0.11	0.18
SREL - max_score	0.60	0.20	**0.30**
`rand`	0.15	0.06	0.08

Table 1: Results for Lexical Match alignment for SYN and SREL sense representations.

Both sense configurations, SYN and SREL, outperform the baseline `rand`. However, the Recall with no filtering (no_threshold) has extremely low levels, ranging from 0.32 for SREL to 0.29 for SYN, pointing out that the two resources use different ways to encode the verb senses. Globally, the SREL sense representation does not perform better than SYN. When no filtering is applied the SREL configuration has an improvement in the Recall (+0.03) but not in Precision (-0.03), signaling that the semantic relations have a limited role in the description of verb senses and for identifying key information encoded in the SCL glosses. The difference in performance of the SREL configuration is not statistically significant with respect to the SYN configuration ($p > 0.05$). Provided this limited effect of the extended semantic relations, we have decided to select the SYN configuration as the best since it is simpler and with better values for Precision.

To improve the results, we have extended the SYN basic representations with the lexical items of the MWN Italian glosses (+IT)[7]. The results are illustrated in Table 2.

Lexical Match	P	R	F1
SYN+IT - no_threshold	0.36	0.38	0.37
SYN+IT - $\geq$ 0.1	0.38	0.31	0.34
SYN+IT - $\geq$ 0.2	0.51	0.13	0.20
SYN+IT - max_score	0.63	0.23	**0.34**
`rand`	0.15	0.06	0.08

Table 2: Results for Lexical Match alignment adding the Italian MWN glosses.

The extension of the basic sense representations with additional data is positive. In particular, it improves the alignment (for the no-threshold results, F1=0.37 vs. F=0.35 for SREL and F1=0.34 for SYN) as they introduce information which better represents the sense definition than the synset words in the bag of words and overcomes missing information in the WN 3.0 annotated glosses. The positive effect of the original Italian data points out a further issue for our task, namely that the derivation of sense representations of MWN synsets by means of synset words (including the sense annotated glosses of WN 3.0) is not equivalent to having at disposal the original glosses.

Concerning the filtering methods, the maximum score filter provides the best results for Precision at a low cost in terms of Recall, with F1 scores ranging between 0.34 (SYN+IT) to 0.29 (SYN).

5.2.2 Sense Similarity Results

The results for the Sense Similarity obtained from the Personalized Page Rank algorithm are illustrated in Table 3.

Similarly to the Lexical Match, the Sense Similarity approach outperforms the baseline `rand`. Overall, the differences in performance with the

[7] The Italian MWN glosses for the items in the Golds are present for 24% senses of the verbs

Semantic Match	**P**	**R**	**F1**
Most Frequent Sense	0.21	0.05	0.08
Most Frequent + Correct Sense	0.33	0.05	**0.09**
Most Frequent + Correct + Vector Similarity	0.34	0.02	0.04
`rand`	0.15	0.06	0.08

Table 4: Results for Semantic Match experiments.

Similarity Measure	**P**	**R**	**F1**
PPR - no_threshold	0.10	0.9	0.19
PPR - ≥ 0.1	0.47	0.25	**0.32**
PPR - ≥ 0.2	**0.66**	0.16	0.26
PPR - max_score	0.42	0.20	0.27
`rand`	0.15	0.06	0.08

Table 3: Results for automatic alignment based on Similarity Score.

Lexical Match results are not immediate. In general, as the Recall value for no threshold filtering shows, almost all aligned sense pairs of the gold are retrieved, outperforming the Lexical Match approach. This difference is related to the different nature of the sense descriptions, i.e. a *semantic* representation based on a lexical knowledge graph, which is able to catch semantically related items out of the scope for the Lexical Match approach.

By observing the figures, we can notice that the simple cut-off thresholds provide better results with respect to the maximum score. The best F1 score (F1=0.32) is obtained when setting the cosine similarity to 0.1, though Precision is less than 0.50 (namely, 0.47). When compared with threshold value of 0.1 of the Lexical Match, Sense Similarity yields the best Precision (P=0.47 *vs.* P=0.42 for Verb SYN, P=0.38 for Verb SYN+IT, and P=0.40 for Verb SREL). Similar observations can be done when the threshold is set to 0.2. In this latter case, Sense Similarity yields the best Precision score with respect to all other filtering methods and the Lexical Match results obtained with maximum score (P=0.66 *vs.* P=0.59 for Verb SYN, P=0.63 for Verb SYN+IT, and P=0.60 for Verb SREL). The better performance of the simple cut-off thresholds with respect to the maximum score is due to the fact that aligning senses by means of semantic similarity provides a larger set of alignment pairs and facilitates the identification of multiple alignments, i.e. one-to-many.

5.2.3 Semantic Match Results

In Semantic Match we ran three different experiments, namely Most Frequent Sense, where the assignment of the semantic type of the SF slot fillers is based on the most frequent sense; Most Frequent + Correct Sense, where the assignment of the semantic type of the SF slot fillers is based on the most frequent sense and on the annotated sense for the MultiSemCor data, where available, and, finally, Most Frequent + Correct + Vector Similarity, where the assignment of the semantic type of the SF slot fillers is the same as in Most Frequent + Correct Sense plus an additional filtering for nominal SF fillers based on the vector pair WN similarity measure implemented in the `WordNet::Similarity` package[8].

The results obtained are disappointing. With the exception of Precision, all experiment configurations obtain Recall values lower than the baseline `rand`, suggesting that this approach, though linguistically and theoretically sound, suffers from serious flaws. Both Lexical Match and Sense Similarity outperforms this methods even when no filtering is applied.

For this approach, the low levels for Precision and Recall cannot be explained by means of "lexical gaps" or filtering methods. On the basis of manual analysis of the false negative and false positive data, we could claim that the main reasons for these results are due to:

- the reduced number of examples of in the SCL and their nature as "lexicographic" examples of use;
- the high variability in the syntactic realizations of the complements;
- missing annotated senses in the MultiSemCor corpus;
- parsing errors; and
- the difficulty in acquiring complete SFSs from the MultiSemCor data due to the pres-

[8]http://wn-similarity.sourceforge.net/

ence of SF slot fillers realized by pronouns whose assigment of the semantic type depends on their (anaphoric) resolutions.

In addition to this, the low levels of Precision are also due to the coarse-grained categories of the semantic types of the nominal slot fillers. For instance, the SCL examples of use of two different fundamental senses of the verb "*aprire*" [to open], namely "*aprire il rubinetto*" [to open the tap] and "*aprire la porta*" [to open the door] were all wrongly mapped to the same MWN synset, i.e. v#00920424 "*cause to open or to become open; "Mary opened the car door"*". To keep these senses separated, finer-grained semantic features for describing the semantic types of their nominal fillers, here both "noun.artifact", should be employed. The use of vector pairs WN similarity is an attempt into this direction which, however, resulted unsuccesful.

5.2.4 Merging the Approaches

As the three approaches are different in nature both with respect to the creation of the sense descriptions (simple bag of words *vs.* semantic representation *vs.* frame structures) and to the methods with which the alignment pairs are extracted, we have developed a further set of experiments by merging together the results obtained from the Lexical Match, Sense Similarity, and Semantic Match. As parameters for the identification of the best results we have taken into account the Precision and F1 values. We have excluded the presence of Italian data from the sense descriptions of the Lexical Match approach due to their sparseness. As for the Sense Similarity approach, we have selected the cut-off threshold at 0.2. For the Semantic Match we have selected the Most Frequent + Correct configuration. As for the merging we obtained four data sets: SYN+ppr02, which meges the Lexical Match and Sense Similarity methods, SYN+SM, which merges Lexical Match and Semantic Match, ppr02+SM, which merges Sense Similarity and Semantic Match, and SYN+ppr02+SM, which merges all three methods. The results are reported in Table 4.

The combination of the best result yields the best performance with respect to the stand-alone approaches. In particular, we obtain an F1=0.47 for SYN-ppr02, with an improvement of 18 points with respect to SYN, of 21 points with respect to Sense Similarity with threshold 0.2, and of 38 points with respect to Semantic Match. Furthermore, it is interesting to observe that the F1 score for SYN+SM (F1=0.33) and ppr02+SM (F1=0.31) are higher that those of SYN with maximum score filter (F1=0.29) and PPR - 0.2 (F1=0.26), suggesting that there is a kind of complementarity among the three alingment methods. However, the alignments from the Semantic Match method are noisy with respect to those obtained from Sense Similarity and Lexical Match. When merging the three methods together, SYN+ppr02+SM, we do not register any improvement but a lowering of the performances with the exception of Recall. This calls for a careful use of such data in this task, suggesting that simpler aligning methods are more robust.

Merged	P	R	F1
SYN+ppr02	**0.61**	0.38	**0.47**
SYN+SM	0.48	0.25	0.33
ppr02+SM	0.52	0.22	0.31
SYN+ppr02+SM	0.50	0.38	0.43

Table 4: Results for automatic alignment merging the best results from the three approaches.

6 Conclusion and Future Work

This paper reported on experiments on the automatic alignment of verb senses from two different resources when few data are available. In particular, the lack of Italian glosses in MWN and the absence of any kind of structured information in the SC lexicon posed a serious issue for the straightforward application of state-of-the-art techniques for sense alignment.

We explored three different methods for achieving sense alignment: Lexical Match, Sense Similarity, and Semantic Match. In all cases, we are facing low scores for Recall which point out issues related to data sparseness in our lexica. By comparing the results of the three approaches, we can observe that i.) the Sense Similarity yields the best Precision; ii.) Lexical Match, including minimal semantically related items (i.e. SYN) is a dumb but powerful approach for this kind of tasks; iii.) Semantic Match suffers from data sparseness and also from a certain mismatch between corpus data and lexicographic examples. This latter aspect impacts on the application of more complex approaches grounded on linguist theories to automatic methods for sense alignment. It also calls for an extension of the amount of manually annotated data and better methods of semantic typing of the SF slot fillers, as the poor results of Most Frequent + Correct + Vector Similarity show. Furthermore, lexicographic examples of use from SCL, and probably most of the other lexicographic dictionaries, are rather simple and not always prototypical with respect to the actual sense realization in real corpus data. Distributional approaches on SFS acquisition could be helpful to improve this method, provided that reliable ways for assigning SFSs to verb senses encoded in existing resources are developed.

Finally, Sense Similarity based on PPR and Lexical Match qualify as real complementary methods for achieving reliable sense alignments in a simple way and when dealing with few data. Our merged approach provides satisfying results with an overall F1=0.47. The alignment of verb senses is not a simple task as verbs tend to have more abstract definitions than nouns and rely on semantic relations such as entailment which are still poorly encoded in existing resources. Future work will concentrate on the aligned sense pairs obtained by SYN+ppr02 to experiment techniques to reduce the sense descriptions in MWN and in SCL to boostrap better sense alignments, and on the exploitation of crowdsourcing on pre-aligned data to collect additional information on SF structures.

References

G. Attardi and F. Dell'Orletta. 2009. Reverse revision and linear tree combination for dependency parsing. In *Proceedings of Human Language Technologies: The 2009 Annual Conference of the North American Chapter of the Association for Computational Linguistics, Companion Volume: Short Papers*, Boulder, Colorado.

L. Bentivogli and E. Pianta. 2005. Exploiting parallel texts in the creation of multilingual semantically annotated resources: the MultiSemCor Corpus. *Natural Language Engineering*, 11:247–261, 8.

I. Chiari, A. Gangemi, E. Jezek, A. Oltramari, G. Vetere, and L. Vieu. 2013. An open knowledge base for italian language in a collaborative perspective. In *Proceedings of DH-case13, Collaborative Annotations in Shared Environments: metadata, vocabularies and techniques in the Digital Humanities*.

M. Ciaramita and M. Johnson. 2003. Supersense tagging of unknown nouns in WordNet. In Michael Collins and Mark Steedman, editors, *Proceedings of the 2003 Conference on Empirical Methods in Natural Language Processing*, pages 168–175.

A. Eneko and A. Soroa. 2009. Personalizing PageRank for Word Sense Disambiguation. In *Proceedings of the 12th conference of the European chapter of the Association for Computational Linguistics (EACL-2009)*, Athens, Greece.

E. Jezek and V. Quochi. 2010. Capturing coercions in texts: a first annotation exercise. In *Proceedings of the Seventh conference on International Language Resources and Evaluation (LREC'10)*, pages 1464–1471, Valletta, Malta. European Language Resources Association (ELRA).

A. Lenci, G. Lapesa, and G. Bonansinga. 2012. Lexit: A computational resource on italian argument structure. In *Proceedings of the Eighth conference on International Language Resources and Evaluation (LREC'12)*, pages 3712–3718.

M. Lesk. 1986. Automatic sense disambiguation using machine readable dictionaries: how to tell a pine code from an ice cream cone. In *Proc. of 5th Conf. on Systems Documentation*. ACM Press.

C. Masolo, A. Gangemi, N. Guarino, A. Oltramari, and L. Schneider. 2002. Wonderweb deliverable D17: the wonderweb library of foundational ontologies. Technical report.

M Matuschek and I. Gurevych. 2013. Dijkstra-wsa: A graph-based approach to word sense alignment. *Transactions of the Association for Computational Linguistics (TACL)*, 2:to appear.

R. Mihalcea. 2007. Using Wikipedia for automatic word sense disambiguation. In *Human Language Technologies 2007: The Conference of the North American Chapter of the Association for Computational Linguistics; Proceedings of the Main Conference*, Rochester, New York.

R Navigli and S. Ponzetto. 2012. BabelNet: The automatic construction, evaluation and application of a wide-coverage multilingual semantic network. *Artificial Intelligence*, 193:217–250.

R. Navigli. 2006. Meaningful clustering of senses helps boost word sense disambiguation performance. In *Proceedings of the* 44th *Annual Meeting of the Association for Computational Linguistics joint with the* 21st *International Conference on Computational Linguistics (COLING-ACL)*, Sydney, Australia.

E. Niemann and I. Gurevych. 2011. The peoples web meets linguistic knowledge: Automatic sense alignment of Wikipedia and WordNet. In *Proceedings of the 9th International Conference on Computational Semantics*, pages 205–214, Singapore, January.

A. Oltramari, G. Vetere, I. Chiari, E. Jezek, F.M. Zanzotto, M.Nissim, and A. Gangemi. 2013. Senso Comune: A collaborative knowledge resource for italian. In I. Gurevych and J. Kim, editors, *The Peoples Web Meets NLP, Theory and Applications of Natural Language Processing*, pages 45–67. Springer-Verlag, Berlin Heidelberg.

E. Pianta, L. Bentivogli, and C. Girardi. 2002. MultiWordNet: developing an aligned multilingual database. In *First International Conference on Global WordNet*, Mysore, India.

E Pianta, C. Girardi, and R. Zanoli. 2008. TextPro Tool Suite. In *Proceedings of the Sixth International Conference on Language Resources and Evaluation (LREC-08)*, volume CD-ROM, Marrakech, Morocco. European Language Resources Association (ELRA).

G. Rigau and E. Agirre. 1995. Disambiguating bilingual nominal entries against WordNet. In *Proceedings of workshop The Computational Lexicon, 7th European Summer School in Logic, Language and Information*, Barcelona, Spain.

D. Roland and D. Jurafsky. 2002. Verb sense and verb subcategorization probabilities. In S. Stevenson and P. Merlo, editors, *The Lexical Basis of Sentence Processing: Formal, Computational, and Experimental Issues*, pages 325–346. John Benjamins, Amsterdam.

A. Roventini, N. Ruimy, R. Marinelli, U. Marisa, and M. Michele. 2007. Mapping concrete entities from PAROLE-SIMPLE-CLIPS to ItalWordNet: Methodology and results. In *Proceedings of the 45th Annual Meeting of the Association for Computational Linguistics Companion Volume Proceedings of the Demo and Poster Sessions*, Prague, Czech Republic, June.

M. Ruiz-Casado, E. Alfonseca, and P. Castells. 2005. Automatic assignment of Wikipedia encyclopedic entries to WordNet synsets. In *Proceedings of the Third international conference on Advances in Web Intelligence*, AWIC'05, Berlin, Heidelberg. Springer-Verlag.

Abduction for Discourse Interpretation: A Probabilistic Framework

Ekaterina Ovchinnikova
USC/ISI
4676 Admiralty Way
Marina del Rey, CA 90292
katya@isi.edu

Andrew S. Gordon
USC/ICT
12015 Waterfront Drive
Los Angeles, CA 90094-2536
gordon@ict.usc.edu

Jerry Hobbs
USC/ISI
4676 Admiralty Way
Marina del Rey, CA 90292
hobbs@isi.edu

Abstract

Abduction allows us to model interpretation of discourse as the explanation of observables, given additional knowledge about the world. In an abductive framework, many explanations can be constructed for the same observation, requiring an approach to estimate the likelihood of these alternative explanations. We show that, for discourse interpretation, weighted abduction has advantages over alternative approaches to estimating the likelihood of hypotheses. However, weighted abduction has no probabilistic interpretation, which makes the estimation and learning of weights difficult. To address this, we propose a formal probabilistic abductive framework that captures the advantages weighted abduction when applied to discourse interpretation.

1 Introduction

In this paper, we explore discourse interpretation based on a mode of inference called *abduction*, or inference to the best explanation. Abduction-based discourse processing was studied intensively in the 1980s and 1990s (Charniak and Goldman, 1989; Hobbs et al., 1993). This framework is appealing because it is a realization of the observation that we understand new material by linking it with what we already know. It instantiates in discourse understanding the more general principle that we understand our environment by coming up with the best explanation for the observables in the environment. Hobbs et al. (1993) show that abductive proofs can be efficiently exploited for a whole range of natural language pragmatics problems, such as word sense disambiguation, anaphora and metonymy resolution, interpretation of noun compounds and prepositional phrases, and detection of discourse relations. As applied to discourse interpretation, abduction was shown to have advantages over deduction, a more classical mode of inference (Ovchinnikova, 2012). One serious advantage concerns treatment of incomplete knowledge. In the cases when it is impossible to provide it with all the knowledge which is relevant for interpretation of a particular piece of text, deductive reasoners fail to find a prove. Instead of a deterministic yes/no proof abduction provides a way of measuring in how far the input formula was proven and which of its parts could not be proven.

In the early 90s, research on abduction-based discourse processing resulted in good theoretical work and in interesting small-scale systems, but it faced three difficulties: 1) parsers were slow and not accurate enough, so that inference had no place to start, 2) inference processes were neither efficient nor accurate enough, 3) there was no large knowledge base designed for discourse processing applications. In the last two decades, the first of these difficulties has been addressed by progress in statistical parsing, e.g. (McClosky et al., 2006; Huang, 2008; Bos, 2011). Recently, efficient reasoning techniques were developed that overcome the second difficulty (Inoue and Inui, 2011; Inoue et al., 2012b). Finally, it has been shown that there exists sufficient knowledge about the world – at a level of precision that enables its translation into formal logic – available in a variety of resources (Ovchinnikova et al., 2011; Ovchinnikova, 2012). These advances have recently been capitalized upon in several large-scale applications of abduction to discourse processing tasks (Inoue and Inui, 2011; Ovchinnikova et al., 2011; Ovchinnikova, 2012; Inoue et al., 2012a).

In an abductive framework, often many explanations can be provided for the same observation. In order to find the best solution for our pragmatic problem, we need to be able to choose the best, i.e. the most probable, explanation. Several approaches were proposed for estimating the likelihood of alternative abductive explanations: cost-based abduction (Charniak and Shimony, 1990), weighted abduction (Hobbs et al., 1993), abduction based on Bayesian Networks (Pearl, 1988; Charniak and Goldman, 1989; Raghavan and Mooney, 2010), abduction based on Markov Logic Networks (Kate and Mooney, 2009).

In this paper, we show that weighted abduction employing a cost propagation mechanism (see Section 3) and favoring low-cost explanations has certain features relevant for discourse processing that other approaches do not have (see Section 4). The main such feature is the approach to unification, i.e. associating two entities with each other, so that their common properties only need to be proved or assumed once (see Section 2). Weighted abduction favors explanations with the maximum number of unifications. Thus, it favors those explanations that link parts of observations together and supports discourse coherence, which is crucial for discourse interpretation.

There is not yet any work on linking weights in weighted abduction to probabilities, which makes the estimation and learning of the weights difficult. In this paper, we show that the original cost propagation mechanism in weighted abduction as informally introduced in (Hobbs et al., 1993) cannot be interpreted in terms of probabilities. However, we can still capture features of weighted abduction desirable for discourse processing in a formal probabilistic framework based on Bayesian Networks. As a result, we obtain a theoretically sound probabilistic abductive framework favoring explanations relevant for discourse interpretation.

2 Abduction

Abduction is inference to the best explanation. Formally, logical abduction is defined as follows:
Given: Background knowledge B, observations O, where both B and O are sets of first-order logical formulas,
Find: A hypothesis H such that $H \cup B \models O, H \cup B \not\models \perp$, where H is a set of first-order logical formulas.

Observation O is usually a conjunction of existentially quantified propositions (Charniak and Goldman, 1989; Hobbs et al., 1993; Raghavan and Mooney, 2010):

$$\exists x_1, ..., x_k, ..., y_1, ..., y_l (q_1(x_1, ..., x_k) \wedge ... \wedge q_n(y_1, ..., y_l)).$$

We extend the notion of observation by allowing inequalities ($x \neq y$) as conjuncts. Sometimes inequalities follow from the natural language syntax. For example, if we read *There is a cat on the mat. Another cat is on the table*, we immediately know that there are two different cats mentioned. This text can be logically represented as follows:

$$\exists x_1, x_2, y_1, y_2 (cat(x_1) \wedge on(x_1, y_1) \wedge mat(y_1) \wedge cat(x_2) \wedge on(x_2, y_2) \wedge table(y_2) \wedge x_1 \neq x_2)).$$

Background knowledge B is a set of first-order logic formulas. In order to keep the inference process computationally tractable, B is often restricted to a set of Horn clauses (Charniak and Shimony, 1990; Hobbs et al., 1993; Kate and Mooney, 2009; Raghavan and Mooney, 2010). Thus, each background axiom has the form

$$P_1 \wedge ... \wedge P_n \rightarrow Q,$$

where all variables on the left-hand side are universally quantified with the widest possible scope and all variables occurring on the right-hand side only are existentially quantified. We weaken this restriction allowing multiple literals on the right-hand side of the background axioms because of the importance of the context and compositionality for discourse interpretation. For example, in order to express the fact that a testing process can be called "dry run", we use the following axiom:

$$\forall x, y, e, z, u (process(x) \wedge of(x, e) \wedge test(e, z, u) \rightarrow dry(x) \wedge run(x)).$$

Breaking this axiom into two different axioms (one implying that the process is dry and the other implying that it is a run) will result in loosing the binding of the arguments of *dry* and *run*.

We allow inequalities ($x \neq y$) as conjuncts in the background axioms. Inequalities can be used to represent incompatibility. For example, the axiom below represents the fact that the arguments of the relation *parent_of* refer to different objects:

$$\forall x, y (parent\_of(x, y) \rightarrow x \neq y).$$

The two main inference operations in abduction are backchaining and unification. *Backchaining* is the introduction of new assumptions given an observation and background knowledge. For example, given $O = q(A)$ and $B = \{\forall x(p(x) \rightarrow q(x))\}$, there are two candidate hypotheses: $H_1 =$

$q(A)$ and $H_2 = p(A)$. We say that $p(A)$ *explains* $q(A)$ in H_2. If an atomic proposition is included in a hypothesis (*hypothesized*) and not explained, then it is *assumed*, e.g., $q(A)$ is assumed in H_1.

Unification is merging of propositions with the same predicate name by assuming that their arguments are same.[1] For example, $O = \exists x, y(p(x) \wedge p(y) \wedge q(y))$. Given this observation, the propositions $p(x)$ and $p(y)$ are unifiable. Thus, there is a hypothesis $H = \exists x(p(x) \wedge q(y) \wedge x = y)$.

Both operations (backchaining and unification) can be applied as many times as possible to generate a possibly infinite set of hypotheses. The generation of the set of hypotheses $\mathcal{H}$ initialized as an empty set can be formalized as follows.

Backchaining

$$\frac{\bigwedge_{i=1}^{n} P_n \rightarrow \bigwedge_{j=1}^{m} Q_j \in B \text{ and } O \wedge H \models \bigwedge_{j=1}^{m} Q_j \text{ and } O \wedge H \wedge \bigwedge_{i=1}^{n} P_n \not\models \bot, \text{ where } H \in \mathcal{H}}{\mathcal{H} := \mathcal{H} \cup \{H \wedge \bigwedge_{i=1}^{n} P_n\}}$$

Unification

$$\frac{O \wedge H \models p(X) \wedge p(Y) \text{ and } O \wedge H \wedge X = Y \not\models \bot, \text{ where } H \in \mathcal{H}}{\mathcal{H} := \mathcal{H} \cup \{H \wedge X = Y\}}$$

3 Estimating Hypothesis Likelihood

Often many hypotheses can be constructed for the same observation. In order to find the best solution for our pragmatic problem, we need to choose the best, i.e. the most probable, hypothesis. Several approaches were proposed for estimating the likelihood of alternative abductive explanations.

Charniak and Shimony (1990) propose cost-based abduction. In this framework, the likelihood of a hypothesis depends on the probability of the assumed atomic propositions to be true.

Another popular approach to abduction is based on Bayesian Networks (Pearl, 1988; Charniak and Goldman, 1989; Raghavan and Mooney, 2010). In this framework, abductive explanations are represented by a directed graph constituting a Bayesian net, such that the nodes of the graph correspond to atomic predications and the edges connect explanations with the predications they explain. Each node has an associated conditional probability $P(A|B)$, where B is an explanation of A. Given the constructed Bayesian net, the best abductive hypothesis is selected using standard methods, which assign values to the unobserved nodes in the network that maximize the posterior probability of the joint assignment given the observations.

One more approach developed by (Kate and Mooney, 2009) is based on Markov Logic Networks (MLNs) (Richardson and Domingos, 2006). In this approach, a weight is assigned to each background axiom that reflects the strength of a constraint it imposes on the set of possible worlds. The higher the weight, the lower the probability of a world that violates the axiom. An MLN can be viewed as a set of templates for constructing Markov networks. Originally, MLNs employ deductive reasoning. Kate and Mooney (2009) adapt MLNs for abductive inferences by introducing reverse implications for every axiom in the knowledge base and adding mutual exclusivity constraints on the transformed axioms.

Finally, weighted abduction (Hobbs et al., 1993) proposes a cost propagation mechanism for selecting best hypotheses. In this framework, each atomic observation is assigned a positive real-valued cost. Atomic antecedents in the background axioms are assigned positive real-valued weights. If an axiom $\alpha = P \rightarrow Q$ is applied then the cost of each newly introduced literal p in P is equal to the sum of the costs of the literals in Q multiplied by the weight of p in α. For example, given the axiom $\forall x(p(x)^{0.9} \wedge s(y)^{0.1} \rightarrow q(x))$ and the observation $q(A)^{\$10}$, the literal $p(A)$ costs $\$10 \times 0.9 = \$9$ and the literal $s(y)$ costs $\$10 \times 0.1 = \$1$. When two literals are unified, the result of their unification is assigned the minimum of their costs. For example, given the observation $p(x)^{\$10} \wedge p(y)^{\$20}$ there is a hypothesis $x = y^{\$10}$. The cost of the hypothesis is equal to the sum of the costs of the assumptions. Each unification reduces the overall cost of the hypothesis, while an application of an axiom can increase or decrease the overall cost depending on whether its total weight is less or greater than 1. There is not yet any work on interpreting the weighted abduction cost propagation in terms of probabilities. Therefore the minimal cost hypothesis does not necessarily correspond to the most probable one.

All mentioned approaches to estimating the likelihood of abductive hypotheses have a common problem. The problem is that they all imply certain assumptions that cannot be proved or disproved practically because of the absence of the gold standard (collection of correct proof graphs)

[1]Note that the abduction unification mechanism is different from how unification is usually understood in computer science and logic, because it allows us to assume equalities of constants.

that is obviously very difficult to obtain. Cost-based abduction implies that the likelihood of a hypothesis depends on the joint likelihood of the assumptions only and that the assumptions are mutually independent. Abduction based on Bayesian Networks implies that the truth of the literals depends on their direct explanations only. MNL-based abduction implies that the probability of a background axiom to hold does not depend on the observation. All mentioned framework imply that unifications always hold.

In order to successfully apply abductive inference to pragmatic tasks, we should formulate the underlying independence assumptions with a good understanding of our domain of interest (in our case, it is discourse interpretation) and design a probabilistic framework correspondingly.

4 Abduction for Discourse Processing

Weighted abduction has three features, missing in other abduction-based frameworks, that are especially relevant for discourse processing. In this section, we discuss these features.

Unification The first feature is related to the unification inference. Weighed abduction prefers hypotheses with the maximum number of unifications. Therefore, it favors those explanations that link parts of observations together and thus support discourse coherence.

Suppose we want to construct an interpretation for the sentence *John composed a sonata.* The verb *compose* has two readings, 1) the "put together" reading (e.g., *The party composed a committee*, and 2) the "create art" reading. Suppose there are the following axioms:

1) $put\_together(e, x_1, x_2) \wedge collection(x_2) \rightarrow compose(e, x_1, x_2)$

2) $create\_art(e, x_1, x_2) \wedge work\_of\_art(x_2) \rightarrow compose(e, x_1, x_2)$

3) $sonata(x) \rightarrow work\_of\_art(x)$

Axioms (1) and (2) correspond to the two readings of *compose*. Axiom (3) states that a sonata is a work of art. Weighted abduction favors Axiom (2) over (1) for the observed sentence, because unification of *sonata* resulting from the application of Axioms 2 and 3 with the observable *sonata* reveals the implicit discourse redundancy and supports linking the meanings of *compose* and *sonata*.

As mentioned above, weighted abduction implies unconditional unification. In the discourse interpretation context, unification is one of the principal methods by which coreference is resolved. A naive approach to coreference in an inference-based framework is to unify propositions having the same predicate names unless it implies logical contradictions (Hobbs et al., 1993; Bos, 2011). However, in situations when knowledge necessary for establishing contradictions is missing, the naive procedure results in overmerging. For example, given $O = \exists x, y(animal(x) \wedge animal(y))$, we do not want to assume that x equals y when $dog(x) \wedge cat(y)$ are observed. For *John runs and Bill runs*, with the observations $O = \exists x, y(John(x) \wedge run(x) \wedge Bill(y) \wedge run(y))$, we do not want to assume that John and Bill are the same individual just because they are both running. If we had complete knowledge about incompatibility (*dog* and *cat* are disjoint, people have unique first names), the overmerging problem might not occur because of logical contradictions. However, it is not plausible to assume that we would have an exhaustive knowledge base. A proposal to introduce weighted unification is described in (Inoue et al., 2012a), where unification costs depend on the semantic relation (synonymy vs. antonymy), modality and polarity, and shared properties of the unified literals.

Observations costs The second feature concerns the unequal treatment of atomic observations depending on their initial cost. Hobbs et al. (1993) mention that costs reflect the demand for propositions to be proved. Those propositions that are most likely to be linked referentially to other parts of the discourse are expensive to assume. This idea is illustrated by an example provided in (Blythe et al., 2011). Suppose there are two sentences.

The smart man is tall.

The tall man is smart.

The logical representation for each of them is $\exists x(smart(x) \wedge tall(x) \wedge man(x))$. But certain syntactic features attached to propositions (e.g., definite article) influence the probability of the propositions to be explained or assumed. In the first sentence we want to prove $smart(x)$ to anchor the sentence referentially. Then $tall(x)$ is new information to be assumed. Blythe et al. (2011) suggest having a high cost on $smart(x)$ to force the proof procedure to find this referential anchor. The cost on $tall(x)$ will be low, to allow it to be assumed without expending effort in trying to locate that fact in background knowledge. For the second sentence, the case is the reverse.

Suppose we know that educated people are smart and big people are tall, and furthermore that John is educated and Bill is big and both of them are men. This knowledge is formalized as follows:

$\forall x(educated(x) \rightarrow smart(x))$
$\forall x(big(x) \rightarrow tall(x))$
$educated(John), big(Bill), man(John), man(Bill)$

In weighted abduction, the best interpretation for the first sentence is that the smart man is John, because he is educated, and the cost for assuming he is tall is paid. The interpretation to avoid is one that says x is Bill; he is tall because he is big, and the cost of assuming he is smart is paid. Weighted abduction with its differential costs on observables favors the first and disfavors the second.

Weighted conjuncts in the antecedents The third feature of weighted abduction is related to the weights of the conjuncts in the antecedents of the background axioms. Hobbs et al. (1993) say that the weights correspond to the "semantic contribution" each conjunct makes to its consequent and discuss the following example:

$\forall x(car(x) \wedge \textit{no-top}(x) \rightarrow convertible(x))$

Hobbs et al. (1993) assume that *car* contributes more to *convertible* than *no-top*, therefore the former should have a higher weight forcing its explanation. Thus, given a convertible mentioned in text, we will probably intend to link it to some other mentioning of a car rather than to a mentioning of an object with no top.

5 Graph Representation of Hypotheses

In this section, we introduce a formalization allowing us to estimate probabilities of abductive hypotheses in Section 6. We follow (Charniak and Shimony, 1990) and represent the set of all possible hypotheses as an AND/OR directed acyclic graph (AODAG).

Definition 1 *An AODAG is a 3-tuple $< G, l, o >$, where:*

1. *G is a directed acyclic graph, $G = (V, E)$.*
2. *l is a function from V to {AND, OR}, called the label. A node labeled AND is called an AND node, etc.*
3. *$o \subseteq V$ is a set of observed nodes.*

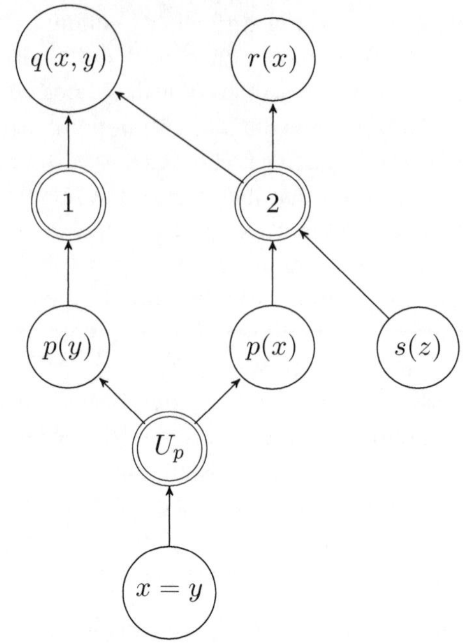

Figure 1: AODAG for the running example.

Consider an observation $O = \exists x, y(q(x, y) \wedge r(x))$ and the background knowledge B:

1) $\forall y(p(y) \rightarrow \exists x(q(x, y)))$
2) $\forall x, z(p(x) \wedge s(z) \rightarrow \exists y(q(x, y) \wedge r(x)))$

The AODAG in Fig. 1 is constructed by applying backchaining and unification to observation O. The nodes marked with a double circle represent inference operations: backchaining using Axioms 1 ("1" node) and 2 ("2" node) as well as unification ("U_p" node). Note that all operation nodes are AND nodes. All literal nodes are OR nodes. The notation $u \searrow v$ is used to say that u is an immediate parent of v. In our example, node "1" is a parent of $q(x, y)$ or $1 \searrow q(x, y)$.

Definition 2 *A truth assignment for an AODAG is a function f from V to $\{T, F\}$. A truth assignment is a model if the following conditions hold:*

1. *If $v \in o$ then $f(v) = T$.*
2. *If $v \notin o$ and v is an AND node then one of the following statements hold:*
   - *(a) $f(v) = F$ and $\exists u \searrow v : f(u) = F$.*
   - *(b) $f(v) = T$ and $\forall u \searrow v : f(u) = T$.*
3. *If $v \notin o$ and v is an OR node then one of the following statements hold:*
   - *(a) $f(v) = T$ and $\exists u \searrow v : f(u) = T$.*

(b) $f(v) \in \{T, F\}$ *and* $\forall u \searrow v : f(u) = F$.

4. *If* $\exists v_1, .., v_n$ *such that for all* $i \in \{1, .., n\} : v_i$ *is* $x_i = x_{i+1}$ *and* $\exists v_0$ *equal to* $x_1 \neq x_{n+1}$ *then* $f(v_0) \wedge f(v_1) \wedge ... \wedge f(v_n) = F$.

Condition 1 in Definition 2 ensures that observables are true in every model. Condition 2 ensures that an operation node is true if the result of this operation is true. Otherwise, an operation node is false. Condition 3 ensures that a literal node is true if one of its explanations is true. Otherwise, it can be either true or false. We rely on the "open world" assumption, i.e., we do not assume that the knowledge base contains all possible facts about the world. Thus, assumptions can be made without explanations. Condition 4 rules out inconsistencies that result from an equality and an inequality of the same variables. It rules out truth assignments that assign T to both equality chains $x_1 = x_2 ... = x_{n+1}$ and an inequality $x_1 \neq x_{n+1}$.

It is easy to see that the set of hypotheses corresponds to the set of models of the AODAG. Given Definition 2, the truth assignment
$M = \{(q(x, y), T), (r(x), T), (1, T), (p(y), T), (2, F), (p(x), F), (s(z), F), (U, F), (x = y, F)\}$
is a model of the example AODAG. It corresponds to the hypothesis $p(y) \wedge r(x)$. The nodes in a model that are assigned the truth value T and have no parents with the truth value T are called *assumptions* in this model. If $u \searrow v$ and both u and v are assigned the truth value T in a model, then u *explains* v in this model. For example, $r(x)$ is an assumption in the model M above, whereas $q(x, y)$ is explained by Axiom 1 in M.

6 Probabilities and Independence Assumptions

Now we are ready to estimate the likelihood of abductive hypotheses relevant for discourse interpretation. Let us associate a random variable from the set $\{X_1, ..., X_n\}$ with each of v nodes in an AODAG. The variables X_i ($i \in \{1, ..., n\}$) take values from the set $\{T, F\}$. If $f(v_i) = T$ then $X_i = T$; otherwise $X_i = F$. The joint probability distribution of the set $\{X_1, ..., X_n\}$ is as follows:

$$P(X_1, ..., X_n) = \prod_{i=1}^{n} P(X_i | \pi_i), \qquad (1)$$

where X_i is conditioned on π_i that denotes all other variables from the set $\{X_1, ..., X_n\}$ on which X_i depends. The question is how to define π_i for each X_i. In order to do it, we need to make independence assumptions.

As discussed in Section 4, the cost propagation mechanism in weighted abduction results in the following model preferences:

1. Other things being equal, a model that results from application of more reliable axioms is favored.

2. Other things being equal, a model that contains more true unification nodes is favored.

3. Other things being equal, a model that explains referential observables is favored.

Let us formulate independence assumptions reflecting the above model preferences. We can use the local Markov property: each variable is conditionally independent of its non-descendants given its immediate parent variables. But we also need a special account for unifications, because any true unification raises the likelihood of the corresponding model.

One option is to say that every axiom node in an AODAG also depends on its parent unification nodes. For example, nodes 1 and 2 in the example AODAG depend on the node U_p. However, given more observables there could be more unifications resulting from axiom applications. For example, if we add observable $s(t)$ then the application of Axiom 2 can result in one more unification ($t = z$). Given a set of golden AODAG models, one can compute all possible unifications resulting from a particular axiom. Alternatively, we can say that it does not matter unifications of which literals result from an axiom; the only thing that matters is how many unifications are there. In order to implement this second option, we introduce one more type of random variables associated with an AODAG: $numbU_v$ is associated with each axiom node v. It takes values from the set $\mathbb{N}$ and stands for the number of true unifications that are parents of v.

In order to account for referentiality, we introduce another type of random variables Ref_v associated with each literal node v in an AODAG. It takes values from the set $\{T, F\}$. If v is a referential observable or it has a referential observable as its child, then $Ref_v = T$; otherwise $Ref_v = F$. Each axiom application depends on whether its immediate children are referential or not.

We associate random variables X_{node_name} with each node of our example AODAG. In addition,

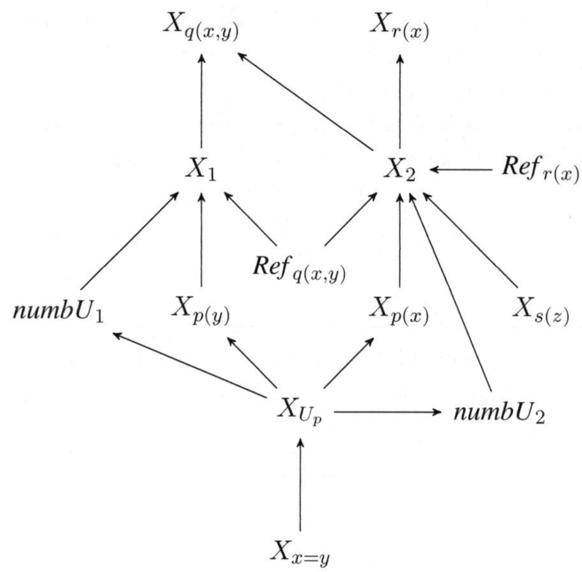

Figure 2: Bayesian network for the running example AODAG.

we introduce random variables $numbU_1$, $numbU_2$, $Ref_{q(x,y)}$ and $Ref_{r(x)}$. Fig. 2 shows the corresponding Bayesian network for the example AODAG that has the following joint probability distribution:

$$P(X_{x=y}) * P(X_{U_p}|X_{x=y}) * P(X_{p(y)}|X_{U_p}) * \\ P(X_{p(x)}|X_{U_p}) * P(X_{s(z)}) * P(numbU_{p(y)}|X_{U_p}) * \\ P(X_1|X_{p(y)}, numbU_{p(y)}, Ref_{q(x,y)}) * \\ P(X_2|X_{p(x)}, X_{s(z)}, numbU_{p(x),s(z)}, Ref_{q(x,y)}, Ref_{r(x)}) * \\ P(X_{q(x,y)}|X_1, X_2) * P(X_{r(x)}|X_2) * \\ P(numbU_{p(x),s(z)}|X_{U_p}) * P(Ref_{q(x,y)}) * P(Ref_{r(x)})$$

Now we can estimate the probability of all abductive hypotheses or compute the best hypothesis a using standard method for computing Most Probable Explanation (Pearl, 1988) that maximizes the posterior probability of the joint assignment given the observations (values of variables $X_{q(x,y)}$, $X_{r(x)}$, $Ref_{q(x,y)}$, $Ref_{r(x)}$ in our example). If conditional probability tables need to be learned, we can use standard algorithms: Expectation Maximization (Dempster et al., 1977; Langseth and Bangsø, 2001; Ramoni and Sebastiani, 2001) and Markov Chain Monte Carlo methods (Liao and Ji, 2009).

7 Linking Costs and Weights in Weighted Abduction to Probabilities

Section 6 gives us a probabilistic approach to abduction that preserves the relevant discourse interpretation features of weighted abduction, so now we want to see what are the relationships between weights and probabilities across these two frameworks. Consider our running example again. Suppose $cost(q(x,y)) = c_1$, $cost(r(x)) = c_2$, weight of $p(y)$ in Axiom 1 is w_1, and weights of $p(x)$ and $s(z)$ in Axiom 2 are w_2 and w_3 correspondingly. There are 5 hypotheses for the given observation. According to the cost propagation scheme, the hypotheses are assigned the following costs.

$H_1 = q(x,y) \wedge r(x)$
$cost(H_1) = c_1 + c_2$
$H_2 = p(y) \wedge r(x)$
$cost(H_2) = w_1 * c_1 + c_2$
$H_3 = p(x) \wedge s(z)$
$cost(H_3) = w_2 * (c_1 + c_2) + w_3 * (c_1 + c_2)$
$H_4 = p(y) \wedge p(x) \wedge s(z)$
$cost(H_4) = w_1 * c_1 + w_2 * (c_1 + c_2) + w_3 * (c_1 + c_2)$
$H_5 = p(y) \wedge p(x) \wedge s(z) \wedge y = x$
$cost(H_5) = min(w_1 * c_1, w_2 * (c_1 + c_2)) + w_3 * (c_1 + c_2)$

The corresponding AODAG has 5 models:

$M_1 = \{(q(x,y), T), (r(x), T), (1, F), (p(y), F), (2, F), (p(x), F), (s(z), F), (U, F), (x = y, F)\}$
$M_2 = \{(q(x,y), T), (r(x), T), (1, T), (p(y), T), (2, F), (p(x), F), (s(z), F), (U, F), (x = y, F)\}$
$M_3 = \{(q(x,y), T), (r(x), T), (1, F), (p(y), F), (2, T), (p(x), T), (s(z), T), (U, F), (x = y, F)\}$
$M_4 = \{(q(x,y), T), (r(x), T), (1, T), (p(y), T), (2, T), (p(x), T), (s(z), T), (U, F), (x = y, F)\}$
$M_5 = \{(q(x,y), T), (r(x), T), (1, T), (p(y), T), (2, T), (p(x), T), (s(z), T), (U, T), (x = y, T)\}$

Our goal is to find function g such that

$$\forall i \in \{1,..,5\} : cost(H_i) = g(P(M_i)). \quad (2)$$

The hypothesis cost is a sum of the assumption costs (e.g., $cost(H_1) = c_1 + c_2$). Can we derive costs of atomic literals from the probabilities of these literals to be assumed? The smaller the cost, the bigger the probability that the literal is assumed. The event when no axioms are applied to the literal node v is denoted by $Assume(v)$. If we set g to the negative logarithm, then summing costs will be equal to multiplying probabilities:

$$cost(v) = -log(P(Assume(v))). \quad (3)$$

Model M_1 refers to the event when no axioms are applied: $Assume(q(x,y)) \cap Assume(r(x))$. Obviously, the events $Assume(q(x,y))$ and

$Assume(r(x))$ are not independent, because Axiom 2 is applicable to both $q(x,y)$ and $r(x)$. Therefore we get the following contradiction:

$$cost(H_1) = cost(q(x,y)) + cost(r(x)) = \\ -log(P(Assume(q(x,y)) * P(Assume(r(x))) \\ \neq \\ -log(P(Assume(q(x,y) \cap Assume(r(x))) = \\ -log(P(M_1)).$$

We cannot link the sum of costs of atomic literals to the product of the probabilities of these literals to be assumed, because the assumption events are not independent. Therefore we have to reject Eq. 3. Suppose we selected c_1 and c_2 so that

$$c_1 + c_2 = -log(P(Assume(q(x,y)) \cap \\ Assume(r(x))) = -log(P(M_1)).$$

Can we then link axiom weights to probabilities? Model M_3 refers to the situation when only Axiom 2 is applied. It has the following probability[2]:

$$P(M_3) = P(X_1 = F \cap X_2 = T \cap \\ X_{p(y)} = F \cap X_{p(x)} = T \cap X_{s(z)} = T \cap \\ X_{U_p} = F | X_{q(x,y)} = T, X_{r(x)} = T).$$

Since $cost(H_3) = (w_2 + w_3) * (c_1 + c_2)$, we can try to link $w_2 + w_3$ to the probability of Axiom 2 to be applied. But in order to compute $P(M_3)$ the value of $cost(H_3)$ is also required to accommodate the probability of Axiom 1 not to be applied. Thus, instead of one axiom weight for each axiom α we need to have a table of conditional weights depending on all other axioms that can be applied in combination with α. This is not the case in weighted abduction.

The discussion above shows that we need conditional probabilities that cannot be linked to atomic literal costs and weights, because variables assigned to the atomic literal nodes are *not independent*. The question remains open if it is possible to tune weights and costs so that least cost hypotheses in weighted abduction correspond to the most pragmatically relevant (and the most probable) explanations. This is an empirical question and the answer to it depends on a particular application.

The fact that costs and weights in weighted abduction cannot be linked to probabilities does not make the framework inapplicable to discourse interpretation or any other task. One can see costs and weights as being parameters that need to be tuned in a practical setting. Inoue and Inui (2011) show that it is possible to represent weighted abduction as a linear constraint optimization problem and learn costs and weights in a large-margin learning procedure (Inoue et al., 2012b) including unification cost learning (Inoue et al., 2012a).

However, the problem remains how to set prior values for costs and weights before starting the learning. Furthermore, it is impossible to interpret learned values, which results in the choice of the best hypothesis being unpredictable.

8 Conclusion

Abduction allows us to model interpretation of discourse as the explanation of observables given knowledge about the world. In an abductive framework, many explanations can be constructed for the same observation. Therefore, an approach to estimating the likelihood of the alternative explanations is required.

In this paper, we showed that the cost propagation mechanism in weighted abduction has advantages over alternative approaches when applied to discourse interpretation. However, costs and weights in weighted abduction have no probabilistic interpretation, which makes their estimation and learning difficult. We proposed a formal framework for computing likelihood of abductive hypotheses with an account of variable inequalities and probabilistic unification. We discussed independence assumptions relevant for discourse processing. We showed that the cost propagation mechanism cannot be interpreted in terms of probabilities, but that features of weighted abduction relevant for discourse interpretation can be still captured in a probabilistic framework.

Future work concerns implementation of the probabilistic abductive framework proposed in Section 6 and its comparison with weighted abduction as tested on specific discourse processing tasks, such as recognizing textual entailment or coreference resolution; see (Ovchinnikova et al., 2011; Inoue et al., 2013) and (Inoue et al., 2012a) for applications of abduction to these tasks.

Acknowledgments

We thank Chris Wienberg for his valuable comments. This research was supported by ONR grant N00014-13-1-0286.

[2]For simplicity, we ignore the referential variables.

References

J. Blythe, J. R. Hobbs, P. Domingos, R. J. Kate, and R. J. Mooney. 2011. Implementing weighted abduction in markov logic. In *Proc. of IWCS'11*, pages 55–64, Oxford, England.

J. Bos. 2011. A survey of computational semantics: Representation, inference and knowledge in wide-coverage text understanding. *Language and Linguistics Compass*, 5(6):336–366.

E. Charniak and R. P. Goldman. 1989. A Semantics for Probabilistic Quantifier-Free First-Order Languages, with Particular Application to Story Understanding. In N. S. Sridharan, editor, *IJCAI'89*, pages 1074–1079. Morgan Kaufmann.

E. Charniak and S. E. Shimony. 1990. Probabilistic semantics for cost-based abduction. In *Proc. of the 8th National Conference on AI*, pages 106–111.

A. P. Dempster, N. M. Laird, and D. B. Rubin. 1977. Maximum likelihood from incomplete data via the EM algorithm. *Journal of the Royal Statistical Society: Series B*, 39:1–38.

J. R. Hobbs, M. Stickel, D. Appelt, and P. Martin. 1993. Interpretation as abduction. *Artificial Intelligence*, 63:69–142.

L. Huang. 2008. Forest reranking: Discriminative parsing with non-local features. In *Proc. of ACL'08*, pages 586–594.

N. Inoue and K. Inui. 2011. ILP-Based Reasoning for Weighted Abduction. In *Proc. of AAAI Workshop on Plan, Activity and Intent Recognition*.

N. Inoue, E. Ovchinnikova, K. Inui, and J. R. Hobbs. 2012a. Coreference Resolution with ILP-based Weighted Abduction. In *Proc. of COLING'12*, pages 1291–1308.

N. Inoue, K. Yamamoto, Y. Watanabe, N. Okazaki, and K. Inui. 2012b. Online large-margin weight learning for first-order logic-based abduction. In *Proc. of the 15th Information-Based Induction Sciences Workshop*, pages 143–150.

N. Inoue, E. Ovchinnikova, K. Inui, and J. R. Hobbs. 2013. Weighted abduction for discourse processing based on integer linear programming. In *Plan, Activity, and Intent Recognition*.

R.J. Kate and R. J. Mooney. 2009. Probabilistic abduction using markov logic networks. In *Proc. of PAIR'09*, Pasadena, CA.

H. Langseth and O. Bangsø. 2001. Parameter learning in object-oriented bayesian networks. *Ann. Math. Artif. Intell.*, 32(1-4):221–243.

W. Liao and Q. Ji. 2009. Learning bayesian network parameters under incomplete data with domain knowledge. *Pattern Recognition*, 42(11):3046–3056.

D. McClosky, E. Charniak, and M. Johnson. 2006. Effective self-training for parsing. In *Proc. of HLT-NAACL'06*.

E. Ovchinnikova, N. Montazeri, T. Alexandrov, J. R Hobbs, M. McCord, and R. Mulkar-Mehta. 2011. Abductive Reasoning with a Large Knowledge Base for Discourse Processing. In *Proc. of IWCS'11*, pages 225–234, Oxford, UK.

E. Ovchinnikova. 2012. *Integration of World Knowledge for Natural Language Understanding*. Atlantis Press, Springer.

J. Pearl. 1988. *Probabilistic Reasoning in Intelligent Systems: Networks of Plausible Inference*. Morgan Kaufmann.

S. Raghavan and R. Mooney. 2010. Bayesian abductive logic programs. In *Proc. of Star-AI'10*, pages 82–87, Atlanta, GA.

M. Ramoni and P. Sebastiani. 2001. Robust learning with missing data. *Machine Learning*, 45(2):147–170.

M. Richardson and P. Domingos. 2006. Markov logic networks. *Machine Learning*, 62(1-2):107–136.

Word Similarity Using Constructions as Contextual Features[1]

Nai-Lung Tsao
National Central University
No.300, Jhongda Rd. Jhongli City,
Taoyuan County 32001, Taiwan
beaktsao@stringnet.org

David Wible
National Central University
No.300, Jhongda Rd. Jhongli City,
Taoyuan County 32001, Taiwan
wible@stringnet.org

Abstract

We propose and implement an alternative source of contextual features for word similarity detection based on the notion of lexicogrammatical construction. On the assumption that selectional restrictions provide indicators of the semantic similarity of words attested in selected positions, we extend the notion of selection beyond that of single selecting heads to multiword constructions exerting selectional preferences. Our model of 92 million cross-indexed hybrid n-grams (serving as our machine-tractable proxy for constructions) extracted from BNC provides the source of contextual features. We compare results with those of a grammatical dependency approach (Lin 1998), testing both against WordNet-based similarity rankings (Lin 1998; Resnik 1995). Averaged over the entire set of target nouns and 10-best candidate similar words, Lin's approach gives overall similarity results closer to WordNet rankings than the constructional approach does, while the constructional approach overtakes Lin's in approximating WordNet similarity for target nouns with a frequency over 3000. While this suggests feature sparseness for constructions that resolves with higher frequency nouns, constructions as shared contextual features render a much higher yield in similarity performance in approximating WordNet similarity than grammatical relations do. We examine some cases in detail showing the sorts of similarity detected by a constructional approach that are undetected by a grammatical relations approach or by WordNet or both and thus overlooked in benchmark evaluations.

1. Introduction

Distributional approaches to semantics have contributed substantially to computational techniques for detecting or judging the semantic similarity of words for a wide range of applications. Such approaches work from the assumption that the distribution (or the set of contexts) of a word reflect the meaning of that word and, accordingly, that words with similar distributions have similar meanings (Harris 1954; 1968; Miller and Charles 1991; Lenci 2008, inter alia). Computational work taking such a distributional approach involves two dimensions: (1) some operationalization of the notion 'context' used in determining a word's distribution, and (2) some means of measuring similarity between or among sets of contexts that constitute a word's distribution. Such work typically involves extracting from a reference corpus the contexts of the candidate words, under some specified definition of context, and rendering these contexts as feature vectors in a vector space that can in turn be compared for (dis)similarity. In this paper we propose a novel construal of context and contextual features in determining word similarity distributionally and describe and evaluate an implementation of it.

A motivating premise for our approach is that in comparing words by comparing quantitative measures of their distributions, certain details of these distributions and the contexts that constitute them are obscured. For numerous applications, such as query expansion, document similarity judgment and document classification, this opacity may be irrelevant. There are, however, applications where the loss of some of this obscured detail comes at a cost, that is, where it may become relevant to ask for a pair or set of words not only 'How similar are they?' but 'How are they similar?' While current distributional approaches generally focus on the first question, we would like to build on those results to explore ways to further address the second.

2. The Basic Approach

Central to any implementation of distributional lexical semantics is the notion of context, or, as

[1] This research was supported by Taiwan's National Science Council through Grant #NSC 100-2511-S-008-005-MY3

Harris referred to this, a word's "environments" (1954, p. 146). Computational work on word similarity has operationalized context typically as features. These include unordered sets of co-occurent words attested within some window of proximity to the target word, i.e., bag-of-words (Dagan et al. 1993; Ng and Lee 1996; Tumuluru et al. 2012), ordered sequences of words, i.e., n-grams (Damashak 1995; Jones et al. 2006; Sahlgren et al. 2008; DeVine and Bruza 2010), ordered sequences of POS categories and collocations co-occurring with the target word (Ng and Lee 1996) and co-occurring words that stand in specified grammatical relation to the target word (Hindle 1990; Ruge 1992; Grefenstette 1994; Lin 1997, 1998; Geffet and Dagan 2009, inter alia). Distributional semantic work on word similarity over the past three decades has shown relatively little variety in how context has been operationalized, falling under one of these few types just mentioned. Probably the most linguistically sophisticated construal of context among these is the use of grammatical relations such as subject-verb, object-verb, adjective-noun as the contextual features. Crucial for us, these approaches that take grammatical relations as contextual features constitute, as Dagan (2000) points out, "a statistical alternative to traditional notions of selectional constraints and semantic preferences" (p. 3). Thus, as a feature of the noun *cell* reported in Lin (1998), the triples *cell, subject-of, absorb* and *cell, object-of, attack* indicate the selection of the noun *cell* by the verb *absorb* as its subject argument and by *attack* as its (direct) object argument. It is worth noting here that these grammatical relations (or selectional preferences) are head to head (that is, lexeme to lexeme) relations; a particular verb or preposition, for example, is seen as selecting for a particular semantic class (or set of classes) of noun.

The work reported here shares this assumption that semantic selection is a potentially rich source for identifying similar words. We suggest, however, that semantic selection is not always head-driven. More specifically, we explore an approach to detecting semantically restricted positions that are governed by larger multiword units. In other words, we consider the possibility of positions that are selected by something more like a construction (roughly along the lines of Fillmore et al. 1988; Goldberg 2006; inter alia) rather than a lexical head. For example, taking discrete grammatical relations as a feature, standing in object relation to the transitive verb *remove* would be one feature that various nouns could share, nouns attested as object of *remove*. If, however, we expand the notion of selection beyond single heads as the selecting expression such as a single verb, we create the possibility of not simply the verb *remove* as the contextual feature of its objects, as in (1), but also of that noun slot taking the more enriched context in (2) as a feature.

(1) remove [noun]
(2) undergo surgery to remove a [noun]

While taking (2) rather than (1) as the contextual feature of the [noun] slot would of course reduce dramatically the set of nouns attested in that slot, our motivating assumption is that it offers the possibility of narrowing the semantic class of nouns we would expect to find there. At the same time, and of equal interest to us, (2) provides a more articulated, fleshed out context.

Here perhaps the relevance of constructional selection and a constructional approach to contextual features for some applications can be made a bit clearer. Thesaurus construction is a fundamental domain of word similarity application which itself feeds numerous other applications. One area of such applications for thesauri where contextual detail becomes relevant is language learning. For language learners seeking to expand their vocabulary, a decontextualized list of discrete synonyms is of limited value, as attested by the uses that learners can create when relying on traditional thesauri. What does constitute a potentially useful source of traction for mastering unknown words from known ones, however, is access to exactly which multiword patterns of behavior of the known word generalize to the unknown word(s) and which patterns do not. Such patterning may elude what can be captured even by grammatical relations. The noun *place* stands in the grammatical relation of object to the verb *take* in both *take place* (as in *occur*) and *take the place of* (as in *replace*). Of course, it could be assumed that contributions of such nuanced differences come out in the wash when taken with broader distributional trends from sufficiently large corpora. We would like to consider the alternative possibility that incorporating such nuance as part of the contextual features used in statistical approaches to distribution can contribute to word similarity research.

In what follows we describe one specific implementation of detecting constructional selection to determine word similarity and compare it to an approach that uses head to head grammatical relations (subject-verb; object-verb, etc.). Since Lin (1998) is the most widely referenced approach using grammatical dependencies as a feature type for word similarity detection (Padó and Lapata 2007; Geffet and Dagan 2009; Kotlerman et al. 2009 ; inter alia), we run an implementation of Lin (1998) as our point of comparison to a grammatical relations approach. We first describe our method and then Lin's in section 3, and then in section 4 report and compare results produced from these two approaches applied to the same set of nouns.

3. Methods

3.1. An Implementation of the Constructional Approach

The challenge posed by our approach is how to automatically identify positions that are semantically selected. Since we are trying to identify selectional preferences imposed not by lexical heads but by multiword lexico-grammatical constructions, extracting head-to-head grammatical relations (e.g., subject-verb) will not suffice. That is, we need an enriched version of context and contextual features. To motivate our means of identifying constructional selection, an example in (3) can show the sort of linguistic phenomenon we aim to detect.

(3) have no [noun] but [to verb]

There are 325 tokens in BNC (British National Corpus) that instantiate this pattern (e.g., *have no choice but to accept...*). Crucially, considering the [noun] slot in those 325 tokens, 323 of them are tokens of just three distinct nouns: *choice* (freq: 137), *option* (freq: 110), *alternative* (freq: 76). Clearly, these three nouns are semantically similar. This semantic similarity could be fortuitous or it could reflect that this position is subject to selectional preference. Pursuing this latter possibility, the question is what might be the source of the semantic preference. It cannot plausibly be attributed to a specific lexical head, say an argument-taking predicate; in (3) that would be the semantically uninformative light verb *have*. Hence, this sort of semantic selection will fly below the radar of grammatical dependency approaches to semantic similarity. We suggest that the noun slot in (3) is semantically selected by the entire surrounding construction: *have no ____ but [to verb]*. This surrounding construction we will take as a shared feature of the three nouns attested: *choice*, *option*, *alternative*. We call this phenomenon *constructional selection*.

The challenge now can be stated as how to automatically identify loci of constructional selection, paradigms like the noun slot in (3), which are semantically restricted yet not by a lexical head. For this, we first need a means of identifying candidate constructions from corpora. We do this using the notion of hybrid n-gram from Wible and Tsao (2010) as the machine-tractable proxy, and then identify positions within them that exhibit semantic selection. We describe these two steps in turn.

Hybrid N-grams and Semantically Selected Slots

We operationalize the class of contexts that potentially exhibit constructional selection with the notion of hybrid n-gram (Tsao and Wible 2009; Wible and Tsao 2010). Hybrid n-grams are a variation of n-gram which, in addition to lexemes or specific word forms as grams, also admit part-of-speech category labels as a gram type. Thus, in addition to a traditional tri-gram *consider yourself lucky*, a hybrid tri-gram would also include *consider yourself [adj],* a more abstract version that thereby describes the tokens *consider yourself lucky* and *consider yourself fortunate*, for example. Hybrid n-grams would also include *consider [reflx prn] [adj]*, *[verb] [reflx prn] lucky*, and so on. A requirement we impose on hybrid n-grams for our language model is that they must each include one lexical gram (at least one gram that is either a lexeme or a specific word form of a lexeme). In this sense, all hybrid n-grams are lexically anchored. (See Wible and Tsao (2010) for details on hybrid n-gram extraction.)

Our language model consists of all hybrid n-grams from 3 to 6 grams in length extracted from BNC. As with any n-gram model spanning more than one value of n, there is substantial redundancy in our first-pass model, which is magnified because of our inclusion of more abstract part-of-speech grams. To mitigate the effects of this redundancy, we prune more abstract counterparts of a more specific hybrid n-gram when the more specific version accounts for 80% or more of the tokens of the more abstract one. Thus *point [prep] view* is pruned since more than 80% of its tokens in BNC are cases of the more specific *point of view*. Likewise we prune shorter n-grams in cases where 80% of their tokens are also tokens of the n+1 counterpart hybrid n-gram. Thus, *the other hand* is pruned because a threshold proportion of its tokens are part of the longer *on the other hand*. (See Wible and Tsao 2010 for details on extraction and pruning of hybrid n-grams.) To prevent a proliferation of unhelpful contexts such as *of the [noun]*, we further require that the hybrid n-gram must contain at least one lexical content word in addition to the target noun slot. The fully pruned version of the model contains 92 million unique hybrid n-grams.

Detecting Selectional Preferences in Hybrid N-gram Contexts

The pruned model of 92 million hybrid n-grams serves as the pool of candidate contexts we use to determine both the distribution of a word and its similarity to the distribution of other words. Two words share a context in case they are attested in the same gram or slot in a hybrid n-gram; that is, the two words share this contextual feature. Thus, *option* and *choice* have the shared feature of being occupants of the [noun] slot in *have no [noun] but [to verb]*. Put in structuralist terms, the words *option* and *choice* share a precise context as members of the same paradigmatic slot within a syntagmatic sequence.

As we noted with the pattern in (3) above, not all slots (or paradigms) in hybrid n-grams are selective. Thus, we need some further means of identifying those that are. Recall the two slots in the hybrid n-gram in (3) (repeated here) differ in selectivity and thus suggest the sort of distinction we need to make to identify selectionally restrictive slots (of the pattern's 325 tokens, only 5 different nouns account for the 325 noun tokens but 172 different verbs for the 325 tokens filling the [to verb] slot).

(3) have no [noun] but [to verb]

To identify the selective slots, we require that a word must account for at least 10% of the tokens attested in that specific slot of that hybrid n-gram in order for that hyrbrid n-gram to qualify as a contextual feature of that word. Accordingly, for two words to share a contextual feature, they must each account for 10% of the tokens attested in the same slot in the same hybrid n-gram. Thus, *trouble* and *problem* share a contextual feature by virtue of each accounting for minimally 10% of the tokens attested in the [noun] slot of the hybrid n-gram: *have a lot of [noun] with. Trouble* occurs in 12 of the 32 tokens of this construction and *problem* in 4 of the 32.

Recall that we further require shared contexts contain, in addition to the target noun slot, at least one lexical content word to avoid a massive proliferation of uninformative shared contexts such as: *and the [noun]*.

It is worth noting here that our means of identifying contexts that have selectionally restrictive slots makes no reference to semantic knowledge sources such as WordNet (Miller 1995) or other thesauri, but relies simply on frequency distribution profile of words attested in a paradigm slot. Note also that there could be a variety of ways to identify selective slots within hybrid n-grams, and our use of the 10% occupancy threshold is a first and basic approximation.

We measure similarity between two words by simply determining the number of shared contextual features, operationalized as shared membership in the same selective slots within the same hybrid n-gram. The set of nouns we consider are all and only the nouns found in WordNet and that have a frequency in BNC $\geq$ 100. We exclude from consideration compound nouns found in WordNet. This leaves us with 12,061 nouns. For every pair of such nouns, we calculate a similarity score for a target word t as follows:

$$\frac{\log(|P|) * \log(|C|)}{\log(f(w))}$$

, where $|P|$ is the number of unique shared contexts or hybrid n-grams between two words, $|C|$ is the number of unique shared lexical collocates occurring in the set of shared contexts and w is the frequency of the candidate similar word.

The reason we take into account $|C|$, the number of unique shared collocates, is basically to reward lexical diversity across shared contexts on the assumption that greater diversity within the circle of 'mutual friends' for two words indicates greater similarity of those two words. Consider the target noun *wealth* and two of its candidate similar nouns—*range* and *lack*—which have the same value of $|P|$, the same number of shared contexts with *wealth*; (11 contexts each). There are seven different collocates in the eleven contexts shared by *wealth* and *range* (e.g., *draw* in *draw on a [wealth/range/...] of; available* in *the [wealth/range/...] of [noun] available from*), but there are only three distinct collocates in the eleven contexts shared by *wealth* and *lack* (e.g. *experience* in *his [wealth/lack...] of experience*). Including $|C|$ in our equation is a means of differentiating these otherwise indistinguishable cases.

Using similarity scores calculated with the above equation, we can generate for each of the 12061 target nouns a ranked list of similar nouns. In this paper we consider only the 10-best similar nouns created by these rankings. While Lin 1998 uses 200-best, and 10-best will certainly yield lower recall and hurt evaluation scores against benchmarks, we find little motivation for considering more than 10 similar nouns in light of the fact that, for example, WordNet averages under 2 words per synset for all its nouns, even for high frequency nouns.

3.2. Lin's Approach

To compare our constructional selection results with a head-driven selectional approach that uses grammatical dependency, we implement Lin (1998) using BNC as the reference corpus as a representative of the latter.

Lin's version requires a parsed corpus in order to extract the grammatical relations as contextual features. For this we use Link parser (Sleator and Temperley 1993) to parse BNC and extract all head-to-head dependency relations as triples: word 1, rel, word 2. Lexical categories of the words extracted for dependency relations were noun, verb, adj, adv, prep. From these triples we retain only those that include a noun and filter out redundancies (for example, for a token dependency 'brown dog' Link parser extracts two triples 'brown modif dog' and 'dog noun-mod brown' but we retain only the latter). About 78 million such triples are extracted and retained. We measure word association strength between the two words in each triple using the following MI measure from Lin (1998).

$$I(w, r, c) = \log \frac{\|w, r, c\| \times \|*, r, *\|}{\|w, r, *\| \times \|*, r, c\|}$$

where w is the target word, r is the dependency relation (subject of; object of, etc.), and c is a collocate standing in relation r to word w. $\|w, r, c\|$ denotes the frequency of the relational triple in parsed BNC. When w, r, or c is replaced by the wild card(*), the frequency of the relational triples that match the rest of the pattern is summed up. For example, $\| cell, subject-of, * \|$ is the total number of occurrences of *cell-subject* relationships for any c in parsed BNC.

Taking all nouns found in WordNet with frequency in BNC ≥ 100 (compound nouns excluded), for each pair of such nouns we calculate a similarity score following Lin (1998) with the following equation:

$$\frac{\sum_{(r,c)\in T(w_1)\cap T(w_2)} \left(I(w_1, r, c) + I(w_2, r, c)\right)}{\sum_{(r,c)\in T(w_1)} I(w_1, r, c) + \sum_{(r,c)\in T(w_2)} I(w_2, r, c)}$$

where $T(w)$ is the set of pairs (r, c) such that $I(w, r, c)$ is positive.

Using similarity scores calculated accordingly, we can generate for each target noun a ranked list of similar nouns.

4. Evaluation and Comparison [2]

We first consider here the extent of overlap in the 10-best results produced by the constructional and relational approaches, then compare both constructional and relational approaches as they approximate word similarity scores derived from WordNet, and finally elaborate on specific illustrative cases.

4.1. Comparison of Overlap in Results: Constructional and Relational Approaches

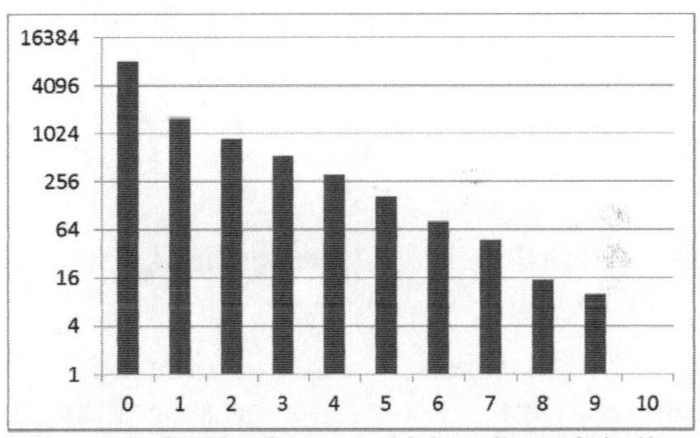

Figure 1. Overlap between 10-best lists of similar words by Lin (1998) and construction approach

For each of the two approaches, we generated rankings of similar words for all 12061 target nouns found in WordNet (compounds excluded) and with a minimum frequency of 100 in BNC. Figure 1 shows the comparison for overlap of the 10-best lists, with the x axis showing the number of similar nouns out of the two 10-best lists with increasing overlap from left to right (from 0 to 10 overlapping similar words from the two methods) and the y axis representing the number of target nouns whose 10-best similar words show that amount of overlap. As the figure makes apparent, the two approaches yield widely

[2] Similarity rankings available at http://www.stringnet.org

divergent results, with well over half of the 12061 nouns tested showing no overlapping similar words from the two 10-best lists.

We should note that our purpose for comparing results of our approach with Lin's here is not to use Lin's as a benchmark for our method to aspire to. Rather, we are interested in the differences in that come of using head-to-head grammatical dependencies as in Lin's method compared to using constructional selection as the contextual feature type that reflects word similarity as in ours. Before discussing these differences, we first compare the performances of the two approaches to similarity results based on WordNet.

4.2. Comparisons with WordNet-based Similarity Results

Method of Comparison

Here we compare the automatically generated results of the constructional approach (cxnl) and the relational approach (rlnl) each to similarity results based on the handcrafted resource, WordNet (wn). We first need similarity results from WordNet. For this, we use WordNet 3.0 (Miller 1995) and the following word similarity measure applied to WordNet from Lin (1997):

$$\mathrm{sim}_{\mathrm{wnc}}(c_1, c_2) = \max_{c \in \mathrm{super}(c_1) \cap c \in \mathrm{super}(c_2)} \frac{2 \log P(c)}{\log P(c_1) + \log P(c_2)}$$

$$\mathrm{sim}_{\mathrm{wn}}(w_1, w_2) = \max_{c_1 \in S(w_1) \cap c_2 \in S(w_2)} (\mathrm{sim}_{\mathrm{wnc}}(c_1, c_2))$$

where $S(w)$ is the set of senses of word w in WordNet, super(c) is the set of super-ordinate classes of concept c in WordNet. The probability of a concept is estimated by the sense tag count information in WordNet. We use Resink's approach (1995) to estimate the probabilities. The probability of a concept subsumes all probabilities of its descendants in WordNet.

With the WordNet-based similarity, we have word similarity results on the same noun set for three different approaches: construction-based (cxnl), grammatical relation–based (rlnl), and WordNet-based (wn). We use Lin's approach (1998) to measure two pair-wise correlations of results: cxnl-wn; rlnl-wn. The correlation for a pair of methods is arrived at following Lin (1998). For a target word, two similar word lists based on two methods are represented as follows:

method 1: $(w_1, s_1), (w_2, s_2), \ldots, (w_n, s_n)$

method 2: $(w'_1, s'_1), (w'_2, s'_2), \ldots, (w'_n, s'_n)$

where w is a candidate similar word and s is the similarity score between the target word and w.

The set of similar words and similarity scores for each target word schematized above can be taken as a vector, the features of that vector being the pairings of similar word and similarity score $(w_1, s_1)\ldots(w_n, s_n)$. The similarity between the results of two methods is taken as the cosine of these two vectors for each target word averaged across all target words, as defined in the following equation:

$$\frac{\sum_{w_i = w'_j} s_i s'_j}{\sqrt{(\sum_{i=1}^{n} s_i^2)(\sum_{j=1}^{n} s'^2_j)}}$$

We apply this equation to two pairings of methods for comparison: constructional:WordNet (cxnl:wn) and relational:WordNet (rlnl:wn).

Results and Discussion of WordNet Comparisons

The overall similarity scores for the pairings of approaches (see below) show the grammatical relations approach approximating WordNet-based similarity results more closely than the constructional approach does.

cxnl-wn: 0.0411
rlnl-wn: 0.0565

Figure 2 represents the similarity to WordNet results of the constructional and relational methods broken down into frequency bands for target words (frequency in BNC). The y axis represents cosine averages of constructional:WordNet results and relational:WordNet results, i.e., the similarity of these two approaches to WordNet-based results, and the x axis is the frequency of the target words receiving these similarity scores. What is worth noting in Figure 2 and not apparent from the overall scores is that the constructional approach performance catches up to the relational approach at a frequency of 3000 and overtakes it for frequencies above that.

This raises the question of how the trend here would play out with higher frequencies from a larger corpus. In this regard, we also consider the average number of features responsible for these scores under the two different methods. This is shown in Figure 3.

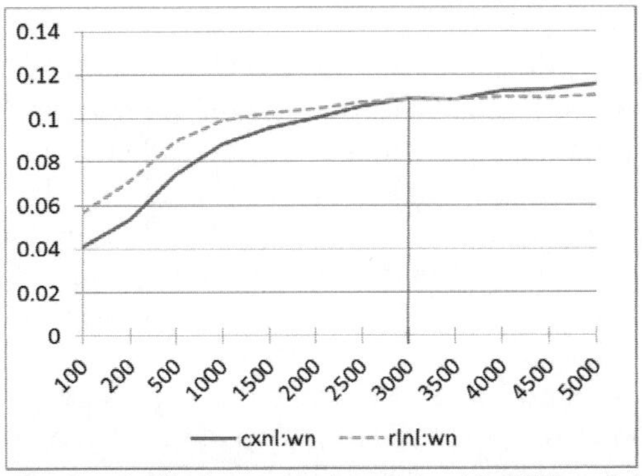

Figure 2. similarity score (y axis) with WN and frequency of target nouns (x axis)

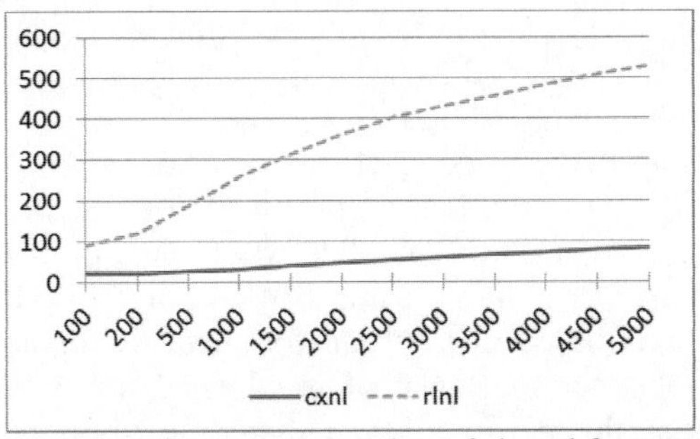

Figure 3. x axis: average number of shared features of 10-best sim nouns; y axis: frequency of target noun.

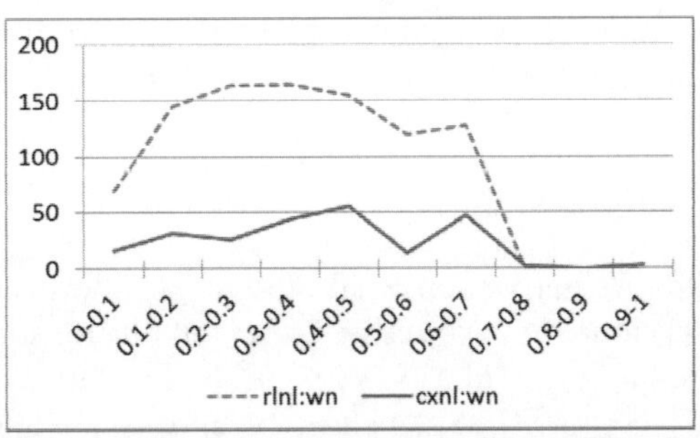

Figure 4. x axis: score of approximation to WN similarity results; y axis: number of shared features for 10-best sim nouns

While Figure 2 might suggest that the constructional approach is relatively data-hungry and suffers from feature sparseness at the lower frequency levels, another perspective on this is suggested by Figure 3 and Figure 4, which show a notable difference in the "yield" of similarity performance by the two different sorts of features; i.e., constructions compared to grammatical relations as features. Notably, Figure 3 shows a comparatively sharp rise in the number of features used by the relational approach, reaching over 500 for the high frequent words, whereas the number of constructional features rises gradually and remains well under 100 for all levels of frequency. This suggests a relatively healthy 'return on investment' (ROI) or what we might call 'feature yield' for constructions as contextual features.

Some Specific Suggestive Cases

In considering the results above, it is important to remember that we are not aspiring to superiority to previous distributional approaches on some single linear scale of performance, though this impression is hard to avoid under the need to offer some comparative evaluation. What we would like to suggest, rather, is that a constructional approach of the sort we propose shows sensitivity to similarities between (among) words that current distributional approaches have not, similarities worth trying to capture. This latter purpose raises difficulties since, we will argue here, the traditional benchmarks for evaluating word similarity results (i.e., traditional thesauri or WordNet) are also less attuned to some of the dimensions of semantic similarity that our approach seems able to capture.

To shed some light on what these different approaches contribute, we consider results for two different target nouns: *deal* and *ground*

Rank	Constructional Method	Grammatical Relation Method
1	*floor	land
2	reason	field
3	basis	site
4	fact	area
5	cause	surface
6	term	*floor
7	way	water
8	bed	building
9	garden	space
10	issue	path

Table 1. Ranked 10-best similar nouns for *ground* from constructional vs grammatical relation methods

Rank	Constructional Method	Grammatical Relation Method
1	*amount	*agreement
2	*lot	contract
3	bit	arrangement
4	*agreement	*lot
5	degree	proposal
6	source	move
7	lack	plan
8	thing	scheme
9	sense	offer
10	range	*amount

Table 2. Ranked 10-best similar nouns for *deal* from constructional vs grammatical relation methods

For the target noun *ground,* the 10-best lists of our construction method and Lin's grammatical dependency method, shown in Table 1, have only one similar word in common: *floor*. But note the complementarity of the two lists. What we would call true positives from Lin's list that we miss include: *land*, *field*, *site*, *area*, *surface*. On the other hand, what we would consider true positives from the constructional list includes: *reason*, *basis*, *cause*. These are apparently similar in more figurative, metaphorical senses missing from the grammatical dependency list in this case. While WordNet's ranks *reason* and *basis* as the two top similar nouns for *ground*, *cause* is missed by WordNet, its similarity to *ground* receiving a score of 0.

For the target noun *deal*, the ranked list of 10-best similar words generated by Lin and the list generated by our constructional method have only 3 nouns in common, as shown in Table 2.

Focusing on where results of the two methods diverge, it is worth noticing the constructional contexts that *deal* shared with some of the words from its 10-best list that did not appear on the dependency relation or WordNet list. The noun *bit* ranks 3rd in similarity to *deal* under the construction approach but 142nd under Lin and 84th under WordNet. A few of the 92 hybrid n-grams that are shared features of *deal* and *bit* (accounting for more than 10% each of the tokens in the [noun] slot), are given in (4-10):

(4) take a [adj] [noun] of time
(5) make a [adj] [noun] of difference
(6) have a [adj] [noun] of money
(7) under a [adj] [noun] of pressure
(8) be a [adj] [noun] older than
(9) not make a [adj][noun] of
(10) get a fair [noun] of

To see the potential contribution of hybrid n-grams as a feature type for detecting similar words, we can ask whether these instances of shared contexts in (4-10) would be detectable under context construed as, say, n-grams or head-to-head grammatical dependencies or collocation. We consider only (4) in some detail.

The noun slot in (4) selects for both *deal* and *bit*. This hybrid n-gram is instantiated by 53 tokens in BNC; 22 of them with the noun *deal*, 7 of them with *bit* (and 19 of them with the noun *amount*—a conspicuous clue to the sense that *bit* and *deal* share in common here). But would that slot select for these same nouns if we reduced the contextual features to one single selecting head or collocate? The noun slot heads the object NP of the verb *take* in (4), so *take* would be the candidate verb selecting *bit* or *deal* as its object. But the light verb *take* does not select either of these nouns as object.*Take* is in fact part of a V-N collocation here, the N of the collocation being *time* in *take...time*, not the intervening [noun] slot where *bit* and *deal* occur. This excludes selection by or collocation with the verb as responsible for the selection here. Nor does the [adj] slot serve as collocate. Neither *bit* or *deal* is selected by the adjective; it is not a specific adjective here but an open adjective slot, and crucially, there is virtually no overlap in the adjectives that co-occur with *bit* and with *deal* in this context (the only shared adjective is 'good', one token each co-occurring with *bit* (freq = 7) and *deal* (freq = 22)).

Note that a version of this context in (4) rendered as a traditional n-gram made of only lexical grams and no POS slots would not select *bit* and *deal* here in the same slot and therefore detect no shared distribution for them. It requires the abstract POS slot of the hybrid n-gram to capture this portion of their shared distribution.

This covers the relations that could be captured by head to head grammatical dependencies, collocations, and n-grams. Similar considerations would show the contribution of the hybrid n-grams in (5-10) as a sampling.

5. Conclusion

An alternative construal of context in terms of the notion of construction could enrich the sorts of semantic similarity susceptible to detection. Lin's grammatical dependency approach yields substantial results that our approach misses and for which we have no straightforward means of emulating. Nor is it our intention to attempt that. Rather, and on the other hand, our results suggest that construing contextual features as multiword lexico-grammatical wholes can uncover loci of semantic selection that attract similar words. Evaluation against WordNet-based results shows also that despite an appearance of feature sparseness, constructions are comparatively potent indicators of similarity, requiring fewer features to yield similarity results approximating benchmarks. Future work could determine whether constructions reward the use of larger corpora with increased yield in similarity judgments.

References

Ido Dagan. 2000. Contextual word similarity. *Handbook of Natural Language Processing*, 459-475.

Ido Dagan, Shaul Marcus, and Shaul Markovitch. 1993 Contextual word similarity and estimation from sparse data. In *Proceedings of the 31st annual meeting on Association for Computational Linguistics*, pp. 164-171. Association for Computational Linguistics, 1993.

Marc Damashek. 1995. Gauging similarity with n-grams: Language-independent categorization of text. *Science, 267*(5199), 843-848.

Lance De Vine and Peter Bruza. 2010. Semantic oscillations: Encoding context and structure in complex valued holographic vectors. In *Proceedings of AAAI Fall Symposium on Quantum Informatics for Cognitive, Social, and Semantic Processes*.

Charles J. Fillmore, Paul Kay, and Mary Katherine O'Connor. 1988. Regularity and Idiomaticity in Grammatical Constructions: the Case of *Let Alone*. *Language* 64: 501–538.

Maayan Geffet and Ido Dagan. 2009. Bootstrapping distributional feature vector quality. *Computational Linguistics, 35*(3), 435-461.

Adele Goldberg. 2006. *Constructions at Work: The Nature of Generalization in Language*. Oxford: Oxford University Press.

Gregory Grefenstette. 1994. *Explorations in Automatic Thesaurus Discovery*. Kluwer Academic Press, Boston, MA.

Zellig Sabbettai Harris. 1954. Distributional structure. *Word* 10:146–162.

Zellig Sabbettai Harris. 1968. *Mathematical structures of Language*. New York: Wiley.

Donald Hindle. 1990. Noun classification from predicate-argument structures. In *Proceedings of the 28th annual meeting on Association for Computational Linguistics* (pp. 268-275). Association for Computational Linguistics.

Michael N. Jones, Walter Kintsch, and Douglas J.K. Mewhort. 2006. High-dimensional semantic space accounts of priming. *Journal of memory and language*, 55(4), 534-552.

Lili Kotlerman, Ido Dagan, Idan Szpektor and Maayan Zhitomirsky-Geffet. 2009. Directional distributional similarity for lexical expansion. In *Proceedings of the ACL-IJCNLP 2009 Conference Short Papers* (pp. 69-72)

Alessandro Lenci. 2008. Distributional semantics in linguistic and cognitive research. in Lenci Alessandro. (ed.), From context to meaning: Distributional models of the lexicon in linguistics and cognitive science, special issue of the *Italian Journal of Linguistics*, 20/1: 1-31.

Dekang Lin. 1997. Using syntactic dependency as local context to resolve word sense ambiguity. In *Proceedings of ACL/EACL-97*, pages 64-71, Madrid, Spain, July.

Dekang Lin. 1998. Automatic retrieval and clustering of similar words. In *Proceedings of the 17th international conference on Computational linguistics-Volume 2*, pp. 768-774.

George A. Miller. 1995. WordNet: A Lexical Database for English. *Communications of the ACM* Vol. 38, No. 11: 39-41

George A. Miller and Walter G. Charles. 1991. Contextual correlates of semantic similarity. *Language and Cognitive Processes* 6 (1): 1–28.

Hwee Tou Ng, and Hian Beng Lee. 1996 Integrating multiple knowledge sources to disambiguate word sense: An exemplar-based approach. In *Proceedings of the 34th annual meeting on Association for Computational Linguistics*, pp. 40-47.

Sebastian Padó and Mirella Lapata. 2007. Dependency-based construction of semantic space models. *Computational Linguistics, 33*(2), 161-199.

Phil Resnik. 1995. Using information content to evaluate semantic similarity in a taxonomy. *In Proceedings of the 14th International Joint Conference on Artificial Intelligence(IJCAI-95).*

Gerda Ruge. 1992. Experiments on linguistically-based term associations.*Information Processing & Management, 28*(3), 317-332.

Magnus Sahlgren, Anders Host, and Pentti Kanerva. 2008. Permutations as a means to encode order in word space. In *Proceedings of the 30th Annual Meeting of the Cognitive Science Society* (pp. 1300–1305).

Daniel Sleator and Davy Temperley. 1993. Parsing English with a Link Grammar. *Third International Workshop on Parsing Technologies.*

Nai-Lung Tsao and David Wible. 2009. A method for unsupervised broad-coverage lexical error detection and correction. In *Proceedings of the Fourth Workshop on Innovative Use of NLP for Building Educational Applications* (pp. 51 54)

Anand Karthik Tumuluru, Chi-Kin Lo and Dekai Wu. 2012. Accuracy and robustness in measuring the lexical similarity of semantic role fillers for automatic semantic MT evaluation. In *Proceedings of the 26th Pacific Asia Conference on Language, Information, and Computation* (pp. 574-581)

David Wible and Nai-Lung Tsao. 2010. StringNet as a computational resource for discovering and investigating linguistic constructions. In *Proceedings of the NAACL HLT Workshop on Extracting and Using Constructions in Computational Linguistics* (pp. 25-31)

Inference for Natural Language

Amal Alshahrani
School of Computer Science
Universit of Manchester
Manchester M13 9PL, UK
amal.alshahrani@postgrad.manchester.ac.uk

Allan Ramsay
School of Computer Science
Universit of Manchester
Manchester M13 9PL, UK
Allan.Ramsay@manchester.ac.uk

Abstract

The main aim of this study is to develop a natural language inference (NLI) engine that is more robust than typical systems that are based on post-Montague approaches to semantics and more accurate than the kinds of shallow approaches usually used for textual entailment, The term robustness is concerned with processing as many inputs as possible successfully, and the term accuracy is concerned with producing correct result. In recent years, several approaches have been proposed for NLI. These approaches range from shallow approaches to deep approaches. However, each approach has a number of limitations, which we discuss in this paper. We argue that all approaches to NLI share a common architecture, and that it may be possible to overcome the limitations inherent in the existing approaches by combining elements of both kinds of strategy.

1 Introduction

In order to understand natural language, we need to know a lot about the world and be able to draw inference (Ovchinnikova, 2012). For instance, to answer the query "Was Shakespeare the author of Romeo and Juliet?" from the following text: *"Romeo and Juliet* is one of Shakespeare's early *tragedies.* The *play* has been highly praised by critics for its language and dramatic effect" we need background knowledge such as: (i) Tragedies are plays. (ii) Shakespeare is a playwright; playwrights write plays. (iii) Plays are written in some language and have dramatic effect.

Hence without background knowledge, answering the query would be impossible.

Tackling this task will open the door to applications of these ideas in various areas of Natural Language Processing (NLP) (Dale, Moisl and Somers, 2000) such as question answering (QA), information extraction (IE), summarisation, and semantic search.

Many approaches have been suggested in the literature to achieve this goal. These approaches can be divided into two groups:

Shallow approaches, which are based on lexical overlap, pattern matching, distributional similarity and others (Dagan and Glickman, 2004).

These approaches have a number of limitations and difficulties. In particular,

- They may not take semantic representation into account.
- They may not be sound.
- They cannot easily make use of complex background knowledge.

Deep approaches, which are based on semantic analysis, lexical and world knowledge, logical inference and others (Blackburn et al., 2001).

These approaches have a number of limitations and difficulties For instance,

- Compositional translation to logical form requires syntactic analysis which conforms to a grammar expressed as a set of rules. Such analyses are very hard to obtain for freely occurring texts.
- For complex sentences, logical forms often turn out to be extremely verbose, and hence are difficult for standard theorems provers to handle.
- Vast amounts of additional knowledge are required.

This kind of deep approach can succeed in restricted domains, but it fails badly on open domain problems.

2 Proposed system

It is widely assumed that shallow and deep approaches of NLI have completely different structure (MacCartney, 2009). However, if you look at the left and right-sides of Figure (1), you can see that at a very gross level of abstraction they can be decomposed into the same three major steps. They start with a pre-processing stage (stage A) which analyses the syntactic structure of input as some kind of parse tree. Then the second step (stage B) is responsible for normalising these trees to some format that is suitable for the intended inference engine. Finally, the inference engone (stage C) is responsible for comparing the representations obtained by stage B to see what follows from what was said.

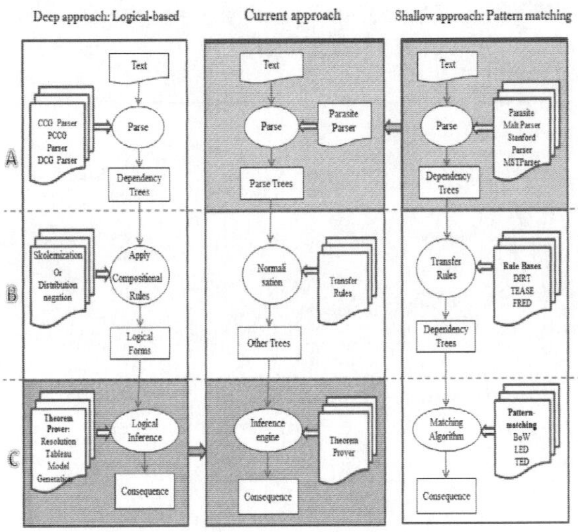

Figure 1: System Architecture.

The differences between the left- and right-hand sides of Figure 1 are that the stage C of the deep approach utilises a standard theorem prover for first-order logic (or some extension thereof), and hence requires stage B to produce formulae of the relevant logic on the basis of the trees produced by stage A. It is, however, extremely difficult to produce such formulae from freely occurring texts, since most parsers that are robust enough to handle texts such as newspaper articles or Wikipedia pages rely on implicit rules that have been extracted from corpora, and it is somewhere between difficult and impossible to attach compositional rules to such inferred parsing rules. Shallow approach are less ambitious about the degree of normalisation that can be achieved, but as a consequence the inference engines that they depend on are less powerful. The goal of the current proposal is to use an adaptation of a standard theorem prover, but to apply it directly, or almost directly, to the dependency trees obtained by the parser.

2.1 Stage A: Structural Analysis

This stage represents the pre-processing of the current system. It is responsible of converting input sentences from natural language expressions into dependency trees. To achieve this goal, we use the PARASITE parser (Ramsay, 1999; Seville and Ramsay, 2001). The advantage of using an in-house parser is that it allows some measure of control over the shape of then output trees—that if, for instance, we believe that it is better for the auxiliaries in a verb chain to be the head of the chain then we can arrange it so that our trees have this shape; and if we decide that the contrary is the case, then we can easily make the change. Controlling the underlying structure of the grammar obviates the need for subsequent transformations during the second stage of the process—to take another example, making the determiner the head of an NP might make sense from the point of view of the inference engine, so if we have control over that decision during the parsing process then we will not have to do anything about it during normalisation.

2.2 Stage B: Normalisation

In any NLI system, the output of the initial structural analysis is likely to produce structures that are not well-matched to the intended inference engine. This is clear for deep approaches, where a considerable amount of machinery is required for transforming parse trees into logical forms, but it is also true for shallow approaches: Alabbas & Ramsay (2012), for instance, showed that induced dependency parsers work better if the head of the first element of a coordinated expression is taken to be the head of the whole coordinated expression, but almost all approaches to inference require the head of such an expression to be the conjunction itself. It is therefore nearly always necessay to carry out some post-processing of the trees produced by the parser before carrying out the third stage of the overall task. In the following sections we describe three such normalisation techniques.

Shallow normalisation

Normalisation in shallow approaches is typically involves producing abstract 'entailment templates' from sets of sentence pairs, where common element of the two sentences in a pair are replaced by variables (Kouylekov and Magnini, 2005).

Numerous systems have been suggested for automatic acquisition of rules, ranging from distributional similarity to finding shared contexts such as *DIRT*[1] (Lin and Pantel, 2001), *TEASE*[2] (Szpektor et al., 2004), and *MSR Paraphrase Corpus (Dolan et al., 2004)*. For example, the normalisation for the sentence (‘*X solves Y*’ implies *‘X finds a solution to Y’*), which is (Templates with variables) is illustrated in Figure 4.

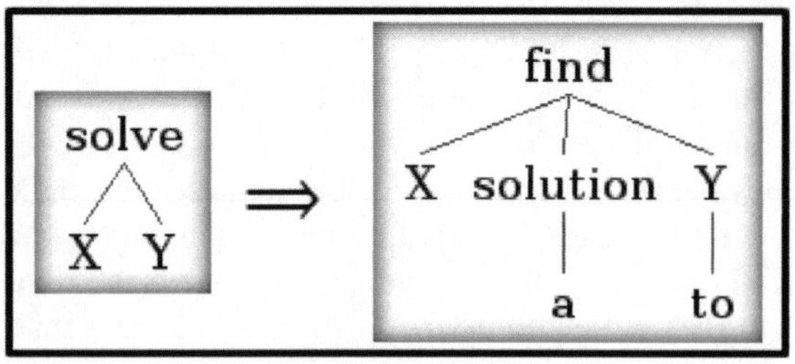

Figure 4: Normalise the sentences ‘*X solves Y ⟹ X finds a solution to Y*’.

Deep normalisation

Normalisation in deep approaches is defined as translation of natural language expressions into formal meaning representations (logical form) (Blackburn et al., 2001). There are a lot of systems available such as conversion to clausal form (Lukasova et al., 2012), Skolemisation (Degtyarev, Lyaletski, and Morokhovets, 1999), distribution of negation and others. For instance, *(John solves the problem → John finds a solution to the problem)*.

The normalization for the previous sentences is:

$$\forall x,y(solve(x,y)) \Rightarrow \exists z(find(x,z) \wedge solution(z) \wedge to(z,y))$$

Our normalization

In our normalization we translate a form of a natural language into a restricted subset of the same natural language,

In our case the first form is a dependency tree, obtained from the parser in stage (A). Such a tree may not be ideal for using with the theorem prover in stage (C). We therefore have to normalise such trees in order to adapt them for use with our chosen theorem proving strategy. Exactly what normalisation is required depends on the nature of the theorem prover. For example in Figure 5 we use the dependency tree in figure 5(b’) to obtain a subset of dependency tree by converting into the form (LHS → RHS) as in Figure 5(c’) and Figure 5(d’), using the rules in Figure 6(b, c, and d). Then in Figure 7&8 we simplified the sub-tree (c) and (d) to obtain the last version of sub-tree (e) & (f) as required for using with our theorem prover.

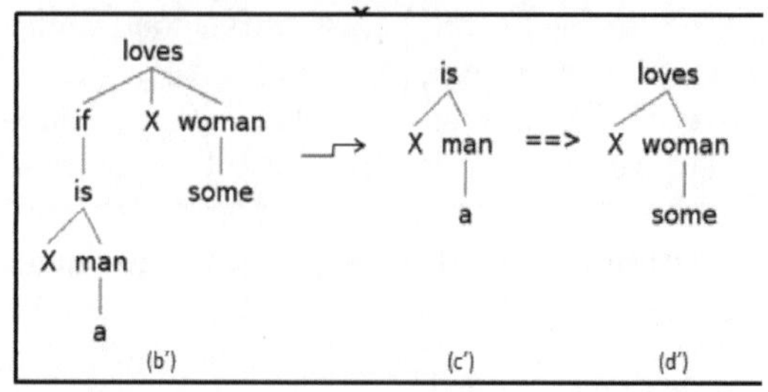

Figure 5: Convert the sentence into the form (LHS (c’) → RHS (d’)).

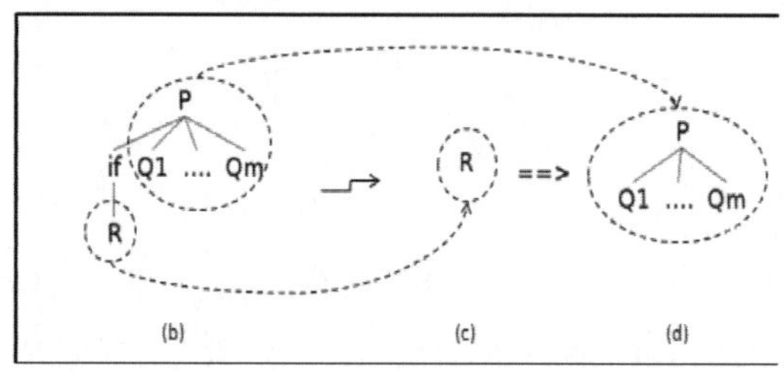

Figure 6: Rule for converting the sentence into the form (antecedent (c) → consequent (d)).

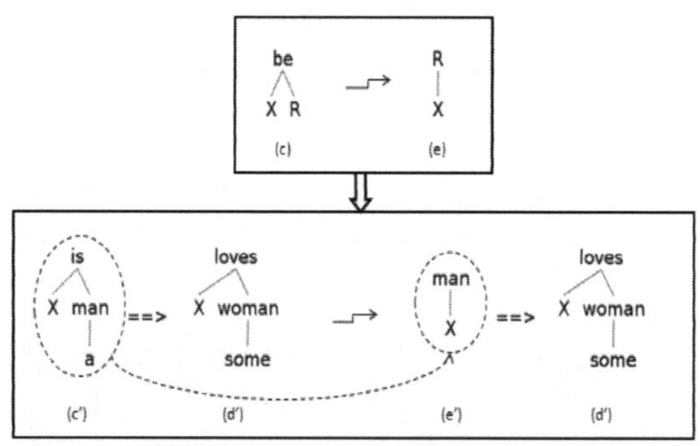

Figure 7:Simplifed subtree(c’) to subtree (e’) by applying the rule in (c) & (e).

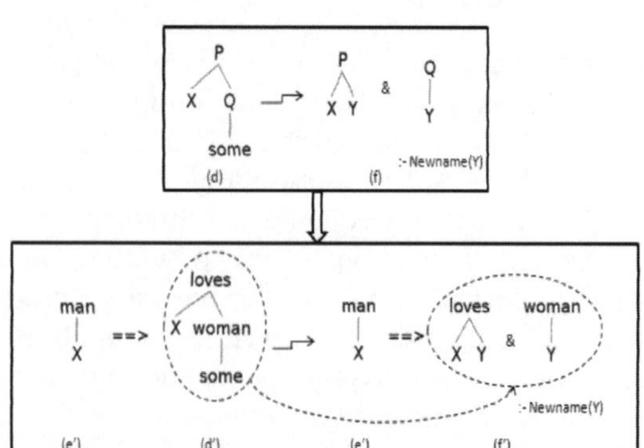

[1] “Discovery of Inference Rules from Text”.
[2] “Textual Entailment Anchor Set Extraction”.

Figure 8:Simplified subtree(d') into sub-tree(f') by applying the rule in (d) & (f).

2.3 Stage C: Inference Engine

The key to the current proposal is the observation that the central step in almost all current theorem provers, namely that given two sequents/clauses A_1 & ... & A_{n1} ==> C_1 *or* ... *or* C_{m1} *or X* and *X'* & A'_1 & ... & A'_{n2} ==> C'_1 *or* ... *or* C'_{m2} where *X* and *X'* can be unified by some unifier σ, you can 'cut' X to obtain σ (A_1 & ... & A_{n1} & A'_1 & ... & A'_{n2} ==> C_1 *or* ... *or* C_{m1} *or* C'_1 *or* ... *or* C'_{m2}).

There are numerous ways of invoking this rule: the key is that for the vast majority of theorem provers this rule is the core of the process.

It is worth noting that the elements of a rule need not be expressions of some formal logic. They usually are, but there is no a priori reason why they should be. They could, for instance, be the rules of a game: a program for playing chess might exploit rules which describe legal board transformations, a program for finding routes might exploit rules which describe links between places, ... In particular, they might be dependency trees.

This is clear enough for simple rules: if we allow natural language utterances to contain variables, then we can easily write rules like

X and Y used to be married if X and Y have got divorced

Rules like this can easily be applied using the standard rule of cut mentioned above. More interestingly, we can also us it to apply essentially higher-order rules such as

P are not Q if P used to be Q

We have previously shown how to extend SATCHMO (Manthey & Bry 1988) to cover intensionality (Ramsay 2001). The same machinery can be exploited to handle higher rules of the kind shown, which is crucial for handling natural language, where intensionality, type-shifting and other higher-order notions are rife.

We also intend to generalise the conditions under which cut applies. The standard rule requires *X* and *X'* to unify. Within the current framework, *X* and *X'* are trees. As such, we can use approximate matching, e.g. allowing *X'* to be subset of *X* to allow for the deletion of modifiers, or by allowing the terms that appear in *X'* to denote subsets of the corresponding terms in *X*.

These two moves will allow us to work directly with dependency trees, without making any assumptions about where these trees came from. We can thus avoid the need to translate into some target formal language: if some element of the antecedent of one rule matches an element of the consequent of another, subject to whatever constraints we put on the matching process, then we can use the rule.

3 Conclusion

We have proposed a strategy for carrying out inference over natural language sentences by applying standard theorem proving technology directly to dependency trees. This circumvents the need to translate from parse trees, of whatever kind, to formal logic, which has proved challenging for over forty years. It does introduce two risks: that the inference chaijns will become unsound, and that inference will become very slow. The first of these can be moderated by varying the conditions under which a partial match is allowed: if only exact matches are allowed, then there will be no risk, but rules which are potentially relevant may be missed, and as more flexibility in the matching process is permitted there will be more chance of mistakes but wider coverage. Similarly, if subtrees are only matched if they are term-unifiable then there should be no loss of speed, and as the conditions for matching are relaxed the process will become slower but more flexible.

Acknowledgements

Allan Ramsay's contribution to this work was supported by Qatar National Research Foundation grant NPRP 09-046-6-001. Amal Alshahran is supported by a grant from the government of the Kingdom of Saudi Arabia.

References

Alabbas, M & Ramsay A M, *Arabic Treebank: from Phrase-Structure Trees to Dependency Trees*, META-RESEARCH Workshop on Advanced Treebanking, LREC 2012, Istanbul, 61--68, 2012

Blackburn, P., Bos, J., Kohlhase, M., & De Nivelle, H. (2001). Inference and computational semantics. *In Computing Meaning* (pp. 11-28). Springer Netherlands.

Dagan, I. and Glickman, O. (2004). *Probabilistic textual entailment: generic applied modeling of language variability.* In Proceedings of the PA CAL Workshop on Learning Methods for Text Understanding and Mining, pp. 26–29, Grenoble, France.

Dale, R., Moisl, H. L., & Somers, H. L. (Eds.). (2000*). Handbook of natural language pr cessing. CRC Press*.

Degtyarev, A. I., Lyaletski, A. V., & Morokhovets, M. K. (1999, January). *Evidence algorithm and sequent logical inference search*. In Logic for Programming and Automated Reasoning (pp. 44-61). Springer Berlin Heidelberg.

Dolan, W. B., Quirk, C., and Brockett, C.. 2004. *Unsupervised Construction of Large Paraphrase Corpora: Exploiting Massively Parallel News Sources*. In Proceedings of COLING 2004.

Kouylekov, M., & Magnini, B. (2005, April). *Recognizing textual entailment with tree edit distance algorithms*. In Proceedings of the First Challenge Workshop Recognising Textual Entailment (pp. 17-20).

Lin, D. and Pantel, P. (2001). *DIRT-discovery of inference rules from text*. In Proceedings of the 7th ACM SIGKDD Conference on Knowledge Discovery and Data Mining, pp. 323–328, San Francisco, California, USA. doi:10.1145/502512.502559.

Lukasova, A., Zacek, M., Vajgl, M., & Kotyrba, M. (2012). *Resolution reasoning by RDF Clausal Form Logic*. International Journal of Computer Science, 9.

MacCartney, B. (2009). *Natural language inference* (Doctoral dissertation, Stanford University).
Manthey, R., & Bry, F. (1988, January). *SATCHMO: a theorem prover implemented in Prolog*. In 9th International Conference on Automated Deduction (pp. 415-434). Springer Berlin Heidelberg.

Ovchinnikova, E. (2012). *Integration of world knowledge for natural language understanding* (Vol. 3). Springer.

Ramsay, A.M., Theorem proving for untyped constructive lambda-calculus: implementation and application, *Logic Journal of the Interest Group in Pure and Applied Logics,* 9(1), 89-106, 2001

Ramsay, A.M., (1999). *Parsing with discontinuous phrases*. Natural Language Engineering, 5(3):271–300,doi:10.1017/S1351324900002242.

Seville, H. and Ramsay, A. (2001). *Capturing sense in intensional contexts*. In Proceedings of the 4th International Workshop on Computational Semantics, pp. 319–334, Tilburg, The Netherlands.

Textual Inference and Meaning Representation in Human Robot Interaction

Bastianelli Emanuele[1], Giuseppe Castellucci[2], Danilo Croce[3], Roberto Basili[3]
[1]DICII, [2]DIE, [3]DII
University of Roma, Tor Vergata
00133 Roma, Italy
{bastianelli,castellucci}@ing.uniroma2.it
{croce,basili}@info.uniroma2.it

Abstract

This paper provides a first investigation over existing textual inference paradigms in order to propose a generic framework able to capture major semantic aspects in Human Robot Interaction (HRI). We investigate the use of general semantic paradigms used in Natural Language Understanding (NLU) tasks, such as Semantic Role Labeling, over typical robot commands. The semantic information obtained is then represented under the *Abstract Meaning Representation*. AMR is a general representation language useful to express different level of semantic information without a strong dependence to the syntactic structure of an underlying sentence. The final aim of this work is to find an effective synergy between HRI and NLU.

1 Introduction

As robots are being marketed for consumer applications (viz. telepresence, cleaning or entertainment) natural language interaction is expected to make them more appealing and accessible to the end user. The latest technologies in speech recognition are available on cheap computing devices, thus enabling different levels of interaction. The first level needed in HRI is the command understanding. This is a challenging task as it consists not only in understanding the utterance meaning, but also in translating it into the robot-specific command. In the recent years, works about the interpretation of natural language (NL) instructions in a specific environments, e.g. allowing a simulated robot to navigate to a specified location, has been oriented to cover a specific subset of the language (Kruijff et al., 2007; Bos and Oka, 2007). This led to very powerful and formalized systems that are, at the same time, very specific and limited in terms of expressiveness. In many NLP tasks where robustness is crucial, e.g. Question Answering as discussed in (Ferrucci et al., 2010), methods based on Statistical Learning (SL) theory have been used to overcome such issues in the support of complex Textual Inference tasks, as in (Chen and Mooney, 2011).

In this paper, instead of focusing on specific language understanding algorithms, we investigate the combination of state-of-the-art textual inference technologies in order to design effective systems for HRI. The final aim of this research is to propose a unifying framework able to capture semantic aspects as these are needed in the HRI area. We foster the idea that many problems tackled and solved in Natural Language Processing, c.g. Semantic Role Labeling (SRL) (Palmer et al., 2010), can be taken into account for HRI. Existing techniques can be used to automatically acquire useful semantic representations to interpret robot commands as investigated in (Thomas and Jenkins, 2012). Let us consider a domotic scenario where a robot receives vocal instructions, e.g. "*take the book on the table*". We think that the command targeted by this utterance can be expressed through the adoption of semantic roles as defined in existing lexical theories, as discussed in (Fillmore, 1985) or (Levin, 1993). Moreover, the generalization level offered by this representation can be improved to better reflect human instructions with the environment where the robots are acting into. For example, we can extend the semantic roles in order to properly capture spatial as well as temporal expressions. These can be crucial for the robot to understand spatial relations between objects in the space or temporal references that are necessary to correctly plan the intended action sequence.

Accordingly, among the investigated theories, we will focus on the use of the Frame Semantics

(Fillmore, 1985) and Spatial Semantics (Zlatev, 2007). While the former aims at addressing the problem of scene and event understanding, the latter specifically focuses on the spatial relations involved. It enables a planning and reasoning module to correctly disambiguate objects in the world the robot is acting into. We propose the use of a general structure to represent all the semantics we are interested in. In fact, a typical problem when working with different representations, is that they are totally independent each other. They are not designed to work together in a more general semantic framework. In order to do it, we investigate the use of a new and appealing representation formalism, i.e. *Abstract Meaning Representation* (AMR) (Banarescu et al., 2013). It allows to express semantics without imposing any strong bias to the original sentence or syntactic structure. The final instantiated AMR annotation could be easily mapped to the commands expressed in the robot language (e.g. the logic form), in a way similar to the one proposed in (Thomas and Jenkins, 2012).

In order to prove the effectiveness of the proposed idea, we evaluated existing natural language technologies not customized to the target HRI scenario. In the rest of the paper, in Section 2 different Natural Language Processing tasks are discussed with respect the HRI area. Finally, in Section 3 the conclusion and future works about a new robotic-centric corpus are derived.

2 From Human Voice to Robot Instructions through NLP

A complete NL processing chain for an agent acting in an environment (real or virtual) should be realized as follow: starting from an utterance, a textual representation is obtained from a generic Automatic Speech Recognizer (ASR) (e.g. the CMU Sphinx (Walker et al., 2004)); morpho-syntactic modules (e.g. Stanford CoreNLP (Klein and Manning, 2003)) are then applied; finally, the semantic information is extracted by semantic parsing processors. Starting from this last information, a specific *mapping module* translates the so represented meaning of a sentence in the corresponding robot command.

In this section, different NLP semantic processing tasks useful for robot instructions understanding are described. An evaluation of each task is addressed using 20 commands typical of an HRI scenario. They come from a larger corpus we are labeling to capture major semantic aspects for HRI. These sentences are manually annotated with respect to syntax, part-of-speech tags, parse trees and semantics, with respect to Frame Semantics (Fillmore, 1985) and Spatial Roles (Kordjamshidi et al., 2012). Annotations have been carried out by two of the authors, while conflicts have been resolved by a third one. In the following, a possible NLU pipeline is discussed.

From Voice to Text. The first step in a robot instruction understanding scenario is the automatic transcription of vocal commands. Transcriptions of the utterances are obtained by the audio signal processing performed by ASRs. The ASR engines are usually classified depending on the technique used to generate the Language Model. Two different approaches can be followed for this purpose. The first one, which is called *command-and-control* and is used in the development of several vocal interfaces for commercial systems (i.e. telephone customer care, reservation systems). It requires a grammar-based language specification, typically through Context Free Grammars. The second approach, called *free-form speech*, relies directly on statistical techniques over very large corpora (millions of words), by computing probabilities of sequences of words. While in command-and-control engines it is possible to enrich the grammar with higher-level information, such as attaching semantic information to each rule, in free-form speech engines an external and independent module to compute the desired representation is needed. The use of a grammar-based approach can simplify the semantic parsing process at the expense of coverage, i.e. the constraints imposed to the set of recognized lexicons and utterances. From this point of view, free-form speech systems cover a wider range of linguistic phenomena. For example, in the work of (Thomas and Jenkins, 2012) the official Google speech APIs of the Android environment is used as a free-form speech engine. A *Word Error Rate* of 24% is measured using the Google speech APIs over the 20 test robot commands. It is a promising result, considering that very few sentences are pronounced by English native speakers.

Morphosyntactic Analysis. The last two decades of NLP research have seen the proliferation of tools and resources that reached a significant maturity after 90's. We evaluated a well known platform for the general language processing chain, that is the Stanford Core NLP platform[1]. It includes tokenization, POS tagging, Named Entity Recognition as well as parsing and is mostly based on statistical, e.g. max-entropy, models for language processing. We want to evaluate the use of these tools to achieve a good command recognition accuracy for a robot. Usually, in NLU morphosyntactic analysis can be crucial to provide features that words alone are not sufficient to express. For example, the dependency parse tree of an utterance could be used in further processing, such as in SRL. We measured the quality of the Stanford parser in terms of *Unlabeled Attachment Score* (UAS) and *Labeled Attachment Score* (LAS) on our 20 test utterances. The former aims at verifying the ability of an algorithm to identify a syntactic relation, while the latter aims at measuring the quality of the relation labeling. We report an accuracy of 87% in UAS and 83% of LAS.

Modeling commands through Semantic Roles. An appropriate theory is necessary in order to capture useful semantics for robot instructions. We argue that Frame Semantics (Fillmore, 1985) could be a good choice to represent different aspects of a robot command. *Frames* are the main structure used to represent and generalize events or actions. They are micro-theories about real world situations (e.g. `movement actions`, such as *moving*, `events`, such as *natural phenomena*, and `properties`, such as *being colored*). Each frame provides its set of semantic roles, i.e. the different elements involved in the situation described by the frame (e.g. an *Agent*). FrameNet (Baker et al., 1998) is a semantic resource reflecting Fillmore's Frame Semantics. In FrameNet lexical entries (such as verbs, nouns or adjectives) are linked to *Frames*, and the roles, expressing the participants in the underlying event, are mapped to *frame elements*. FrameNet has produced an extensive collection of frames as well as a large scale annotated corpus. For example, for the sentence "*take the book on the table*" the following representation is produced: ***take*** [*the book*]$_{Theme}$ [*on the table*]$_{Source}$. In this structure, the different aspects of the TAKING event are highlighted, as the roles THEME and PLACE, suitable for further processing. Frame Semantics can provide a bridge between the linguistic information of a command and its inner robot representation.

We applied Babel, a general purpose SRL system[2] (Croce and Basili, 2011; Croce et al., 2012), to the test sentences. In table 1 results for three different sub-tasks of a SRL chain are reported. In particular, Precision, Recall and F1-Measure are shown for the tasks *Frame Prediction* (FP), *Boundary Detection* (BD), and *Argument Classification* (AC). The first one aims at determining the events evoked in a sentence. The second one is intended to identify the roles involved with respect to a frame. The last one is the task of assigning a label to each role. Performances are lower with respect to the state-of-the-art as, on the one hand, the adopted system was not trained to deal with domain specific phenomena, such as the verb *to be*. On the other hand, the FP badly performed on spoken sentences with jargon expressions, such as "*close the water*", consequently biasing the AC step.

	Precision	Recall	F1-Measure
FP	0.71	0.6	0.65
BD	0.81	0.70	0.75
AC	0.58	0.50	0.54

Table 1: SRL measures on 20 robot commands.

Describing Robot Environment through Spatial Roles. One of the main functions of language is to communicate spatial relationships between objects in the world. Frame Semantics seems inadequate to represent this information at the level of granularity needed by the grounding process of a robotic system. A more specific semantic theory seems thus required and its impact is investigated.

Recently, *Spatial Role Labeling* (SpRL) (Kordjamshidi et al., 2011) was defined as the problem of extracting generic spatial semantics from natural language. The underlying theory is the *holistic spatial semantic theory* (Zlatev, 2007). It defines the basic concepts in the spatial domain of the natural language that help to determine the location or trajectory of motion of a given referent in the discourse. For example, a spatial utterance must address a TRAJECTOR, i.e. the entity whose location is of relevance, or the LANDMARK, i.e. the reference entity in relation to which the location of the trajectory of motion is specified. The SpRL task aims at extracting spatial semantic roles from sentences. Thus, in the sentence "*take the book on the table*", a system should recognize that the preposition "*on*" is the SPATIAL INDICATOR of the relation between "*book*" and "*table*", respectively

[1] `http://nlp.stanford.edu/software/corenlp.shtml`

[2] The system is not domain specific, since it is trained on the FrameNet 1.5 dataset

	Precision	Recall	F1-Measure
SI	0.78	0.84	0.81
TR	0.80	0.61	0.70
TD	0.75	0.75	0.75

Table 2: Spatial Role Labeling results.

a TRAJECTOR and a LANDMARK. These information should help a robotic system to correctly determine which book has to be taken within the physical world, i.e. the one on the table. In table 2 we report performance measures in terms of Precision, Recall and F1-Measure of a Spatial Role Labeler (Bastianelli et al., 2013).These results refer to the SPATIAL INDICATOR (SI), TRAJECTOR (TR) and LANDMARK (LD) (Kordjamshidi et al., 2011) labeling on the 20 test sentences used above.

Expressing Rich Semantic Information through AMR. In order to integrate the information conveyed by the Frame Semantics and the Spatial Semantics, we want to propose a representation flexible and as much as possible close to the domotic domain, i.e. the robot language. The Abstract Meaning Representation (AMR) (Banarescu et al., 2013) is a novel semantic representation language that allows to represent semantics in an abstract way, focusing on concepts, their instances and the relations among them. According to this notation, the meaning of a sentence is represented as a rooted, labeled (acyclic) graph, where the semantic structure is built in a recursive way. In AMR, sentences that have different syntactic structures but basically the same meaning are represented by the same structure. While the AMR proposed in (Banarescu et al., 2013) uses the PropBank frame sets (Palmer et al., 2010), we want to adopt it to embed the semantics coming both from Frame Semantics and Spatial Semantics. The command "*take the book on the table*" will be represented as follows:

```
(t / take – Taking
    : Theme(b / book)
    : Source(t1 / table)
    : location(o / on
            : trajector(b))
            : landmark(t1)))
```

Here, *book* and *table* represent concepts; `b` and `t1` are the instances respectively related. Frame Semantics is represented by the instance `t` of the verb *take*, evoking the frame `Taking`. In a similar way, the two semantic roles `Theme` and `Source` are defined as the instances `b` and `t1`. The spatial relation `location` is defined across the two semantic roles, linking the `b` instance to the `t1` through the preposition *on*. This structure appears to be very agile for computing and for the HRI interface design. It can be seen as the abstraction step in the representation of meaning, used before the final translation into the logic-like formalism. This latter is closer to the robot representation, but more complex to manage. The tree-like structure of AMR makes it very easy to navigate, elaborate and visualize. Furthermore, many consolidated formalism can be derived from this one, as neo-davidsonian Discourse Representation Structures (Bos and Oka, 2007). While DRSs are closest to a possible representation of the world a robot might have, AMR offers a promising degree of abstraction, especially because we want to follow a data-driven approach, without relying on too rigid representations or tools. It seems to embed in a logic-like formalism all the information needed for the symbol grounding process of a robot, such as relation between linguistic objects as well as roles. Actually, a mapping procedure to compile the final AMR representation is under development.

3 Conclusion and Future Work

In this paper, we discussed the possibility of combining state-of-the-art textual inference technologies in the design of HRI architectures. Moreover, we experimented standard NL inference tools to verify the quality achievable by current technologies. This is the first step of a research that aims at defining a unified framework able to capture the major semantic aspects of linguistic utterances within the HRI field. Clearly, many aspects of this challenging research area are underway. A deeper investigation of the semantic theories and representation schemata is still needed. As we are interested in data driven paradigms, we need to improve the adaptation capability of existing technologies and to provide more labeled data for them. At the moment, we collected about 450 audio streams (recorded during the Robocup 2013) expressing generic robot commands from different speakers. We are starting labeling them according to the semantic theories investigated in this paper. We are planning to release the annotated resource, as soon as a significant amount of annotated sentences has been produced. Further evaluations are finally needed to investigate the impact of the error rate through the entire pipeline.

References

Collin F. Baker, Charles J. Fillmore, and John B. Lowe. 1998. The berkeley framenet project. In *Proceedings of the 36th Annual Meeting of the Association for Computational Linguistics and 17th International Conference on Computational Linguistics - Volume 1*, Association for Computational Linguistics '98, pages 86–90, Stroudsburg, PA, USA. Association for Computational Linguistics.

Laura Banarescu, Claire Bonial, Shu Cai, Madalina Georgescu, Kira Griffitt, Ulf Hermjakob, Kevin Knight, Philipp Koehn, Martha Palmer, and Nathan Schneider. 2013. Abstract meaning representation for sembanking. In *Proceedings of the 7th Linguistic Annotation Workshop and Interoperability with Discourse*, pages 178–186, Sofia, Bulgaria, August. Association for Computational Linguistics.

Emanuele Bastianelli, Danilo Croce, Daniele Nardi, and Roberto Basili. 2013. Unitor-hmm-tk: Structured kernel-based learning for spatial role labeling. In *Proceedings of the 7th International Workshop on Semantic Evaluation (SemEval-2013)*, Atlanta, Georgia, USA, June.

Johan Bos and Tetsushi Oka. 2007. A spoken language interface with a mobile robot. *Artificial Life and Robotics*, 11(1):42–47.

David L. Chen and Raymond J. Mooney. 2011. Learning to interpret natural language navigation instructions from observations. In *Proceedings of the 25th AAAI Conference on Artificial Intelligence (AAAI-2011)*, pages 859–865.

Danilo Croce and Roberto Basili. 2011. Structured learning for semantic role labeling. In *AI*IA*, pages 238–249.

Danilo Croce, Giuseppe Castellucci, and Emanuele Bastianelli. 2012. Structured learning for semantic role labeling. *Intelligenza Artificiale*, 6(2):163–176.

David Ferrucci, Eric Brown, Jennifer Chu-Carroll, James Fan, David Gondek, Aditya A. Kalyanpur, Adam Lally, J. William Murdock, Eric Nyberg, John Prager, Nico Schlaefer, and Chris Welty. 2010. Building Watson: An Overview of the DeepQA Project. *AI Magazine*, 31(3).

Charles J. Fillmore. 1985. Frames and the semantics of understanding. *Quaderni di Semantica*, 6(2):222–254.

Dan Klein and Christopher D. Manning. 2003. Accurate unlexicalized parsing. In *Proceedings of ACL'03*, pages 423–430.

Parisa Kordjamshidi, Martijn Van Otterlo, and Marie-Francine Moens. 2011. Spatial role labeling: Towards extraction of spatial relations from natural language. *ACM Trans. Speech Lang. Process.*, 8(3):4:1–4:36, December.

Parisa Kordjamshidi, Steven Bethard, and Marie-Francine Moens. 2012. SemEval-2012 task 3: Spatial role labeling. In **SEM 2012: The First Joint Conference on Lexical and Computational Semantics – Volume 1: Proceedings of the Main Conference and the Shared Task, and Volume 2: Proceedings of the Sixth International Workshop on Semantic Evaluation (SemEval 2012),*, pages 365–373. Association for Computational Linguistics, June.

Geert-Jan M. Kruijff, Hendrik Zender, Patric Jensfelt, and Henrik I. Christensen. 2007. Situated dialogue and spatial organization: What, where... and why? *International Journal of Advanced Robotic Systems*, 4(2).

Beth Levin. 1993. *English Verb Classes and Alternations A Preliminary Investigation.* University of Chicago Press, Chicago and London.

Martha Palmer, Daniel Gildea, and Nianwen Xue. 2010. *Semantic Role Labeling.* Synthesis Lectures on Human Language Technologies. Morgan & Claypool Publishers.

Brian J Thomas and Odest Chadwicke Jenkins. 2012. Roboframenet: Verb-centric semantics for actions in robot middleware. In *Robotics and Automation (ICRA), 2012 IEEE International Conference on*, pages 4750–4755. IEEE.

Willie Walker, Paul Lamere, Philip Kwok, Bhiksha Raj, Rita Singh, Evandro Gouvea, Peter Wolf, and Joe Woelfel. 2004. Sphinx-4: A flexible open source framework for speech recognition.

Jordan Zlatev. 2007. Spatial semantics. *Handbook of Cognitive Linguistics*, pages 318–350.

An empirical classification of verbs based on Semantic Types: the case of the 'poison' verbs

Jane Bradbury
RIILP
University of Wolverhampton
J.Bradbury3@wlv.ac.uk

Ismail El Maarouf
RIILP
University of Wolverhampton
i.el-maarouf@wlv.ac.uk

Abstract

This article proposes a new approach to verb classification based on Semantic Types selected in corpus-based verb patterns. This work draws on Hanks's theory of Norms and Exploitations (Hanks 2013) and applies Corpus Pattern Analysis to a subset of verbs from Levin's 'poison' class, including verbs such as *hang* and *stab*. These patterns are taken from the Pattern Dictionary of English Verbs, which aims at recording prototypical phraseological patterns for the most frequent verbs of English using the British National Corpus.

1 Introduction

This article proposes a new approach to verb classification based on Semantic Types (STs) of the verbs' arguments. This work draws on Hanks's theory of Norms and Exploitations (Hanks 2013) and applies Corpus Pattern Analysis to a subset of verbs from Levin's 'poison' class (class 42.2) [*asphyxiate, crucify, drown, hang, knife, poison, smother, stab, strangle, suffocate:* those verbs available in PDEV at the time of writing], (Levin 1993: 232-233). The patterns are taken from the Pattern Dictionary of English Verbs (PDEV[1]), which records prototypical patterns of use for English verbs in the British National Corpus[2].

This paper focuses on the patterns that relate to the 'literal' (i.e. killing-related) senses of the 'poison' verbs. According to Levin, they 'lexicalize a means component and it is this means that differentiates amongst them'. For example, the verb *poison* entails the notion that an attempt to kill is being made by means of a poisonous substance, whereas the verb *knife* entails the notion of a knife as a means of killing.

Levin argues that the meaning of the verb determines to a large extent its syntactic behaviour. She therefore undertakes the description of English verb classes that share both syntactic alternations and similar meaning. This claim bears comparison with empirical work in Corpus Linguistics, such as Sinclair's account of *yield* (Sinclair 1990: 53-65), where convincing evidence that sense and syntax are closely associated was found. Similar claims are made in Natural Language Processing, especially in distributional models of meaning (Grefenstette 1994; Bieman & Giesbrecht 2011) used in a large number of applications (Cohen & Widdows 2009).

Levin's verb classes have been integrated and extended into a lexical resource for Natural Language Processing (NLP), VerbNet[3] (Kipper et al. 2008) used in applications such as Semantic Role Labelling (Swier et al. 2004). The present paper proposes to create a semantic network from PDEV, by building strings of STs and linking them to verbs. One of the motivations behind this work is that PDEV contains useful information which is absent in NLP resources: while VerbNet analyses the interface between thematic roles (e.g. Agent, Patient) and selectional restrictions (e.g. [+ANIMATE], [+CONCRETE]), PDEV maps clause roles (e.g. Subject, Object) using STs (e.g. [[Human]], [[Location]]).

This paper describes the background and methodology for this work (section 2) and provides a detailed analysis of Levin's claims about the 'poison' verb class (section 3), before describing results obtained from using the semantic network (section 4).

[1] freely available at http://deb.fi.muni.cz/pdev/
[2] available at www.natcorp.ox.ac.uk/
[3] see http://verbs.colorado.edu/verb-index/index.php

2 Methodology

2.1 Background

Corpus Pattern Analysis (CPA) is a new technique for mapping meaning onto words in text (Hanks 2012). The focus of CPA is on analysing large corpora to identify the prototypical syntagmatic and collocational patterns with which words are associated. It has simultaneously given rise to a new theory of language in use, the Theory of Norms and Exploitations (TNE, see Hanks 2013), which can be compared with Pattern Grammar (Hunston and Francis 2000) and Construction Grammar (Goldberg 1995).

PDEV (in progress) aims to provide a well-founded corpus-driven account of verb meaning, using STs to stand as prototypes for collocational clusters occurring in each clause role. Current CPA practice has shown that the scientific concepts from WordNet[4], the most widely used semantic repository, do not map well onto words as they are actually used; this is partly because folk concepts, and not scientific concepts, form the foundation of meaning in natural language (Wierzbicka 1984). For this reason, a new shallow Ontology consisting of 225 STs has been developed for PDEV which contrasts with WordNet in the following key respects:

- WordNet contains many scientific concepts, whereas the PDEV Ontology is modeled on folk concepts, for example, WordNet has over 50 hyponyms for *Animate Being*, whereas PDEV has only 17 STs listed under [[Animate]];
- WordNet is intuition-based whereas the PDEV Ontology is 'corpus-driven' and built from the words upwards.

For each verb in PDEV, a sample of ~250 lines is analysed and phraseological norms, or patterns, identified and then recorded using STs. For example, in the account of pattern 1 of *strangle*, below, the STs [[Human 1]] and [[Human 2]] are used to indicate that, prototypically, it is a human who performs the action of strangling and they typically perform this act upon another human.

(1) [[Human 1]] strangle [[Human 2]]

Where relevant, information about adverbial phrases is recorded as part of the pattern. For example, pattern 1 of *drown*, below, records that this use of *drown* frequently selects an adverbial phrase indicating in which [[Watercourse]] or what type of [[Liquid]] the drowning occurred.

(2) [[Human | Animal]] drown [NO OBJ] (in [[Watercourse]] | in [[Liquid]])

These STs form the basis of the semantic network, which generates semantic strings from patterns and link them to verbs.

2.2 A semantic network for verbs

PDEV allows for a new kind of verb classification, by clustering verbs according to the STs with which they combine across patterns. To explore this method further, PDEV patterns have been simplified to semantic strings, i.e. combinations of types in various pattern positions. More specifically, semantic strings are the result of the following two changes to the PDEV patterns:

- only STs and lexical sets of subjects, objects, adverbials, adverbial functions, and prepositions are kept and concatenated;
- since patterns allow for several alternative STs in the same clause role and for these clause roles to be optional, all combinations are generated.

Based on the analysis of more than 3500 patterns available in the PDEV, the current version of the network totals over 5064 different semantic strings, with 955 of them linking more than one verb (covering over 71% of patterns). This allows the identification of both the different strings a verb combines with and the verbs clustered around each semantic string. For example, the semantic string '[[Human]] verb [[Human]]', accounting for the transitive use of verbs such as *corner* and *sacrifice,* is the largest cluster of the network, with 188 verbs. Lastly, the network offers the possibility of computing the similarity between verbs, using their shared strings, and applying standard distributional methods.

3 Levin's hypotheses

3.1 Instrumental Phrases

Levin hypothesizes that few of the 'poison' verbs 'will select instrumental phrases (IPs), but that where this is the case, the instrumental phrase is a "cognate"'. Table 1 lists the proportion of tokens combining with IPs for each PDEV pattern, focusing on the patterns which relate to the 'literal' (ie killing-related) senses and with a non-instrumental subject, i.e. [[Human]], [[Institution]] or [[Animate]].

[4] see http://wordnet.princeton.edu/

It is notable that only *crucify* and *knife* – verbs where the means is lexicalized unambiguously – generated zero returns. Elsewhere, contrary to Levin's hypothesis, the selection of instrumental phrases is not infrequent. This could be explained by the broadness of the set of instruments lexicalized by verbs such as *stab* or *hang* (see below). It is interesting to compare the three patterns of *hang* illustrated below: '[[Human 1 | Institution]] hang [[Human 2]]' rarely selects an instrumental phrase, presumably because in this context, where the event described is a formally decreed execution, the instrument used (i.e. *rope, gallows*) is unambiguous. However, '[[Human]] hang [NO OBJ] ([Adv[Location]])' and '[[Human]] hang [Self]' both describe 'unofficial' acts where the instrument used cannot be taken for granted, and in both these patterns the verb selects an IP with relatively high frequency.

Levin's hypothesis, that where an instrumental phrase is used it will be a 'cognate', holds, if 'cognate' is taken to mean 'an object with similar physical properties to the object prototypically used to commit the act in question'.

The instrumental phrases for *stab* include cognates such as *carving knife*, *sheath knife*, and *butcher's knife*, along with the less conventional *screwdriver* and *pencil*. For the previously-mentioned 'unofficial' senses of *hang*, the instrumental phrases include, *rope, string, a belt,* and *blanket torn into strips*. The broad and open-ended nature of these lexical sets (i.e. 'anything sharp and pointed', or 'anything long, thin, flexible and rope-like') suggests that where the means lexicalized by a verb is ambiguous, it is not unusual for an instrumental phrase to be selected.

3.2 STs as subjects

Levin hypothesizes that few of the 'poison' verbs 'allow instrumental subjects'.

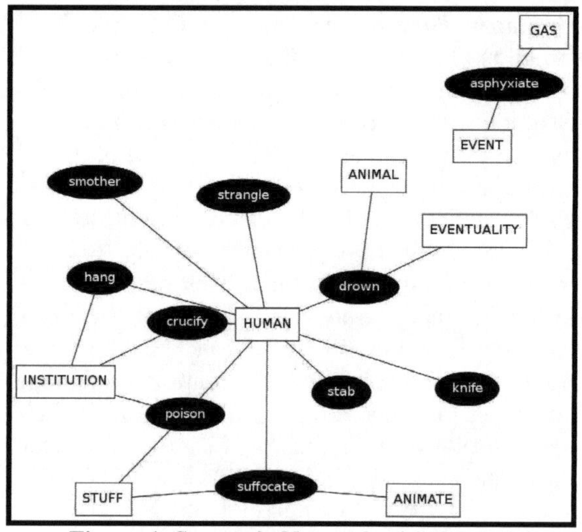

Figure 1. Semantic Network of Subjects

Verb pattern	no of lines with IPs
[[Human 1]] **crucify** [[Human 2]]	0/40
[[Human | Animal]] **drown** [NO OBJ] (in [[Watercourse]] | in [[Liquid]])	25/76*
[[Human]] **drown** [Self]	2/6*
[[Human 1 | Eventuality]] **drown** [[Human 2 | Animal]]	10/51*
[[Human 1 | Institution]] **hang** [[Human 2]]	3/45
[[Human]] **hang** [NO OBJ] ([Adv[Location]])	20/39
[[Human]] **hang** [Self]	12/55
[[Human 1]] **knife** [[Human 2]] (in [[Body Part]] | to {death})	0/22
[[Human 1 | Institution]] **poison** [[Human 2 | Animate]]	5/69
[[Human | Institution | {Stuff = Toxic}]] **poison** [[Location | Watercourse]]	9/31
[[Human 1]] **smother** [[Human 2]]	1/6
[[Human 1]] **stab** [[Human 2]] (in [[Body Part]] | through [[Body Part]]) (to {death})	30/198
[[Human 1]] **strangle** [[Human 2]]	9/84
[[Human | Animate]] **suffocate** [NO OBJ]	10/30**
[[Stuff | Human 1 | Animate 1]] suffocate [[Human 2 | Animate 2]]	6/23**

*This includes references to location where it is [[Watercourse]] or [[Liquid]].

**This includes references to events which caused the suffocation.

Table 1. Instrumental phrases

In order to investigate this aspect further, STs in Subject position have been extracted from the semantic network (Figure 1). As can be seen, both Instrument and Agent roles occur as subjects: the subjects are [[Gas]], [[Stuff]], [[Event]] and [[Eventuality]]. In conformity with Levin's claim, [[Stuff]] accounts for relatively few subjects for *suffocate* (25%) and *poison* (12%). In contrast, in our sample *asphyxiate* was only observed to select [[Gas]] and [[Event]] as subjects. The network also reveals subjects that are neither Agents nor Instruments, represented by the ST [[Eventuality]] (example 3).

(3) A rock-fall into Shimbara Bay caused three **surges** which *drowned* 15,000 people.

Figure 1 also shows how verbs can be grouped according to STs: all verbs except *asphyxiate* select [[Human]] in subject position. In addition, *poison*, *hang* and *crucify* all select [[Human]] and [[Institution]] as subjects.

4 ST-based classification

4.1 Literal senses of 'poison' verbs

The semantic network records a total of 161 semantic strings for the 'poison' verbs, only 28 of which are related to 'killing', and 9 strings cluster two or more verbs. The largest cluster is around the string '[[Human]] verb [[Human]]', which is selected by all verbs with the exception of *asphyxiate* (see 3.2). No strings provide evidence that *asphyxiate* belongs to the 'poison' class, as opposed to e.g. *poison* and *suffocate*, which share three strings.

The network includes strings of '[[Human]] verb [NO OBJ]' for *hang, drown,* and *suffocate*, which are inchoative alternations of the transitive/causative pattern. Levin has these alternations as a separate class ['suffocate' verbs] which only includes *asphyxiate, choke, drown, stifle* and *suffocate*. Levin does not list *hang* as having an inchoative use in the 'killing' sense, but evidence is found in the corpus (40 examples out of 500) as in *He was sentenced to hang*.

Reflexive object uses such as in '[[Human]] verb [SELF]' for *drown* and *hang* have not been identified by Levin (see Obligatorily Reflexive Objects class), but must be accounted for.

Strings that include adverbials are relevant to *knife* and *stab*, which share '[[Human]] verb [[Human]] {to death}' (resultative), and '[[Human]] verb [[Human]] {in [[Body Part]]}'. These adverbial phrases serve to clarify some of the semantic ambiguity that these verbs entail, i.e. whether or not the action resulted in death, and the body part affected; verbs such as *asphyxiate* and *strangle* entail no such ambiguity and are not observed to select these adverbial patterns.

4.2 Extended meanings of 'poison' verbs

The semantic network identifies similarities beyond those previously discussed where the focus has been on strings entailing the notion of 'killing'. Semantic strings extend to non-[[Human]] patients as exemplified by '[[Human]] verb [[Physical Object]]' (*smother, hang*). Here, the verb does not entail 'killing', e.g. *hanging* a lamp or *smothering* burning clothes with blankets.

Moreover, some strings entail metaphorical meanings. For example, *drown* and *smother* share the '[[Sound]] verb [[Sound]]' string; both patterns can be interpreted literally as one [[Sound]] being so loud that another [[Sound]] cannot be heard. *Strangle* and *suffocate* share the string '[[Anything]] verb [[Eventuality]]'; both conveying the notion that an [[Eventuality]] can be hindered or brought to an undesired end by [[Anything]]. The network thus helps to unveil the fact that the similarities between verbs can hold on several dimensions of meaning: whilst the 'poison' verbs also select strings which express a means of killing, some of them share other strings which are not covered in Levin's book.

5 Conclusion and perspectives

This paper has proposed a new approach to verb classification based on strings of STs (selected from a well-founded ontology) extracted from a semantic network based on PDEV patterns. Focusing on the 'poison' verbs has enabled the identification of key differences between this resource and Levin's account. The paper has studied the hypothesis that the 'poison' verbs lexicalize a means, through claims made on syntactic and semantic constraints on prepositional phrases and subjects. The analysis has revealed that this class must be revised in light of corpus evidence, and that sub-groupings can be made.

This work will be extended to:

- systematically explore the network with NLP techniques (e.g. distributional methods) to rank the similarity between verbs;
- investigate degrees of ambiguity in lexicalization focusing on instrumental phrases and instrumental subjects;
- explore metaphorical class extension.

Acknowledgements

We would like to thank Patrick Hanks and anonymous reviewers for their comments on an earlier draft. This work was supported by AHRC grant [DVC, AH/J005940/1, 2012-2015].

References

Chris Biemann and Eugenie Giesbrecht. 2011. *Proceedings of the Workshop on Distributional Semantics and Compositionality*. Portland: ACL. http://www.aclweb.org/anthology/W11-13

Lou Burnard. 1995. *Users' reference guide to the British National Corpus*. Oxford: Oxford University Computing Services.

Trevor Cohen, Dominic Widdows. 2009. Empirical distributional semantics: Methods and biomedical applications. *Journal of Biomedical Informatics*, Volume 42 (2). pp 390-405.

Christiane Fellbaum (1998). *WordNet: An Electronic Lexical Database*. Cambridge MA: MIT Press.

Gill Francis and Susan Hunston. 2000. *Pattern Grammar: A corpus-driven approach to the lexical grammar of English (Studies in Corpus Linguistics)*. Amsterdam: John Benjamins.

Adele Goldberg. 1995. *Constructions: A Construction Grammar Approach to Argument Structure (Cognitive Theory of Language and Culture Series)*. Chicago: University of Chicago Press.

Gregory Grefenstette. 1994. *Explorations in automatic thesaurus discovery*. Boston: KAP.

Patrick Hanks. 2012. How people use words to makes meanings: Semantic Types meet Valencies. In Alex Boulton and James Thomas (eds.) *Input, Process and Product: Developments in Teaching and Language Corpora*. Masaryk, Czech Republic: Masaryk University Press, pp 54-69.

Patrick Hanks. 2013. *Lexical Analysis: Norms and Exploitations*. MIT Press, Cambridge MA.

Karin Kipper, Anna Korhonen, Neville Ryant and Martha Palmer. 2008. A Large-Scale Classification of English Verbs. In *Journal of Language Resources and Evaluation*. 42(1), pp 21-40.

Beth Levin. 1993. *English Verb Classes and Alternations: A Preliminary Investigation*. Chicago CHI : University of Chicago Press.

Robert S. Swier and Suzanne Stevenson. 2004. Unsupervised Semantic Role Labelling. In Proceedings of *EMNLP 2004*. pp. 95-102.

Anna Wierzbicka. 1984. "Apples" are not a "Kind of Fruit": The Semantics of Human Categorization. *American Ethnologist*, Vol 11(2). pp 313-328.

Towards universal quantification in distributional semantic space

Matthew Capetola
Universtity of Oxford Faculty of Linguistics, Philology, and Phonetics
Clarendon Press Institute, Walton Road
Oxford OX1 2HG, United Kingdom
matthew.capetola@wolfson.ox.ac.uk

Abstract

This paper defines a representation of universal quantification within distributional semantic space. We propose a discourse-internal approach to the meaning of limited instances of *every*, highlighting the possibilities and limitations of doing textual logic in a purely distributional framework.

1 Introduction

Research in recent years has moved to applying distributional semantic space models to tasks that deal in more complicated meaning structures like phrases and sentences. The underlying question in those applications is how to model *compositionality*, or the idea that the meaning of a larger linguistic unit is a function of its parts. This has typically amounted to describing a correspondence between the combinatorial operations available for linear algebraic structures, like vector addition and matrix multiplication, and the (hypothetical) compositional operations of natural language (Baroni and Zamparelli, 2010; Coecke et al., 2010; Mitchell and Lapata, 2008).

While this has yielded high performance on semantic tasks like sentiment analysis (Socher et al., 2012; Socher et al., 2013) and paraphrase detection (Mitchell and Lapata, 2008; Mitchell and Lapata, 2010; Blacoe and Lapata, 2012), the issue of capturing textual logic, also inextricably linked to compositionality, remains an open problem. Part of the reason for this is that there exists structural opposition between distributional and formal semantics (Grefenstette, 2013). The benefit of distributional semantics is that its vectors represent meanings with high-dimensional subtlety. This allows us to model the way content words modify each other compositionally, better than we might using the comparably flat meaning representations of formal semantics. However, formal semantics is far better equipped to handle the meanings of function words like quantifiers on both individual and interstitial levels. The syntax of formal calculi unambiguously denotes the interrelation of functional operators in a logical expression. In essence, formal semantics treats content words as properties that obtain of entities in a referent domain, or model world. Quantification is then conceived of as a higher-order operation describing relations between the sets of entities circumscribed by such properties. In this way, a comprehensive semantic system in natural language is comprised of a universe of functions built over a universe of entities (Peters and Westerstahl, 2008).

So while the the distributional framework has been successful precisely by doing away with the set-theoretic approach to semantics (Baroni and Zamparelli, 2010), it faces several foreseeable problems, two of which we focus on here.

1. The meaning of a quantifier expression doesn't appeal to features of the domain of quantification. That is, no matter what entities engaging in whatever kind of verbal relation, the meaning of a quantifier like *every* does not change: it stands for the inclusion relation between sets. (Peters and Westerstahl, 2008).

2. Without a model world, or universe of entities over which to quantify, it is unclear what quantifiers mean.

Considering the above points, there is no *a priori* reason to expect that distributional representations make sense for function words. In light of these issues, recent research has moved towards merging distributional semantics with formal compositional calculi like Lambek calculus, leveraging the distinct strengths of both approaches selectively (Lewis and Steedman, 2013).

This paper begins by highlighting some of the persistent expressive differences between distributional and formal semantics. This will help to motivate a limited definition of the universal quantifier *every*, while remaining within a purely distributional framework. It is our belief that further inquiry into this field despite the initially perceived limitations has the potential to produce theoretically and pragmatically impactful results.

2 Mending the structural opposition?

2.1 Previous work

This paper continues in the line of inquiry which has been previously referred to in the literature as "logic for vectors" (Hermann et al., 2013). It seeks to define the meaning of a function word, and textual logic in general, within distributional semantic space. Hermann et al. (2013) is one of the first papers to concern itself explicitly with the meaning of a function word *not, relative to* distributional representations of content words. This contrasts with the aforementioned distributional-formal hybrid approaches, as well as the recent work of Grefenstette (2013). The latter models truth-functional logic using the operations of tensor calculi, rather than redefining what logical words mean altogether when we move to a distributional context.

Integral to the discussion here, as well as the "tripartite representation" of meaning in Hermann et al. (2013), is the concept of a dual-space representation similar to those of Turney (2012). A dual-space model posits that the mathematical structure of a word is comprised of two block components: a domain and a value. A domain is extracted via similarity metrics, and serves to group a term with others according to overarching semantic similarity in the space (Turney, 2012). Hermann et al. give the example that terms *red* and *blue* have very different values, but share the common conceptual domain *colors*. Important for the ideas here is that semantic domains are defined by appeal to other terms within the same semantic space. Taking this further, we will treat semantic domains as higher-order structures: divisions of the semantic space into subspaces, or sets of concepts.

2.2 Domains vs. ontologies

Previous work has shown that imposition of domain structure on a semantic space model affords some additional expressiveness for defining the meanings of function words. We ought to ask to what extent this is the case. Of particular interest in this section is the relationship between *domain* structure of distributional semantics and *model world* structure of formal semantics.

Consider the sentence *All boys are good* $\equiv \forall x : boy(x) \Rightarrow good(x)$. The quantifier is integral to the logical meaning of this sentence. If we eliminate it, we can express the general notion that the concept *boy* is good, by composing distributional representations of the two lexemes. This however, is not as ontologically rich as the formal interpretation. In a model-theoretic semantics, *boy* serves as an ontological domain of entities which are boys. A distributional model, on the other hand, does not postulate the existence of hypothetical wold that is populated by entities. It intentionally does away with this set-theoretic representation. Keeping this structural assumption, what can the universal quantifier mean?

Now consider the sentences *Every country attended* and *Every color is good*. Unlike *boys*, *colors* and *countries* can serve as hypernyms denoting sets of concepts that are learned in discourse. So while while *red* is indeed a color, it is also lexically and conceptually distinct, and a distributional model would learn a representation for *red* which maintains this duality. In contrast, boys in a model world are distinct by virtue of being separate entities, as opposed to distinct concepts. Similarly, for the sentence *Everything red is good*, the donation of *red* in our model are those things in the world which bear the property of being red. When *red* serves as a conceptual domain however, as in the sentence *All reds are good*, it is referring not to entities, but to the set of concepts denoting shades of red.

Another distinction to be drawn is that that our definition of quantification with *every* must be further-confined to cases in which semantic domains are denoted by count nouns. Count nouns are common nouns that can be enumerated and can appear in both single and plural form. In contrast, for other kinds of semantic domains like *politics*, which is a viable concept under which one could group terms in a semantic space, the meaning of quantification changes in subtle ways. *All politics is interesting* ought to have a very different semantic content than a sentence like *Every country attended*.

These distinctions allow us to define, within disributional space, a notion of quantification over countable concepts, but not quantification over mass nouns, entities, or topical concepts. As a general result, we see that dual-space approaches eschew some of the need for an entity-coded ontological structure. It can be thought that the imposition of domains on a semantic space is a way of reclaiming part of the higher-order structure of an ontology, just not all of it. In general, it would seem that the significance of quantifiers in a semantic model is directly proportional to the descriptive capacity and structural advancement of the ontology of that model.

3 Discursive *every*

Consider the sentence *Red is good*. Ignoring the copula *is*, the meaning of the sentence is, formally, a function application of the meaning of *good* to the meaning of *red*, producing *good(red)*. Now consider the sentence *Every color is good*. The formal semantic interpretation of this sentence is as follows:

1. (a) Every color is good. $\equiv$
   (b) $\{x|color(x)\} \subseteq \{x|good(x)\} \equiv$
   (c) $\forall x : color(x) \Rightarrow good(x)$

What is being said is structurally distinct from the meaning of the first sentence considered, and this is because of the intervention of the function word *every*. As in the formal semantics presented above, the sentence means that for any term bearing the domain *color*, that color is good. The quantifier is said to range over entities for which the property *color* obtains. So, this returns not a single sentential representation, but a set of sentential representations such that the property *good* is applied to the elements contained in the semantic domain *color*:

$\{$*Red is good. Blue is good. ...*$\}$

Provided with our dual-space representation, and assuming $\bullet$ represents our compositional strategy and $*$ represents the Kleene Star, a compact representation of this in vectorial calculi is as follows:

$$\begin{bmatrix} f_{good} \end{bmatrix} \bullet \begin{bmatrix} d_{color} \\ * \end{bmatrix}$$

This example puts forth two claims.

1. A sentence which contains the quantifier *every* is by some measure semantically richer than an unquantified sentence.
2. So presented, universal quantification over conceptual domains does not require postulation of a hypothetical model world. Instead, we can treat it as a function from a sentence in discourse to a set of sentences of lower-order meaning comprised of terms from the same discourse.

Formally, the function mentioned in 2. is as follows:

$$f_{every} : S^2 \rightarrow 2^S$$

Where S^2 represents the set of higher-order sentences as described, and 2^S the power set of the set of lower-order sentences.

The obvious appeal of such a representation is that given a more comprehensive treatment and assuming an appropriate compositional model, the values manipulated in this variety of textual logic are of the same mathematical form as the sentences upon which we wish to do inference. They are themselves sentences.

With this definition, we can more formally express the difference between quantification and this proposed idea of quantification over concepts, revisiting a comparison of the domains *boys* and *colors*. If we have learned M subelements of the domain of *colors*, of the N possible colors in a universe of concepts, then $M \leq N$ and:

- *Every color is good.* $\mapsto \bigcup_{i=1}^{M \leq N} color_i$ *is good.*

In contrast, this does not work for quantification over *boy*, because a distributional representation does not learn separate, indexable representations boy_i. These indexed "boys" would denote separate entities, not separate concepts.

As of now, even for conceptual domains of countable concepts, the definition of f_{every} we've provided has a marked shortcoming. It is limited to the subelements of domains for which our model has learned distributional representations. Leaving the functional value of *every* as defined, we would be treating the semantic space as a static proxy for a more complicated ontological structure. So, for example, if we haven't learned a representation for *cerulean*, the projection from *every color* will not include it. In order to do so, this will likely require a dynamic representation of quantification, perhaps one which is capable of modeling inference on subconcepts predictively, or stochastically.

4 Concluding remarks

Confined to the discussion here, progress needs to be made to extend the applicability of f_{every} towards the goal of dynamic inference. This should be rooted in specific computational semantic tasks. The implications of this approach to quantification should then be brought to bear on more complex issues. Can we conceive of constructing a consistent system of "logic for vectors" such that we can consider more syntactically and semantically complex sentences?

References

M. Baroni and R. Zamparelli. 2010. Nouns are vectors, adjectives are matrices: Representing adjective-noun constructions in semantic space. In *Proceedings of the 2010 Conference on Empirical Methods in Natural Language Processing*, pages 1183–1193. Association for Computational Linguistics.

W. Blacoe and M. Lapata. 2012. A comparison of vector-based representations for semantic composition. In *Proceedings of the 2012 Conference on Empirical Methods in Natural Language Processing*.

Bob Coecke, Mehrnoosh Sadrzadeh, and Stephen Clark. 2010. Mathematical foundations for a compositional distributional model of meaning. *CoRR*, abs/1003.4394.

E. Grefenstette. 2013. Towards a formal distributional semantics: Simulating logical calculi with tensors. In *Proceedings of the Second Joint Conference on Lexical and Computational Semantics*.

Karl Moritz Hermann, Edward Grefenstette, and Phil Blunsom. 2013. "not not bad" is not "bad": A distributional account of negation". *Proceedings of the 2013 Workshop on Continuous Vector Space Models and their Compositionality*, August.

Mike Lewis and Mark Steedman. 2013. Combined logical and distributional semantics. *Transactions of the Association for Computational Lingusitics*, 1:179–192.

J. Mitchell and M. Lapata. 2008. Vector-based models of semantic composition. In *Proceedings of ACL*, volume 8.

J. Mitchell and M. Lapata. 2010. Composition in distributional models of semantics. *Cognitive Science*.

Stanley Peters and Dag Westerstahl. 2008. *Quantifiers in Language and Logic*. OUP, Oxford.

Richard Socher, Brody Huval, Christopher D. Manning, and Andrew Y. Ng. 2012. Semantic Compositionality Through Recursive Matrix-Vector Spaces. In *Proceedings of the 2012 Conference on Empirical Methods in Natural Language Processing (EMNLP)*.

Richard Socher, Alex Perelygin, Jean Wu, Christopher Manning, Andrew Ng, and Jason Chuang. 2013. Recursive models for semantic compositionality over a sentiment treebank. In *Conference on Empericial Methods in Natural Language Processing*.

Peter D. Turney. 2012. Domain and function: A dual-space model of semantic relations and compositions. *J. Artif. Intell. Res. (JAIR)*, 44:533–585.

Alternative measures of word relatedness in distributional semantics

Alina Maria Ciobanu
Faculty of Mathematics
and Computer Science
University of Bucharest
alina.ciobanu@my.fmi.unibuc.ro

Anca Dinu
Faculty of Foreign Languages
and Literatures
University of Bucharest
anca_d_dinu@yahoo.com

Abstract

This paper presents an alternative method to measuring word-word semantic relatedness in distributional semantics framework. The main idea is to represent target words as rankings of all co-occurring words in a text corpus, ordered by their *tf – idf* weight and use a metric between rankings (such as Jaro distance or Rank distance) to compute semantic relatedness. This method has several advantages over the standard approach that uses cosine measure in a vector space, mainly in that it is computationally less expensive (i.e. does not require working in a high dimensional space, employing only rankings and a distance which is linear in the rank's length) and presumably more robust. We tested this method on the standard *WS-353 Test*, obtaining the co-occurrence frequency from the *Wacky* corpus. The results are comparable to the methods which use vector space models; and, most importantly, the method can be extended to the very challenging task of measuring phrase semantic relatedness.

1 Introduction

This paper presents a method of measuring word-word semantic relatedness in the distributional semantics (DS) framework.

DS relies on a usage-based perspective on meaning, assuming that the statistical distribution of words in context plays a key role in characterizing their semantic behavior. The idea that word co-occurrence statistics extracted from text corpora can provide a basis for semantic representations can be traced back at least to Firth (1957): "You shall know a word by the company it keeps" and Harris (1954): "words that occur in similar contexts tend to have similar meanings". This view is complementary to the formal semantics perspective, focusing on the meaning of content words, (such as nouns, adjectives, verbs or adverbs) and not on grammatical words (prepositions, auxiliary verbs, pronouns, quantifiers, coordination, negation), which are the focus of formal semantics. Since many semantic issues come from the lexicon of content words and not from grammatical terms, DS offers semantical insight into problems that cannot be addressed by formal semantics.

Moreover, DS Models can be induced fully automatically on a large scale, from corpus data. Thus, a word may be represented by a vector in which the elements are derived from the occurrences of the word in various contexts, such as windows of words (Lund and Burgess, 1996), grammatical dependencies (Lin, 1998; Padó and Lapata, 2007), and richer contexts consisting of dependency links and selectional preferences on the argument positions (Erk and Padó, 2008).

The task of measuring word-word relatedness was previously performed in DS by using vector space models (see (Turney and Pantel, 2010) for an excellent survey of vector-space models), that is employing high dimensional matrices to store co-occurrence frequency of target words and some set of dimension words, usually highly frequent (but not grammatical) words. The relatedness of two target words was typically given by the cosine of the angle between their vectors. Instead of using vector space models, we propose to represent the target words only by rankings (vectors) of words in their decreasing order of co-occurrence frequency or their *tf – idf* weight. The *tf – idf* weight increases with the number of co-occurrences and with the "selectiveness" of the term - the fewer distinct words it occurs with, the higher the weight.

This proposal has some advantages, as discussed in Approach section. We can measure the semantic relatedness between two target words by computing the distance between the two corresponding rankings, using distances defined on rankings.

In the remaining of the paper we will present our approach, describe the data we have used, compare the results and draw the conclusions.

2 Approach

The method we propose is meant to measure word - word semantic relatedness, in a bag of words model, using 4 different distances (Rank distance, MeanRank distance, CosRank distance and Jaro distance) between rankings. To do so, instead of representing words in vector spaces, we represent them as rankings of co-occurring words ordered after their semantic contribution, i.e. arranged in their raw co-occurrence frequency and, separately, in their *tf – idf* weight. We thus take into consideration all words that co-occurred with a target word, not just a predefined set of dimension words.

We define the Rank distance (variants) and the Jaro distance, as it follows.

A ranking is an ordered list and is the result of applying an ordering criterion to a set of objects. Formally (Dinu, 2005), we have:

Let $\mathcal{U} = \{1, 2, ..., \#\mathcal{U}\}$ be a finite set of objects, named universe (we write $\#\mathcal{U}$ for the cardinality of $\mathcal{U}$). A *ranking* over $\mathcal{U}$ is an ordered list: $\tau = (x_1 > x_2 > ... > x_d)$, where $x_i \in \mathcal{U}$ for all $1 \leq i \leq d$, $x_i \neq x_j$ for all $1 \leq i \neq j \leq d$, and $>$ is a strict ordering relation on the set $\{x_1, x_2, ..., x_d\}$.

A ranking defines a partial function on $\mathcal{U}$ where for each object $i \in \mathcal{U}$, $\tau(i)$ represents the position of the object i in the ranking τ.

The order of an object $x \in \mathcal{U}$ in a ranking σ of length d is defined by $ord(\sigma, x) = |d + 1 - \sigma(x)|$. By convention, if $x \in \mathcal{U} \setminus \sigma$, then $ord(\sigma, x) = 0$.

Given two partial rankings σ and τ over the same universe $\mathcal{U}$, the Rank distance between them is defined as:

$$\Delta(\sigma, \tau) = \sum_{x \in \sigma \cup \tau} |ord(\sigma, x) - ord(\tau, x)|.$$

MeanRank distance is the average value of Rank distance computed when elements are ranked top-down and Rank distance computed when elements are ranked bottom-up.

Given two full rankigs σ and τ over the same universe $\mathcal{U}$ with $\#\mathcal{U} = n$, CosRank distance (Dinu and Ionescu, 2012) is defined as follows:

$$\Delta(\sigma, \tau) = \frac{<\sigma, \tau>}{||\sigma|| \cdot ||\tau||} = \frac{\sum_{x \in \mathcal{U}} ord(\sigma, x) \times ord(\tau, x)}{1^2 + 2^2 + ... + n^2}$$

Jaro distance (Jaro, 1989) is a measure which accounts for the number and position of common characters between strings. Given two strings $w_i = (w_{i1}, ..., w_{im})$ and $w_j = (w_{j1}, ..., w_{jn})$, the number of common characters for w_i and w_j is the number of characters w_{ik} in w_i which satisfy the condition:

$$\exists w_{jl} \; in \; w_j : w_{ik} = w_{jl} \; and \; |k - l| \leq \frac{max(m, n)}{2} - 1$$

Let c be the number of common characters in w_i and w_j and t the number of character transpositions (i.e. the number of common characters in w_i and w_j in different positions, divided by 2). Jaro distance is defined as follows:

$$\Delta(w_i, w_j) = \frac{1}{3} * \left(\frac{c}{m} + \frac{c}{n} + \frac{c - t}{c} \right)$$

We computed straightforwardly the distances between pairs of target words in the Word Similarity 353 Test. *WS-353 Test* is a semantic relatedness test set consisting of 353 word pairs and a gold standard defined as the mean value of semantic relatedness scores, assigned by up to 17 human judges. Finally, we used Spearman's correlation to compare the obtained distances to the gold standard.

One advantage of this technique over the standard application of the cosine measure in vectorial space is that it doesn't have to deal with high dimensional matrices, and thus no techniques of reducing dimensionality of the vector space are required. Rank distance only uses rankings (ordered vectors) of semantically relevant words for each target word. It does not even need that these rankings contain the same words or have the same length (number of words). Computing the four distances between the rankings of two target words is linear in the length of the rankings. Thus, the method is much less computationally expensive than standard vector space models used in distributional semantics for the task of word-word semantic relatedness.

Also, we expect the method to be more robust compared to traditional vector space models, since rankings of features tend to vary less then the raw frequency with the choice of corpus.

But most importantly, it opens the perspective of experimenting with new methods of composing (distributional) meaning by aggregating rankings (Dinu, 2005), instead of combining (adding, multiplying) vectors.

2.1 The data

We used the publicly available *Wacky* corpus (Baroni et al., 2009). The corpus is lemmatized and pos tagged. As it is usual in distributional semantics, we only targeted content words and not grammatical words. Here is the list with the pos tags we have employed:

- JJ adjective, e.g. *green*
- JJR adjective, comparative, e.g. *greener*
- JJS adjective, superlative, e.g. *greenest*
- NN noun, singular or mass, e.g. *table*
- NNS noun plural, e.g. *tables*
- NPS proper noun, plural, e.g. *Vikings*
- RB adverb, e.g. *however, usually, naturally, here, good*
- VV verb, base form, e.g. *take*
- VVD verb, past tense, e.g. *took*
- VVG verb, gerund/present participle, e.g. *taking*
- VVN verb, past participle, e.g. *taken*
- VVP verb, sing. present,non-3d, e.g. *take*
- VVZ verb, 3rd person sing. present, e.g. *takes*

Accordingly, we have extracted from *Wacky* corpus the 10 words window co-occurrence vectors for the words in *WS-353 Test* (Finkelstein et al., 2002). *WS-353 Test* is a semantic relatedness test set consisting of 353 word pairs and a gold standard defined as the mean value of evaluations by up to 17 human judges. The value scale for the test is from 0 to 10: completely unrelated words were assigned a value of 0, while identical words a value of 10. Although this test suite contains some controversial word pairs, and there are other test suits such as in (Miller and Charles, 1991) and (Rubenstein and Goodenough, 1965), it has been widely used in the literature and has become the de facto standard for semantic relatedness measure evaluation. For all the 437 target-words in *WS-353 Test*, we computed the raw co-occurrence frequency $tf_{t,d}$ of terms t (base-word) and d (target-word), defined as the number of times that t and d co-occurred. We preprocessed the data, as it follows:

- we deleted all non-English words;
- we separated hyphenated words and recomputed the weights accordingly;
- we eliminated all other words containing non-letter characters;

Then we standardly processed the raw co-occurrence frequencies, transforming it into the *tf – idf* weight: $w_{t,d} = (1+lgtf_{t,d})*lgN/df_t$, where $N = 437$ (the total number of words we are computing vectors for) and df_t is the number of target words t co-occurs with. The *tf – idf* weight increases with the number of co-occurrences of t and d (co-occurrence frequency) and increases with the "selectiveness" of the term - the fewer distinct words it occurs with, the higher the weight.

We then computed the distances between pairs of target words both for raw frequencies and for *tf – idf* weights, for different lengths of the rankings, starting with a length of only 10 and adding 10 at a time until 2000.

3 Results

We summarize our results in Figure 1: one graphic for experiments with raw frequencies and one for experiments with *tf – idf* weight. On the OX axis we represent the length of the rankings (up to the first 2000 words) and on the OY axis the value of human/machine correlation. We only represent the best 3 performing distances, namely Rank, CosRank and Jaro, along with the standard Cosine distance (for comparison).

Method	Source	Spearman Correlation
Hughes and Ramage (2007)	WordNet	0.55
Finkelstein et al. (2002)	LSA, Combination	0.56
Gabrilovich and Markovitch (2007)	ODP	0.65
Agirre et al. (2009)	Web Corpus	0.65
Agirre et al. (2010)	WordNet	0.69
Gabrilovich and Markovitch (2007)	Wikipedia	0.75
Agirre et al. (2009)	Combination	0.78
This work	Wacky	0.55

Table 1: Comparison with vector space experiments for *WS-353 Test*

For the raw co-occurrence, one observes that until the length of 1000, the best performing distance was Jaro distance, followed by CosRank, Rank, all three of them outperforming Cosine. Between a length of 1000 and 2000, the order reverses and Cosine is the best performing distance. An explanation for this is on the one hand that Jaro and Rank distances need no preprocessing like computing *tf – idf* weight and, on the other, that words ranked on places over a certain threshold (in this case 1000) are, in fact, irrelevant (or even represent noise) for the semantic representation of the target word. For the *tf – idf* weight, the traditional Cosine distance performs best, while CosRank is on the second place.

Overall, it turns out that the differences are minor and that measuring the distances between

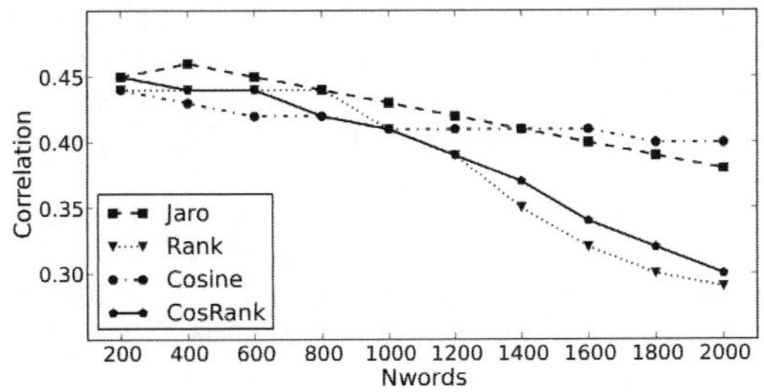

(a) Results for experiments with raw frequencies

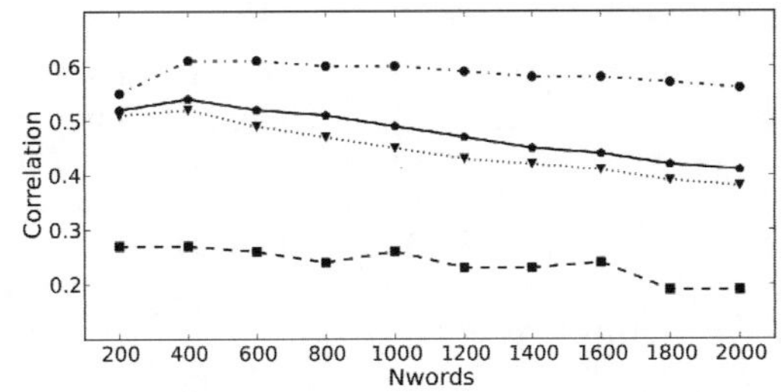

(b) Results for experiments with *tf – idf* weights

Figure 1: Results for experiments on *WS-353 Test* with co-occurrence frequencies from the *Wacky* corpus

rankings instead of vectors is a valid option. The results may thus be further used as baseline for experimenting with this method, like, for instance taking syntactic structure into account.

As we can see in Table 1, the best correlation value of 0.55 (obtained by CosRank computed on the *tf – idf* weights) is identical to the baseline correlation values for the vector space experiments.

When inspecting the worst mismatches between human/machine relatedness judgments between pairs of words, we observed that most of them were following a pattern, namely lower values assigned by humans almost always corresponded to much higher values computed by machine, such in the following examples given in Table 2:

Word Pair	Human Distance	Machine Distance (Jaro)
(month, hotel)	1,81	6,239567
(money,operation)	3,31	6,40989
(king, cabbage)	0,23	4,171145
(coast, forest)	3,15	6,409761
(rooster, voyage)	0,62	4,656631
(governor, interview)	3,25	6,08319
(drink, car)	3,04	5,931482
(day, summer)	3,94	6,576498
(architecture, century)	3,78	5,927852
(morality, marriage)	3,69	5,450308

Table 2: Comparison with vector space experiments for *WS-353 Test*

One can intuitively speculate about the reason of these differences; for instance, the pairs (summer, day) and (king, cabbage) are present in the data as collocations: "summer day" and "king cabbage", which is a very large variety of cabbage. The other pairs ((month, hotel), (money,operation), (rooster, voyage), etc.) seem to allow for explanations based on pragmatic information present in the data.

4 Conclusions and further work

We introduced in this paper an alternative method to measuring word-word semantic relatedness; instead of using vector space models, we proposed to represent the target words only by rankings (vectors) of words in their decreasing order of co-occurrence frequency; we computed the word-word relatedness by four different distances. We tested this method on the standard *WS-353 Test*, obtaining the co-occurrence frequency from the *Wacky* corpus. The Spearman correlation with human given scores are around the baseline for vector space models, so there is hope for improvement. The method is computationally less expensive. Furthermore, it provides a new framework for experimenting with distributional semantic compositionality, since our method can be extended from measuring word-word semantic relatedness to evaluating phrasal semantics. This is in fact one of the most challenging streams of research on distributional semantics: finding a principled way to account for natural language compositionality.

In the future, we will extend the contribution in this paper to evaluating phrase semantics, that differs from all the above methods in that it does not try to learn weights or functions for the vectors, but instead combines or aggregates two vectors containing words ranked in their semantic contribution, in order to obtain a vector for the resulting phrase. When combining two word vectors, one obtains an aggregation set which contains all vectors for which the sum of the distances between them and the two vectors is minimum. The vector in the aggregation set that is closest to the syntactic head of the new phrase is chosen to be the vector representing it. Thus, the syntactic structure of the phrase is taken into account. The word - phrase semantic similarity can be computed as in the experiment reported in this paper and the obtained values compared to some gold standard, like, for instance, in SemEval 2013 task, Evaluating Phrasal Semantics or like the dataset in (Mitchell and Lapata, 2008).

Acknowledgments

This work was supported by the research project PN-II-ID-PCE-2011-3-0959.

References

E. Agirre, E. Alfonseca, K. Hall, J. Kravalova, M. Pasca, and A. Soroa. 2009. A Study on Similarity and Relatedness Using Distributional and WordNet-based Approaches. In *Proceedings of the Conference of the North American Chapter of the Association of Computational Linguistics*, HLT-NAACL '09, pages 19–27.

E. Agirre, M. Cuadros, G. Rigau, and A. Soroa. 2010. Exploring Knowledge Bases for Similarity. In *Language Resources and Evaluation 2010*.

M. Baroni, S. Bernardini, A. Ferraresi, and E. Zanchetta. 2009. The WaCky Wide Web: A Collection of Very Large Linguistically Processed Web-Crawled Corpora. In *Language Resources and Evaluation 43 (3) 2009*, pages 209–226.

L.P. Dinu and R. Ionescu. 2012. Clustering Methods Based on Closest String via Rank Distance. In *14th International Symposium on Symbolic and Numeric Algorithms for Scientific Computing*, SYNASC '12, pages 207–213.

L.P. Dinu. 2005. Rank Distance with Applications in Similarity of Natural Languages. *Fundam. Inform.*, 64(1-4):135–149.

K. Erk and S. Padó. 2008. A Structured Vector Space Model for Word Meaning in Context. In *Proceedings of the Conference on Empirical Methods in Natural Language Processing*, EMNLP '08, pages 897–906.

L. Finkelstein, Evgeniy Gabrilovich, Yossi Matias, Ehud Rivlin, Zach Solan, Gadi Wolfman, and Eytan Ruppin. 2002. Placing Search in Context: The Concept Revisited. *ACM Trans. Inf. Syst.*, 20(1):116–131.

J. Firth. 1957. A Synopsis of Linguistic Theory 1930-1955. *Studies in Linguistic Analysis, Philological Society, Oxford.*

E. Gabrilovich and S. Markovitch. 2007. Computing Semantic Relatedness Using Wikipedia-based Explicit Semantic Analysis. In *Proceedings of the 20th International Joint Conference on Artificial Intelligence*, IJCAI '07, pages 1606–1611.

Z. Harris. 1954. Distributional Structure. *Word*, 10(23):146–162.

T. Hughes and D. Ramage. 2007. Lexical Semantic Relatedness with Random Graph Walks. In *Proceedings of the Joint Conference on Empirical Methods in Natural Language Processing and Computational Natural Language Learning*, EMNLP-CoNLL '07, pages 581–589.

M. A. Jaro. 1989. Advances in Record Linkage Methodology as Applied to the 1985 Census of Tampa Florida. *Journal of the American Statistical Society 84(406)*, pages 414–420.

D. Lin. 1998. Automatic Retrieval and Clustering of Similar Words. In *Proceedings of the 17th International Conference on Computational Linguistics - Volume 2*, COLING '98, pages 768–774.

K. Lund and C. Burgess. 1996. Producing high-dimensional semantic spaces from lexical co-occurrence. *Behavioral Research Methods, Instruments and Computers, 28(2)*, pages 203–208.

G. A. Miller and Walter G. Charles. 1991. Contextual Correlates of Semantic Similarity. *Language and Cognitive Processes*, 6(1):1–28.

J. Mitchell and M. Lapata. 2008. Vector-based Models of Semantic Composition. In *Proceedings of the 46th Annual Meeting of the Association for Computational Linguistics*, ACL '08, pages 236–244.

S. Padó and M. Lapata. 2007. Dependency-Based Construction of Semantic Space Models. *Computational Linguistics*, 33(2):161–199.

H. Rubenstein and J. B. Goodenough. 1965. Contextual correlates of synonymy. *Comunications of the Association of Computing Machinery*, 8(10):627–633.

P. D. Turney and P. Pantel. 2010. From Frequency to Meaning: Vector Space Models of Semantics. *Journal of Artifficial Intelligence Research*, 37:141–188.

Linear Compositional Distributional Semantics and Structural Kernels

Lorenzo Ferrone
University of Rome "Tor Vergata"
Via del Politecnico 1
00133 Roma, Italy
lorenzo.ferrone@gmail.com

Fabio Massimo Zanzotto
University of Rome "Tor Vergata"
Via del Politecnico 1
00133 Roma, Italy
fabio.massimo.zanzotto@uniroma2.it

Abstract

In this paper, we want to start the analysis of the models for compositional distributional semantics (CDS) with respect to the distributional similarity. We believe that this simple analysis of the properties of the similarity can help to better investigate new CDS models. We show that, looking at CDS models from this point of view, these models are strictly related with convolution kernels (Haussler, 1999), e.g.: tree kernels (Collins and Duffy, 2002). We will then examine how the distributed tree kernels (Zanzotto and Dell'Arciprete, 2012) are an interesting result to draw a stronger link between CDS models and convolution kernels.

1 Introduction

Distributional semantics (see (Turney and Pantel, 2010; Baroni and Lenci, 2010)) is an interesting way of "learning from corpora" meaning for words (Firth, 1957) and of comparing word meanings (Harris, 1964). A flourishing research area is compositional distributional semantics (CDS), which aims to leverage distributional semantics for accounting the meaning of word sequences and sentences (Mitchell and Lapata, 2008; Baroni and Zamparelli, 2010; Zanzotto et al., 2010; Guevara, 2010; Grefenstette and Sadrzadeh, 2011; Clark et al., 2008; Socher et al., 2011). The area proposes compositional operations to derive the meaning of word sequences using the distributional meanings of the words in the sequences.

The first and more important feature of distributional semantics is to compare the meaning of different words, a way to compute their similarity. But, when focusing on compositional distributional semantics, methods are presented with respect to the compositional operation of the vectors. A scarce attention is given to how these operations affect the principal objective of the process of compositional distributional semantics: assessing the similarity between two word sequences. This analysis is important as the similarity is generally used even by machine learning models such as the kernel machines (Cristianini and Shawe-Taylor, 2000).

In this paper, we want to start the analysis of the models for compositional distributional semantics with respect to the similarity measure. We focus on linear CDS models. We believe that this simple analysis of the properties of the similarity can help to better investigate new CDS models. We show that, looking CDS models from this point of view, these models are strictly related with the convolution kernels (Haussler, 1999), e.g., the tree kernels (Collins and Duffy, 2002). We will then examine how the distributed tree kernels (Zanzotto and Dell'Arciprete, 2012) are an interesting result to draw a strongest link between CDS models and convolution kernels.

The rest of the paper is organized as follows. Section 2 focuses on the description of two basic binary operations for compositional distributional semantics, their recursive application to word sequences (or sentences) with a particular attention to their effect on the similarity measure. Section 3 describes the tree kernels (Collins and Duffy, 2002), the distributed tree kernels (Zanzotto and Dell'Arciprete, 2012), and the smoothed tree kernels (Mehdad et al., 2010; Croce et al., 2011) to introduce links with similarity measures applied over compositionally obtained distributional vectors. Section 4 draws sketches the future work.

2 Compositional distributional semantics over sentences

Generally, the proposal of a model for compositional distributional semantics stems from some basic vector combination operations and, then, these operations are recursively applied on the parse tree on the sequence of words of the sentences. In the rest of the section, we describe some simple basic operations along with their effects on the similarity between pairs of words and we describe some simple recursive models based on these operations. We finally describe how these simple operations and their recursive applications affect the similarity between sentences.

2.1 Two Basic Composition Operations

As we want to keep this analysis simple, we focus on two basic operations: the simple additive model, (presented in (Mitchell and Lapata, 2008) and cited as a comparative method in many research papers), and the full additive model (estimated in (Zanzotto et al., 2010; Guevara, 2010)).

We analyze these basic operations when resulting composed vectors are used to compute the similarity between two pairs of words. For simplicity, we use the dot product as the similarity measure. Let $a = a_1a_2$ and $b = b_1b_2$ be the two sequences of words and $\vec{a}_1$, $\vec{a}_2$, $\vec{b}_1$, and $\vec{b}_2$ be the related distributional vectors. Let $sim(a_1a_2, b_1b_2)$ be the similarity computed applying the dot product on the vectors $\vec{a}$ and $\vec{b}$ compositionally representing the distributional semantics of a and b.

The Basic Additive model (ADD) (introduced in (Mitchell and Lapata, 2008)) computes the distibutional semantics of a pair of words $a = a_1a_2$ as:

$$ADD(a_1, a_2) = (1 - \alpha)\vec{a_1} + \alpha\vec{a_2}$$

where $0 < \alpha < 1$ weigths the first and the second word of the pair. Then, the similarity between two pairs of words is:

$$sim(a, b) = ADD(a_1, a_2) \cdot ADD(b_1, b_2) =$$
$$(1 - \alpha)^2\vec{a}_1 \cdot \vec{b}_1 + (1 - \alpha)\alpha\vec{a}_1 \cdot \vec{b}_2 +$$
$$(1 - \alpha)\alpha\vec{a}_2 \cdot \vec{b}_1 + \alpha^2\vec{a}_2 \cdot \vec{b}_2$$

that is, basically, the linear combination of the similarities $\vec{a}_i \cdot \vec{b}_j$ between the words composing the sequences. For example, the similarity between sim(animal extracts, beef extracts) takes into consideration the similarity between *animal* (of the first pair) and *extracts* (of the second pair) that can be totally irrelevant.

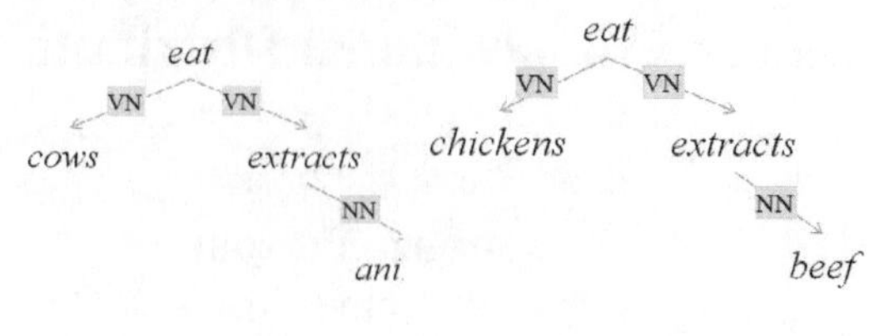

Figure 1: Two sentences and their simple dependency graphs

The Full Additive model (FADD) (used in (Guevara, 2010) for adjective-noun pairs and (Zanzotto et al., 2010) for three different syntactic relations) computes the compositional vector $\vec{a}$ of a pair using two linear tranformations A_R and B_R respectively applied to the vectors of the first and the second word. These matrices generally only depends on the syntactic relation R that links those two words. The operation follows:

$$FADD(a_1, a_2, R) = A_R\vec{a_1} + B_R\vec{a_2}$$

Then, the similariy between two pairs of words linked by the same relation R is:

$$sim(a, b) = FADD(a_1, a_2) \cdot FADD(b_1, b_2) =$$
$$= A_R\vec{a}_1 \cdot A_R\vec{b}_1 + A_R\vec{a}_1 \cdot B_R\vec{b}_2 +$$
$$B_R\vec{a}_2 \cdot A_R\vec{b}_1 + B_R\vec{a}_2 \cdot B_R\vec{b}_2$$

which is a linear combination of similarities between elements such as $A_R\vec{a}_i$, mixing a syntactic factor, the matrix A_R, and a single word of the sequence, a_i. In the above example, sim(animal extracts, beef extracts), (where we consider noun-noun (NN) as the syntactic relation) we also consider a factor (the similarity $B_{NN}\vec{extracts} \cdot A_{NN}\vec{beef}$) that may not be relevant in the similarity computation.

2.2 Recursive application on sentences and its effects on the similarity

The two linear models seems so simple that it is easy to think to recursively extend their application to whole sentences. To explain what is going on and what we are expecting, we will use two sentences as a driving example: *cows eat animal extracts* and *chickens eat beef extracts*. These are similar because both have ***animals*** *eating* ***animal*** *extracts*. This is what we expect the comparison between these two sentences should evaluate. Let

$$sim(T_a, T_b) = \begin{array}{c} RFADD(T_a) \\ \cdot \\ RFADD(T_b) \end{array} = \begin{array}{c} (2A_{VN}\vec{eat} + B_{VN}\vec{cows} + B_{VN}A_{NN}\vec{extracts} + B_{VN}B_{NN}\vec{animal}) \\ \cdot \\ (2A_{VN}\vec{eat} + B_{VN}\vec{chickens} + B_{VN}A_{NN}\vec{extracts} + B_{VN}B_{NN}\vec{beef}) \end{array}$$

Figure 2: Similarity using the recursive full additive model

$x = x_1 \dots x_n$ and $y = y_1 \dots y_m$ be two sentences (or word sequences).

2.2.1 Recursive basic additive model

The recursive basic additive model ($RADD$) is the first model we analyze. We can easily define the model as follows:

$$RADD(x_i x_{i+1} \dots x_n) =$$
$$= (1-\alpha)\vec{x}_i + \alpha RADD(x_{i+1} \dots x_n)$$

where $RADD(x_n) = \vec{x}_n$. Then, $RADD(x)$ is a weighted linear combination of the words in the sentence x, that is:

$$RADD(x) = \sum_{i=1}^{n} \lambda_i \vec{x}_i$$

where $\lambda_i = \alpha^{i-1}(1-\alpha)$ if $i < n$ and $\lambda_n = \alpha^{n-1}$ depends on α and the position of x_i in the sequence.

The similairity between two sentences x and y is then:

$$sim(x,y) = RADD(x) \cdot RADD(y) =$$
$$= \sum_{i=1}^{n} \sum_{j=1}^{m} \lambda_i \lambda_j \vec{x}_i \cdot \vec{y}_j$$

This is the weighted linear combination of the similariy among all the pairs of words taken from the sentences x and y. Given these two sample sentences, this similarity measure hardly captures the similarity in terms of the generalized sentence ***animals*** *eating* ***animal*** *extracts*. The measure also takes into consideration factors such as $\vec{chicken} \cdot \vec{beef}$ that have a high similarity score but that are not relevant for the similarity of the whole sentence.

2.2.2 Recursive Full Additive Model

For the recursive Full Additive Model, we need to introduce a structrured syntactic representation of the sentences. The full additive models (presented in Sec. 2.1) are defined on the syntactic dependency R between the words of the pair. We then use the dependency trees as syntactic representation. A dependency tree can be defined as a tree whose nodes are words and the typed links are the relations between two words. The root of the tree represents the word that governs the meaning of the sentence. A dependency tree T is then a word if it is a final node or it has a root r_T and links (r_T, Rel, C_i) where C_i is the i-th subtree of the node r_T and Rel is the relation that links the node r_T with C_i. The dependency trees of two example sentences are reported in Figure 1.

Stemming from the full additive models (FADD), the recursive FADD (RFADD) can be straightforwardly and recursively defined as follows:

$$RFADD(T) = \sum_i (A_{Rel}\vec{r_T} + B_{Rel} RFADD(C_i))$$

where (r_T, Rel, C_i) are the links originated in the root node r_T.

By recursively applying the model to the first sentence of the example (see Fig. 1), the resulting vector is:

$$RFADD(\text{cows eat animal extracts}) =$$
$$= A_{VN}\vec{eat} + B_{VN}\vec{cows} + A_{VN}\vec{eat} +$$
$$+ B_{VN}RFADD(\text{animal extracts}) =$$
$$= A_{VN}\vec{eat} + B_{VN}\vec{cows} + A_{VN}\vec{eat} +$$
$$+ B_{VN}A_{NN}\vec{extracts} + B_{VN}B_{NN}\vec{animal}$$

A first observation is that each term of the sum has a part that represents the structure and a part that represents the meaning, for example:

$$\overbrace{B_{VN}B_{NN}}^{structure} \underbrace{\vec{beef}}_{meaning}$$

It is possible to formally show that the function $RFADD(T)$ is a linear combination of elements $M_s\vec{w}_s$ where M_s is a product of matrices that represents the structure and $\vec{w}_s$ is the distributional meaning of one word in this structure, that is:

$$RFADD(T) = \sum_{s \in S(T)} M_s \vec{w}_s$$

where $S(T)$ are the relevant substructures of T. In this case, $S(T)$ contains the link chains.

Then, the similarity between two sentences in this case is:

$$sim(T_1, T_2) = RFADD(T_1) \cdot RFADD(T_2) =$$
$$= \sum_{s_1 \in S(T_1), s_2 \in S(T_2)} M_{s_1}\vec{w}_{s_1} \cdot M_{s_2}\vec{w}_{s_2}$$

The similarity between the two sentences T_a =*cows eat animal extracts* and T_b =*chickens eat beef extracts* in Figure 1 is represented in Figure 2. For the above dot product, $B_{VN}A_{NN}\vec{extracts} \cdot B_{VN}A_{NN}\vec{extracts} = 1$ as these addend represents the same piece of structure, $B_{VN}B_{NN}\vec{beef}) \cdot B_{VN}B_{NN}\vec{animal} < 1$ and should be strictly related to the value of $\vec{beef} \cdot \vec{animal}$ as these two parts are representing the branch of the tree describing the objects of the verb in the two sentences. The same should happen for $B_{VN}\vec{cows} \cdot B_{VN}\vec{chickens} < 1$. But, what do we expect for $B_{VN}\vec{cows} \cdot B_{VN}B_{NN}\vec{beef}$? We would like to have a similarity close to $\vec{beef} \cdot \vec{cows}$ or a similarity near 0, as these words appear in a different part of the structure? Going back to the overall goal of evaluating the similarity between the two sentences is clear that the second option should be preferred.

3 Tree Kernels

We here come to the last point we want to describe, the tree kernels (Collins and Duffy, 2002) and some strictly related recent results, the distributed tree kernels (Zanzotto and Dell'Arciprete, 2012) and the smoothed tree kernels (Mehdad et al., 2010; Croce et al., 2011). We want to show that what is computed by the $RADD$ and $RFADD$ is extremely similar to what is computed in tree kernels.

Tree kernels are defined (Collins and Duffy, 2002) as convolution kernels (Haussler, 1999), thus, they are generally defined recursively. But, given two trees T_1 and T_2, these kernels are defined as to compute the dot product between vectors $\Phi(T_1), \Phi(T_2)$, representing the trees in the feature space $\mathbb{R}^n$. Each dimensions (or features) of this huge space $\mathbb{R}^n$ is a relevant subtree t and we can consider that each relevant subtree t has an associated vector $\vec{t}$. The vector $\vec{t}$ is a vector of the orthonormal basis of the space $\mathbb{R}^n$. Then, the function Φ, that maps trees into the space $\mathbb{R}^n$, can be defined as follows:

$$\Phi(T) = \sum_{t \in S(T)} \omega_t \vec{t}$$

where ω_t is a weight assigned to t in the tree T. The tree kernel functions $TK(T_1, T_2)$ then basically computes:

$$TK(T_1, T_2) = \sum_{t_1 \in S(T_1), t_2 \in S(T_2)} \omega_{t_1}\omega_{t_2}\vec{t_1} \cdot \vec{t_2}$$

where $\vec{t_1} \cdot \vec{t_2}$ is the Kronecker's delta between t_1 and t_2, that is: $\vec{t_1} \cdot \vec{t_2} = \delta(t_1, t_2)$.

The equation above is incredibly similar to equation 1 that computes the similarity with the recursive full additive model. There are however two limitations in using tree kernels to encode compositional distributional semantics model: first, standard tree kernels only encode the structure; second, standard tree kernels work in $\mathbb{R}^n$ where n is huge making it infeasible to use such a huge vectors. For the first issue, an interesting line of research are the smoothed tree kernels (Mehdad et al., 2010; Croce et al., 2011) that exploits distributional vectors to compute the similarity among nodes of the trees that contain words. For the second issue an interesting recent result is the distributed tree kernel (Zanzotto and Dell'Arciprete, 2012) that approximates tree kernels by encoding the huge space $\mathbb{R}^n$ in a smaller space $\mathbb{R}^d$, with $d << n$. This allows to encode structural information into small vectors.

4 Conclusions

This paper presents some simple observations on one of the current approaches to compositional distributional semantics, drawing the link with the deeply studied tree kernels and convolution kernels. With this analysis, we aim to show that these approaches are not radically different. Instead, (linear) compositional distributional models can be rephrased as a compact version of some existing convolution kernels.

This paper is not conclusive as it leave open two avenues: first, we need to prove that distributed tree kernel (Zanzotto and Dell'Arciprete, 2012) can also encode distributional informations as described in the smoothed tree kernels (Mehdad et al., 2010; Croce et al., 2011); second, it still leaves unexplored how the similarity between sentences is affected by the other compositional distributional models (Mitchell and Lapata, 2008; Baroni and Zamparelli, 2010; Zanzotto et al., 2010; Guevara, 2010; Grefenstette and Sadrzadeh, 2011; Clark et al., 2008; Socher et al., 2011).

References

Marco Baroni and Alessandro Lenci. 2010. Distributional memory: A general framework for corpus-based semantics. *Comput. Linguist.*, 36(4):673–721, December.

Marco Baroni and Roberto Zamparelli. 2010. Nouns are vectors, adjectives are matrices: Representing adjective-noun constructions in semantic space. In *Proceedings of the 2010 Conference on Empirical Methods in Natural Language Processing*, pages 1183–1193, Cambridge, MA, October. Association for Computational Linguistics.

Stephen Clark, Bob Coecke, and Mehrnoosh Sadrzadeh. 2008. A compositional distributional model of meaning. *Proceedings of the Second Symposium on Quantum Interaction (QI-2008)*, pages 133–140.

Michael Collins and Nigel Duffy. 2002. New ranking algorithms for parsing and tagging: Kernels over discrete structures, and the voted perceptron. In *Proceedings of ACL02*.

Nello Cristianini and John Shawe-Taylor. 2000. *An Introduction to Support Vector Machines and Other Kernel-based Learning Methods*. Cambridge University Press, March.

Danilo Croce, Alessandro Moschitti, and Roberto Basili. 2011. Structured lexical similarity via convolution kernels on dependency trees. In *Proceedings of the Conference on Empirical Methods in Natural Language Processing*, EMNLP '11, pages 1034–1046, Stroudsburg, PA, USA. Association for Computational Linguistics.

John R. Firth. 1957. *Papers in Linguistics*. Oxford University Press., London.

Edward Grefenstette and Mehrnoosh Sadrzadeh. 2011. Experimental support for a categorical compositional distributional model of meaning. In *Proceedings of the Conference on Empirical Methods in Natural Language Processing*, EMNLP '11, pages 1394–1404, Stroudsburg, PA, USA. Association for Computational Linguistics.

Emiliano Guevara. 2010. A regression model of adjective-noun compositionality in distributional semantics. In *Proceedings of the 2010 Workshop on GEometrical Models of Natural Language Semantics*, pages 33–37, Uppsala, Sweden, July. Association for Computational Linguistics.

Zellig Harris. 1964. Distributional structure. In Jerrold J. Katz and Jerry A. Fodor, editors, *The Philosophy of Linguistics*. Oxford University Press, New York.

David Haussler. 1999. Convolution kernels on discrete structures. Technical report, University of California at Santa Cruz.

Yashar Mehdad, Alessandro Moschitti, and Fabio Massimo Zanzotto. 2010. Syntactic/semantic structures for textual entailment recognition. In *Human Language Technologies: The 2010 Annual Conference of the North American Chapter of the Association for Computational Linguistics*, HLT '10, pages 1020–1028, Stroudsburg, PA, USA. Association for Computational Linguistics.

Jeff Mitchell and Mirella Lapata. 2008. Vector-based models of semantic composition. In *Proceedings of ACL-08: HLT*, pages 236–244, Columbus, Ohio, June. Association for Computational Linguistics.

Richard Socher, Eric H. Huang, Jeffrey Pennington, Andrew Y. Ng, and Christopher D. Manning. 2011. Dynamic pooling and unfolding recursive autoencoders for paraphrase detection. In *Advances in Neural Information Processing Systems 24*.

Peter D. Turney and Patrick Pantel. 2010. From frequency to meaning: Vector space models of semantics. *J. Artif. Intell. Res. (JAIR)*, 37:141–188.

F.M. Zanzotto and L. Dell'Arciprete. 2012. Distributed tree kernels. In *Proceedings of International Conference on Machine Learning*, pages 193–200.

Fabio Massimo Zanzotto, Ioannis Korkontzelos, Francesca Fallucchi, and Suresh Manandhar. 2010. Estimating linear models for compositional distributional semantics. In *Proceedings of the 23rd International Conference on Computational Linguistics (COLING)*, August,.

On a Dependency-based Semantic Space for Unsupervised Noun Sense Disambiguation with an Underlying Naïve Bayes Model

Florentina Hristea
University of Bucharest, Department of Computer Science
Academiei 14, Str., Bucharest, Sector 1, C.P. 010014
fhristea@fmi.unibuc.ro

Abstract

Recent studies refocus on usage of the Naïve Bayes model in unsupervised word sense disambiguation (WSD). They discuss the issue of feature selection for this statistical model, when used as clustering technique, and comment (Hristea, 2012) that it still holds a promise for unsupervised WSD. Within the various investigated types of feature selection, this ongoing research concentrates on syntactic dependency-based features, introduced in (Hristea and Colhon, 2012) with respect to adjectives only. We hereby extend the mentioned approach to the case of nouns and recommend the further investigation of this promising feature selection method.

1 Introduction

While the Naïve Bayes model has been widely and successfully used in supervised WSD (Navigli, 2009), its usage in unsupervised WSD has led to more modest disambiguation results and is less frequent. However, more recent studies (Hristea, 2012) state that this statistical model still holds a promise for unsupervised WSD.

The Naïve Bayes model needs to be fed knowledge (of various natures) in order to perform well as clustering technique for unsupervised WSD (Hristea, 2012). Three different sources of such knowledge have been predominantly examined and compared: WordNet (Hristea et al., 2008; Hristea, 2009; Hristea and Popescu, 2009), web N-grams (Preotiuc and Hristea, 2012) and dependency relations (Hristea and Colhon, 2012; Hristea, 2012). While most of these studies discuss all three major parts of speech (nouns, adjectives, verbs), the syntactic dependency-based feature selection method has been applied to adjectives only (Hristea and Colhon, 2012; Hristea, 2012). With the conclusion that the Naïve Bayes model reacts well in the presence of syntactic knowledge of this type and that dependency-based feature selection for the Naïve Bayes model is a reliable alternative to other existing ones. In fact, for the studied adjectives, this type of syntactic feature selection has provided the best disambiguation results (Hristea, 2012). Following the line of reasoning of the mentioned studies, we hereby extend the disambiguation method they propose to nouns, while exemplifying with tests concerning the nouns *line* and *interest*.

Although dependency-based semantic space models have been studied and discussed by several authors (Padó and Lapata, 2007; Năstase, 2008; Chen et al., 2009), to our knowledge, grammatical dependencies have been used in conjunction with the Naïve Bayes model only very recently (Hristea and Colhon, 2012; Hristea, 2012). The latter authors follow the line of reasoning of Padó and Lapata (2007) which they adapt to the particularities of the involved statistical model.

The present study investigates the usage of syntactic features provided by dependency relations as defined by the classical Dependency Grammar formalism (Tesnière, 1959) and as proposed in (Hristea and Colhon, 2012; Hristea, 2012). The semantic space we present to the Naïve Bayes model for unsupervised WSD will be based on dependency relations extracted from natural language texts via a syntactic parser. In order to ensure the same testing setup as the one used in the mentioned studies (Hristea and Colhon, 2012; Hristea, 2012), we shall be making use of a PCFG parser, namely the Stanford parser (Klein and Manning, 2003), for extracting syntactic dependency relations that will indicate the disambiguation vocabulary required by the Naïve Bayes model. When using dependency-based syntactic features this disambiguation vocabulary is formed by taking into account all words that participate in the considered dependencies. Also in order to ensure the same testing setup, we shall be estimating the model parameters using the Expectation-Maximization algorithm (Dempster et al., 1977). Our approach to feature selection is that of implementing a Naïve Bayes model that uses as features *the actual words* occurring in the context window of the target and decreases the existing number of features by selecting a restricted number of such words, as indicated by the chosen dependency relations. The size of the feature set must be reduced in order to decrease the number of parameters which are to be estimated by the EM algorithm for unsupervised WSD.

2 Design of the experiments

Our approach will take into account the final conclusions drawn in (Hristea, 2012) with respect to dependency-based feature selection for the Naïve Bayes model. According to this most recent study, several particularities determined by the involved statistical model stand out. When using the Stanford parser a projective[1] type analysis is recommended. This is in accordance with the classical dependency grammar theory and has previously (Hristea, 2012) improved disambiguation accuracy in the case of adjectives. According to the same study, directionality of the dependency relations counts and the head role of the target (word to be disambiguated) is essential. The type of the dependencies is equally of the essence. It seems sufficient to use first order dependencies (direct relationships between the target and other words). A small number of dependency types should be considered, preferably just one, in order to decrease the number of parameters that will be estimated by the EM algorithm. Some of these conclusions were determined specifically by the nature of the involved statistical model, others by the fact that the Naïve Bayes model is trained with the EM algorithm. For instance, contrary to other authors, who, when discussing the construction of a dependency-based semantic space in general, consider that "directed paths would limit the context too severely" (Padó and Lapata, 2007), Hristea and Colhon (2012) have taken into account both undirected and directed paths - with the latter providing the best test results. The Naïve Bayes model seemed to react strongly to the directionality of dependency relations and considering this directionality was essential when forming the disambiguation vocabulary.

Following this line of work, which is typical for the Naïve Bayes model, when disambiguating the nouns *line* and *interest*, we have considered a *single type* of *first order* dependencies having the target word as *head* and have collected all other words involved in these dependencies in order to form the disambiguation vocabulary.

2.1 Noun experiment

In the case of nouns we have used as test data the *line* corpus (Leacock et al., 1993; Mooney, 1996) and the *interest* corpus (Bruce and Wiebe, 1994). Within the present approach to disambiguation, the value of a feature is given by the number of occurrences of the corresponding word in the given context window (which is hereby represented by the entire sentence). Since the process of feature selection is based on the restriction of the disambiguation vocabulary, it is possible for certain instances not to contain any of the relevant (chosen) words forming this vocabulary. Such instances will have null values corresponding to all features. These instances do not contribute to the learning process. However, they have been taken into account in the evaluation stage of our experiments. Corresponding to these instances, the algorithm assigns the sense for which the value estimated by the EM algorithm is maximal. In order to enable comparison with the mentioned studies, performance is evaluated in terms of accuracy. Also in order to enable comparison with previous work, we have extracted the contexts corresponding to 3 chosen senses of the studied nouns, as shown in Table 1 (for *line*) and Table 2 (for *interest*), respectively. Another reason for performing this reduction to 3 senses was to verify to what extent the existence of a majority sense in the distribution of senses influences the performances of the discussed disambiguation method. Corresponding to the distribution of senses shown in Table 1 (for *line*) and in Table 2 (for *interest*) we have extracted all existing dependency relations using Stanford Parser.

In order to choose a specific type of dependency for the discussed disambiguation method, we have isolated all dependency relations having the target word as head and have classified them according to their frequency and their relevance. (Namely dependencies between the target and dependents which are not content words have been eliminated). The most frequent dependency

[1] Which does not allow the arches denoting the dependency relations to intersect.

relations thus obtained were *amod* (adjectival modifier) and *nn* (noun compound modifier)[2].

Sense	Count
Telephone connection	429 (37.33%)
Formation of people or things; queue	349 (30.37%)
A thin, flexible object; cord	371 (32.28%)
Total count	1149

Table 1 Distribution of the 3 chosen sense of *line*

Sense	Count
Money paid for the use of money	1252 (53%)
A share in a company or business	500 (21%)
Readiness to give attention	361 (15%)
Total count	2113

Table 2 Distribution of the 3 chosen senses of *interest*

We have started by taking into account both these relations since it is not presupposed that the most frequent dependency will provide the best disambiguation result. However, we are interested in frequent dependencies in order to minimize the number of instances having null values corresponding to all features (thus ensuring good corpus coverage). On the other hand, frequent dependencies will provide a greater number of features, resulting in a greater number of parameters that are to be estimated by the EM algorithm. These aspects, which, quite surprisingly, are not of linguistic nature, make the choice of the dependency type to be used in disambiguation a quite delicate one. The present study makes use of the mentioned *amod* and *nn* dependency relations. The disambiguation vocabulary was obtained by retaining all words that are dependents of the target within each of these relations, considered separately. Two distinct disambiguation vocabularies were thus created and tests have been performed corresponding to each of them. The number of contexts and features for each of the considered nouns and dependency relations can be seen in Table 3.

Corpus	line	interest
No. of contexts	1150	2112
No. of senses	3	3
No. of *nn* features	104	65
No. of *amod* features	101	102

Table 3 Corpora features

[2] For both of which see the Stanford Parser Manual (de Marneffe and Manning, 2012).

3 Test results

Performance is evaluated in terms of accuracy, as in (Hristea and Colhon, 2012; Hristea, 2012). In the case of unsupervised disambiguation defining accuracy is not as straightforward as in the supervised cased. The objective is to divide the given instances of the ambiguous word into a specified number of sense groups, which are in no way connected to the sense tags existing in the corpus. These sense groups are then mapped to the sense tags of the annotated corpus. The mapping that results in the highest classification accuracy is chosen. The discussed test results will represent the average accuracy and standard deviation obtained by the learning procedure over 1000 random trials while using the entire sentence as context window and a threshold ε having the value 10^{-9}. As in (Hristea and Colhon, 2012; Hristea, 2012), apart from accuracy, the following type of information is also provided: number of features resulting in the experiment and percentage of instances having only null features.

At the first stage of our experiment, we have performed 100 random trials, both for *line* and for *interest*, corresponding to the *nn* and the *amod* relations, respectively. We have analyzed the obtained results after 10% of the intended tests in order to observe the differences between the two involved dependency relations. These results are presented in Table 4.

After the first 100 random trials, the differences between results obtained with the two considered relations have become visible.

Target word	Relation	No. of features	Accuracy
line	*amod*	101	.544±.08
	nn	104	.579±.08
interest	*amod*	102	.684±.08
	nn	65	.686±.07

Table 4 Test results for *line* and *interest* after 100 random trials

Corresponding to both nouns the obtained accuracy is higher in the case of the *nn* dependency relation. For *line* the "*nn* accuracy" is significantly higher. This has determined us to perform the remaining 900 random trials using the *nn* relation, in the case of both nouns. The obtained test results are shown in Table 5.

Let us note that the *nn* and *amod* relations have a similar frequency in the *line* corpus, while the frequency of the *amod* relation is significantly higher within the *interest* corpus[3].

Target word	No. of features	Percentage of instances having only null features	Accuracy
line	104	15.7	.584±.09
interest	65	38.2	.683±.07

Table 5 Disambiguation accuracy corresponding to the *nn* dependency relation after 1000 random trials

In spite of this, a higher disambiguation accuracy seems to be obtained using the *nn* dependency relation. In the case of *interest* this can be expected since the number of resulting features is smaller, minimizing the number of parameters that are to be estimated by the EM algorithm. In the case of *line* this observation does not hold, but the difference between the number of resulting features is not significant (see Table 4). The final obtained disambiguation results clearly show that the dependency relation which is most frequently occurring in a corpus is not necessarily the most relevant one for unsupervised WSD of this type.

3.1 Further analysis of the results

We have compared the disambiguation accuracy obtained when performing syntactic dependency-based feature selection with that resulting when using other types of features, proposed by the relatively recent literature: semantic WordNet (WN) features (Hristea et al., 2008) and N-gram features (Preotiuc and Hristea, 2012). These authors report test results for the noun *line*.

In the case of the three chosen senses of *line*, the best reported accuracy when using WN features was 0.591 ± .06, obtained with 229 features and with only 15.1% instances having only null features. The N-grams feature selection method reports as highest accuracy 0.547%, obtained for a context window of size 5 and for the 5-*line*-100 feature set[4]. As shown in Table 5, the best obtained dependency-based accuracy is 0.584 ± .09, a result which, at first glance, would encourage us to prefer semantic WN-based feature sets.

We have further performed tests for the three chosen senses of *interest* using both mentioned feature selection methods and within the same testing setup.

In the case of *interest*, WN feature selection results in a maximum accuracy of 0.587 ± 3.3 when using 18 features that ensure 15.9% corpus coverage. Corresponding to N-gram feature selection we have performed tests with the set of features that had provided the best result for *line*. The obtained accuracy was 44.15% ± 1.97%. With respect to *interest* dependency-based feature selection clearly outperforms both these methods (see Table 5).

In fact, we can state that this type of syntactic feature selection is recommended in the case of both studied nouns. Since corresponding to *line* the number of features used in disambiguation by WN feature selection is much greater (more than double) than the one provided by dependency relations. Which makes us believe that, when moving to 6 senses of line, namely to more fine-grained disambiguation, accuracy will drop severely if using this method. In the case of *interest*, where the number of resulting features is low, one should notice the very low corpus coverage. This is probably due to the fact that the synsets corresponding to the three chosen senses of *interest* do not have many semantic relations in WordNet. Due to possible very reduced corpus coverage, we cannot recommend a feature selection method relying solely on the number of WN relations corresponding to a specific synset.

4. Conclusions and future work

So far, syntactic dependency-based feature selection for unsupervised WSD with an underlying Naïve Bayes model seems a reliable alternative to other existing ones. It has already been recommended for adjectives (Hristea, 2012). Concerning nouns, our next step will be to use it for more fine-grained sense disambiguation, namely in the case of all 6 senses of *line* and of *interest*. Using other test data is also intended. The choice of the dependency type to be used in noun disambiguation should also be subject to further investigation, especially in establishing if a connection exists between the frequency of occurrence of a dependency type and disambiguation accuracy. Augmenting the role of linguistic knowledge in informing the construction of this semantic space is also a future goal.

[3] In the subcorpus corresponding to the three chosen senses of *line* the *amod* relation occurs 1638 times while the *nn* relation occurs 1657 times. In the *interest* subcorpus the *amod* relation occurs 5410 times while the *nn* relation occurs 4634 times.

[4] Preotiuc and Hristea (2012) use the following notation: *n-w-t* represents the set containing the top *t* words occurring in N-grams together with the word *w*.

References

Bruce, Rebecca and Janyce Wiebe. 1994. Word-sense disambiguation using decomposable models. In *Proceedings of the 32nd Annual Meeting of the Association for Computational Linguistics,* pages 139-145, Las Cruces, New Mexico.

Chen, Ping, Wei Ding, Chris Bowes, and David Brown. 2009. A fully unsupervised word sense disambiguation method using dependency knowledge. In *Proceedings of Human Language Technologies: The 2009 Annual Conference of the North American Chapter of the Association for Computational Linguistics*, pages 28-36, Boulder, Colorado.

Dempster, Arthur, Nan Laird and Donald Rubin. 1977. Maximum Likelihood from Incomplete Data via the EM Algorithm. *Journal of the Royal Statistical Society. Series B (Methodological)*, 39(1):1-38.

Hristea, Florentina, Marius Popescu, and Monica Dumitrescu. 2008. Performing Word Sense Disambiguation at the Border Between Unsupervised and Knowledge-based Techniques. *Artificial Intelligence Review*, 30(1):67-86.

Hristea, Florentina. 2009. Recent Advances Concerning the Usage of the Naïve Bayes Model in Unsupervised Word Sense Disambiguation. *International Review on Computers and Software*, 4(1):58-67.

Hristea, Florentina and Marius Popescu. 2009. Adjective Sense Disambiguation at the Border Between Unsupervised and Knowledge-based Techniques. *Fundamenta Informaticae*, 91(3-4):547-562.

Hristea, Florentina and Mihaela Colhon. 2012. Feeding Syntactic Versus Semantic Knowledge to a Knowledge-lean Unsupervised Word Sense Disambiguation Algorithm with an Underlying Naïve Bayes Model. *Fundamenta Informaticae*, 119(1):61-86.

Hristea, Florentina. 2012. *The Naïve Bayes Model for Unsupervised Word Sense Disambiguation. Aspects Concerning Feature Selection*. SpringerBriefs in Statistics Series, Springer.

Klein, Dan and Christopher Manning. 2003. Accurate unlexicalized parsing. In *Proceedings of the 41st Annual Meeting of the Association for Computational Linguistics*, pages 423-430, Sapporo, Japan.

Leacock, Claudia, Geoffrey Towell, and Ellen Voorhees. 1993. Corpus-based statistical sense resolution. In *Proceedings of the ARPA workshop on Human Language Technology,* pages 260-265, Princeton, New Jersey.

de Marneffe, Marie-Catherine and Christopher Manning. 2012. Stanford typed dependencies manual. Technical Report, Stanford University.

Mooney, Raymond. 1996. Comparative experiments on disambiguating word senses: An illustration of the role of bias in machine learning. In *Proceedings of the Conference on Empirical Methods in Natural Language Processing*, pages 82-91, Philadelphia, PA.

Nastase, Vivi. 2008. Unsupervised All-words Word Sense Disambiguation with Grammatical Dependencies. In *Proceedings of the Third International Joint Conference on Natural Language Processing*, pages 757-762, Hyderabad, India.

Navigli, Roberto. 2009. Word Sense Disambiguation: a Survey. *ACM Computing Surveys*, 41(2):1-69.

Padó, Sebastian and Mirella Lapata. 2007. Dependency-based Construction of Semantic Space Models. *Computational Linguistics*, 33(2):161-199.

Preotiuc-Pietro, Daniel and Florentina Hristea. 2012. Unsupervised Word Sense Disambiguation with N-Gram Features. *Artificial Intelligence Review*, doi:10.1007/s10462-011-9306-y.

Tesnière, Lucien. 1959. *Eléments de Syntaxe Structurale*. Klincksieck, Paris.

Automatic classification of patterns from the Pattern Dictionary of English Verbs

Ismaïl El Maarouf
University of Wolverhampton
i.el-maarouf@wlv.ac.uk

Vít Baisa
Masaryk University
Lexical Computing Ltd
xbaisa@fi.muni.cz

Abstract

The paper presents a supervised approach to semantic parsing, based on a new semantic resource, the Pattern Dictionary of English Verbs (PDEV). PDEV lists the most frequent patterns of English verbs identified in corpus. Each argument in a pattern is semantically categorized with semantic types from the PDEV ontology. Each pattern is linked to a set of sentences from the British National Corpus.

The article describes PDEV in details and presents the task of pattern classification. The system described is based on a distributional approach, and achieves 66% in Micro-average F1 across a sample of 25 of the most frequent verbs.

1 Introduction

This paper reports the results of Natural Language Processing (NLP) experiments in semantic parsing, based on a new semantic resource, the Pattern Dictionary of English Verbs (PDEV) (Hanks, 2013). This resource is the output of Corpus Pattern Analysis (CPA; (Hanks, 2004)), a corpus lexicography technique for mapping meaning onto words in text. CPA analyses the prototypical syntagmatic patterns with which words in use are associated. The patterns emerge from the analysis of corpus concordance lines and careful attention to linguistic context clues is applied to characterize pattern elements and to distinguish between patterns. Only in a second step is an "implicature" (i.e. a meaning) mapped onto a pattern. In other words, CPA is driven by syntagmatic patterns, not meaning.

Given these two features (pattern-driven and corpus-driven), this resource is unique in its kind, across languages. However, while CPA has made contributions to lexicography and to linguistics, no experiments have yet been made in NLP to use PDEV in applications such as Information Extraction or Statistical Machine Translation.

The present paper proposes to make use of PDEV as a resource for the semantic processing of text. It describes its structure in detail (section 2) and proposes the task of Pattern classification as a first step in semantic parsing (section 3). Contributions are summarized in section 4.

2 Background

2.1 Corpus Pattern Analysis

PDEV is built using the CPA methodology, which draws on Corpus Linguistics (Sinclair, 1991), and is inspired by semantic theories such as the Generative Lexicon (Pustejovsky, 1995), Frame Semantics (Fillmore, 1985) and Preference Semantics (Wilks, 1975). As a methodology for building lexical resources, CPA takes the position that words are only meaningful in context: words in isolation tend to be ambiguous while word patterns are rarely so. While this may seem self-evident, it has important implications for lexical semantics, which are developed in the Theory of Norms and Exploitations (TNE) (Hanks, 2013). According to TNE, it is a fallacy to attempt the definition of words independently and outside of context. Words should be described according to, and along with, the patterns in which they are found in real language use.

CPA builds typical phraseological patterns from corpora, by clustering corpus tokens (labelling them) according to the similarity of their context. The similarity is evaluated in different steps.

- Syntactic analysis involves the identification of the main structures such as idiomatic expressions, phrasal uses, transitive/intransitive patterns, causative/inchoative alternations, and argument/adjunct discrimination.

nb	%	Pattern & primary implicature
1	7%	[[Plant]] blossom [NOOBJ] *[[Plant]] produces flowers or masses of flowers*
2	87%	[[Eventuality | Psych]] blossom [NOOBJ] (into [[Anything = Good]]) *[[Eventuality | Psych]] develops in a promising way or into something that is expected or desired*

[[Psych]] refers to Psychological Entities and includes Emotions, Attitude and Goal.

Figure 1: Patterns for the verb *blossom*

- Semantic analysis involves the use of semantic features shared by collocates in each argument position. For example, Semantic Types (ST; e.g. [[Human]], [[Building]], [[Event]]) are used to represent the prototypical properties shared by the collocates found in a specific pattern position.

Since PDEV patterns represent abstractly several features of tokens from a large sample, they are rarely fully instantiated in an example: actual examples most often instantiate part of a pattern (e.g. subject ellipsis).

2.2 The structure of patterns

PDEV is created using three main tools: a corpus interface, i.e. The SketchEngine[1] (Kilgarriff et al., 2004), an ontology of semantic types[2], and the pattern dictionary[3]. PDEV lexicographers use the British National Corpus[4] (BNC), a large reference corpus containing various text types in British English (100 million words).

A verb pattern includes arguments such as Subject and Object. Each argument can be described according to determiners, semantic types, contextual roles, and lexical sets:

- Determiners account for distinctions between "*take place*" and "*take **his** place*".
- Semantic types account for distinctions such as "building [[**Machine**]]" and "building [[**Relationship**]]".
- Contextual roles account for distinctions such as "[[Human=**Film Director**]] shoot" and "[[Human=**Sports Player**]] shoot".
- Lexical sets account for distinctions such as "reap the **whirlwind**" and "reap the **harvest**".

[1] https://the.sketchengine.co.uk

[2] http://nlp.fi.muni.cz/projekty/cpa/public_onto.html

[3] http://deb.fi.muni.cz/pdev

[4] http://www.natcorp.ox.ac.uk/

Figure 1 shows an example of the PDEV entry of the verb *to blossom*. Both patterns are intransitive; the first has the semantic type [[Plant]] as subject and may be classified as the literal meaning even though it is comparatively rare. The criterion that distinguishes the second pattern, which may be classified as a conventional metaphor, is the semantic type ([[Eventuality]] or [[Psych]]). Pattern 2 also includes an optional prepositional phrase as additional context clue.

(1) The Times noted **fruit trees** which had begun to *blossom ...*
(2) The **silk trade** *blossomed* in Blockley...

Pattern 2 (example 2) illustrates an alternation of semantic types. It means that in the whole set of lines tagged as "blossom 2", subjects are either [[Eventuality]] or [[Psych]]. A semantic type provides the relevant semantic value of all words in context. They are, in practice, controlled generalizations of corpus observations.

Each pattern is described with (i) a primary implicature which elaborates the meaning of the pattern and (ii) percentages. Percentages are obtained by dividing the number of tagged lines over a random sample (the size of the sample depends on the frequency of a verb, usually 250 corpus lines).

3 Pattern classification

3.1 Description of the experiment

An important task performed by semantic parsers is Word Sense Disambiguation (WSD), in which systems predict the senses of words in text. WSD experiments (Navigli, 2009) have used WordNet[5] as a sense repository but we decided to explore how PDEV patterns could be used in this context.

As each pattern is linked to a set of lines, the present task of *pattern classification* requires systems to identify the correct pattern for each verb token. Our experiment was carried out on 25 verbs

[5] http://wordnet.princeton.edu/

$$\text{Macro-F1} = \frac{1}{|C|} \cdot \sum_{k=1}^{|C|} \frac{(1+\beta) \cdot Precision_k \cdot Recall_k}{\beta \cdot (Precision_k + Recall_k)}$$

$$with \beta = 1 \quad (1)$$

with comparatively high frequency in the BNC, on a range of patterns. The dataset contains 20418 verb tokens and was split using the following stratified sampling method: tokens were randomly selected from each verb pattern separately, using a 0.8:0.2 ratio, making sure that in extreme cases, where the set included less than 4 instances, the training set would always contain at least as many examples as in the test set.

Two evaluation metrics were used: Micro-average (Micro-F1) and Macro-average F-score (Macro-F1). Micro-F1 can be computed by counting False and True positives and negatives across classes. Micro-F1 can be complemented with Mac-F1 which gives an estimate of the performance of systems in discriminating patterns (by giving equal weight to classes rather than to instances; see equation (1)).

The baseline was generated by applying the majority class (most frequent) found in the training set, to the test set. Since the dataset is highly biased in terms of label frequency, the baseline Micro-F1 is quite high (0.62 across verbs). However, the baseline reaches 0.12 in Macro-F1.

3.2 Bootstrapping system

The system used for this task is a solution available in the Sketch Engine (Kilgarriff and Rychly, 2010), a corpus query system allowing users to explore corpus concordances. This system bootstraps from an existing automatic thesaurus (Grefenstette, 1994; Lin, 1998) to assign a label to a given verb token. The thesaurus is based on a regular grammar which identifies collocates linked to a verb through a syntactic relation (such as *subject*). The system applies the grammar to extract dependency triples of the form $||w, r, w'||$, where w is a lemma linked to another lemma w' by a relation r. Each triple is weighted with an association score based on the set of extracted triples, as described in equation (2). A distance measure described in equation (3) is then applied to words sharing similar contexts (Rychlý and Kilgarriff, 2007).

The bootstrapping algorithm uses the thesaurus scores to predict a label for each token. For each verb token v of the test set, it compares its contexts (r, w') to the contexts (r, w) labelled as k in the training set (of frequency over 1). The score for each token, results from the sum of the contexts having the best score as described in equation (4).

This method relies on the hypothesis that tokens sharing identical context should be labelled identically. It therefore does not normally discriminates cases where the same context is tagged with two different labels. This occurs only rarely. Two thresholds have been tested, `minscore`, the minimal score returned by the algorithm, and `mindiff`, the minimal difference between the best score and the second best score.

3.3 Results

The bootstrapping system was tested on several combinations of parameters `mindiff` and `minscore`. The best combination was `mindiff` = 0.1, thus a low difference between the first two scores returned by the algorithm, and `minscore` = 0.9, thus a high score threshold.

Table 1 shows that, on average, the system beats the baseline on both Micro-F1 and Macro-F1. While the difference (diff) between the system and the baseline in Micro-F1 is low, it is much higher for Macro-F1, which shows that the bootstrapping system is not biased towards the majority class.

Detailed analysis revealed that the bootstrapping generally suffers from fairly low recall, but has a very satisfying precision on average (Micro-Prec/Micro-Rec = 0.86/0.56; Macro-Prec/Macro-Rec = 0.56/0.41).

Conclusion

This article has presented new results for the classification of verb patterns from the Pattern Dictionary of English Verbs (PDEV). The latter is an interesting resource for semantic parsing as it is a corpus-based meaning repository with links to patterns of use. The tagged corpus of the PDEV has been used on a task of pattern classification similar to Word Sense Disambiguation, which is potentially beneficial to many Natural Language Processing applications.

The system used in this experiment is a bootstrapping algorithm relying on a distributional thesaurus and is a solution available in the

Verb	nb of Pat	Test size	Micro-Average F1			Macro-Average F1		
			System	Baseline	Diff	System	Baseline	Diff
blow	43	194	59	21	+38	40	10	+30
break	37	211	64	11	+53	41	3	+38
smile	29	101	37	79	-42	27	7	+20
laugh	18	160	45	65	-20	45	7	+38
sleep	16	168	62	79	-17	49	6	+43
object	14	123	59	88	-29	61	15	+46
breathe	12	203	62	40	+22	46	32	+14
arouse	11	102	90	94	-4	53	31	+22
beg	10	208	67	31	+36	52	5	+47
arm	10	177	70	61	+9	55	8	+47
smoke	8	248	65	96	-31	26	3	+23
wake	8	132	74	60	+14	53	30	+23
forge	7	117	54	33	+21	38	29	+9
rush	6	141	69	53	+16	43	8	+35
talk	6	79	42	73	-31	19	22	-3
call	5	168	57	32	+25	36	19	+17
say	4	216	82	86	-4	44	3	+41
enlarge	4	154	75	91	-16	26	13	+13
cry	4	119	55	57	-2	60	0	+60
import	4	100	73	92	-19	25	15	+10
explain	4	93	80	58	+22	80	23	+57
cross	3	437	66	51	+15	54	0	+54
speed	3	180	82	73	+9	20	2	+18
throw	3	165	78	30	+48	59	1	+58
arrest	3	100	88	97	-9	35	15	+20
MEAN	11	164	66	62	+4	43	12	+31

Table 1: Results for the pattern classification task

$$\text{AScore(w,r,w')} = \log \frac{||w, r, w'|| \cdot ||*, *, *||}{||w, r, *|| \cdot ||*, *, w'||} \cdot \log(||w, r, w'|| + 1) \tag{2}$$

$$\text{Dist(w,w')} = \frac{\sum_{(tuple_i, tuple_j) \in \{tuple_w \cap tuple_{w'}\}} AS_i + AS_j - (AS_i - AS_j)^2/50}{\sum_{tuple_i \in \{tuple_i \cup tuplej\}} AS_i} \tag{3}$$

$$\text{score}_{v,k} = \sum_{(w,r)} \sum_{(w',r)} \max \left(\text{Dist}_{w,w'} \cdot \frac{\sum_{(w,r,k)}}{\sum_{(w,r)}} \right) \tag{4}$$

SketchEngine. Results showed that the system beats the baseline on average and has a high precision, which makes it a potentially interesting tool for NLP applications. Various grammars or methods to generate thesaurus contexts need to be tested in order to improve the system's recall without sacrificing precision. In the future, the system will also be analysed on a larger set of verbs.

Acknowledgements

We would like to thank Patrick Hanks, Jane Bradbury, and anonymous reviewers for their comments on an earlier draft. This work was supported by AHRC grant [DVC, AH/J005940/1, 2012-2015]. It has also been partially supported by the Ministry of Education of Czech Republic within the LINDAT-Clarin project LM2010013.

References

Charles J. Fillmore. 1985. Frames and the semantics of understanding. *Quaderni di Semantica*, 6(2):222–254.

Gregory Grefenstette. 1994. *Explorations in Automatic Thesaurus Discovery (The Springer International Series in Engineering and Computer Science)*. Springer.

Patrick Hanks. 2004. Corpus pattern analysis. In *Euralex Proceedings*, volume 1, pages 87–98.

Patrick Hanks. 2013. *Lexical Analysis: Norms and Exploitations*. MIT Press.

Adam Kilgarriff and Pavel Rychly. 2010. Semi-automatic dictionary drafting. In Gilles-Maurice de Schryver, editor, *Oxford Handbook of Innovation*. Menha Publichers, Kampala.

Adam Kilgarriff, Pavel Rychly, Pavel Smrz, and David Tugwell. 2004. Itri-04-08 the sketch engine. *Information Technology*, 105:116.

Dekang Lin. 1998. Automatic retrieval and clustering of similar words. In *Proceedings of the 17th international conference on Computational linguistics-Volume 2*. Association for Computational Linguistics.

Roberto Navigli. 2009. Word sense disambiguation: A survey. *ACM Comput. Surv.*, 41(2):10:1–10:69.

James Pustejovsky. 1995. *The Generative Lexicon*. MIT Press.

Pavel Rychlý and Adam Kilgarriff. 2007. An efficient algorithm for building a distributional thesaurus (and other sketch engine developments). In *Proceedings of the 45th Annual Meeting of the Association for Computational Linguistics Companion Volume Proceedings of the Demo and Poster Sessions*, pages 41–44, Prague, Czech Republic. Association for Computational Linguistics.

John Sinclair. 1991. *Corpus, concordance, collocation*. Oxford University Press.

Yorick Wilks. 1975. A preferential, pattern-seeking, semantics for natural language inference. *Artif. Intell.*, 6(1):53–74.

Extending the Semantics in Natural Language Understanding

Michael Marlen
Kansas State University
msm6666@ksu.edu

David Gustafson
Kansas State University
dag@ksu.edu

Abstract

Natural Language understanding over a set of sentences or a document is a challenging problem. We approach this problem using semantic extraction and building an ontology for answering questions based on the data. There is more information in a sentence than found by extracting out the visible terms and their obvious relations between one another. Keeping track of inferences, quantities, inheritance, properties, and set related information is what gives this approach the advantage over alternatives. Our methodology was tested against the FraCas Test Suite with near perfect results for the sections: Generalized Quantifiers, Plurals, Adjectives, Comparatives, Verbs, and Attitudes. The results indicate that extracting the visible semantics as well as the unseen semantics and their interrelations using an ontology to logically provide reliable and provable answers to questions validating our methodology.

1 Introduction

There has yet to be a system that is fully capable of understanding English. We define understanding as the ability to reason by successfully mapping an ontology onto a preexisting ontology built from the premises. This is demonstrated using the FraCaS Test Suite problems that are presented in English (Cooper, 1996). Sukkarieh (2003) showed that the FraCas Test Suite is widely regarded as the gold standard for Natural Language Understanding systems. Our research moves closer to solving the problems presented in the FraCas Test Suite by allowing for multiple premises to be presented using an open world framework.

Our system takes multiple premises and attempts to answer a question correctly based on the premises.

We understand that with Natural Language Understanding, appropriate domain knowledge is important. So background knowledge (additional premises) for certain problems are provided as natural language. The assumption for our work is that there is sufficient domain knowledge available to interpret the semantics of the propositions. This would be needed for any test set where the set of premises does not describe some of the relationships that are generally understood to be known by a human reader. We'd like to be able to obtain domain knowledge and general knowledge from reading internet sources, such as Wikipedia. Currently, we just provide background domain information to the system as part of the problem statements such as those contained within the FraCaS Test Suite.

The system currently focuses on the language contained within the FraCaS Test Suite. In addition, our work only considers the subset of natural language (English) from which a parser can produce a valid grammar tree from problems contained within the FraCaS Test Suite. This subset allows us to test what is possible for our methodology while not having to deal with an invalid or incomplete parse. While it is not the focus of this paper, there are ways of ruling out particularly bad parses, such as when the StanfordNLP parser produces an incomplete parse tree. If the premises are unable to be parsed successfully the user could be asked to reword the premises and / or question and try again. Currently, we ignore these problems.

The reason for this is to identify if it is possible to generate sufficient knowledge to reason over to be able to answer the questions contained within the test suite and if so, it could be extended further to be tested against other test suites or even more real world scenarios.

2 Related Work

There is work in many areas in Natural Language Understanding, from statistical analysis of language (Manning et al., 1999), to predicate logic based systems, or natural logic (MacCartney et al. 2007). The first type of system, the statistical based, comes in many different varieties such as feature analysis, Bayesian priors, domain-based features, etc. (Rosario et al., 2001; Pantel et al., 2006; Nastase, 2006; Turney, 2010). There is a problem with the prepositional logic type systems as well. Those systems only work in the realm of true and false and do not leave any room for non-Boolean related queries. Natural

Logic requires both premises and a working hypothesis to try to find an answer through entailment checking the validity of the statement.

Other work on textual entailment includes (Dagan et al. 2005; Giampiccolo et al. 2007).

There is work in understanding the semantic meaning and modeling semantics as shown in (Grefenstette, 2011; Baroni, 2010; Mitchell, 2010).

Additionally, there is work using ontologies to learn from text as shown in (Buitelaar, Cimiano, Magini 2005). Our work draws on the layered cake approach presented in their book.

Other research areas include entailment inference (Schubert et al., 2010) and the use of episodic logics (Schubert et al., 2000), as well as relationship extraction done by Romano (2006).

The FraCaS Test Suite contains 346 NLI problems, divided into nine sections, each focused on a specific category of semantic phenomena (Cooper, 1996; MacCartney et al., 2008). MaCartney and Manning achieve rather good results, however they removed problems with multiple premises as well as those without a hypothesis (MacCartney et al., 2007; MacCartney et al., 2008). MacCartney's work, worked well with single premise statements.

3 Methodology

The best way to understand how the system works is by taking a look at the high level algorithm shown in Figure 1. This depicts the steps the system must take to achieve an understanding.

```
1. For each premise: Parse the premise and generate
   ordered list of grammar trees
   a. For each grammar tree for a given premise[1]
      i.  Generate intermediate object by pattern
          matching each set of children for all
          non-leaf nodes[2] //These intermediate ob-
          jects will hold additional generated in-
          formation
      ii. Normalize words; nouns become singular,
          verbs become present tense[3]
     iii. While there are changes to be made
          1. Apply POS/word rules to intermediate
             object.
          2. Push information into temporary ontol-
             ogy
          3. Type match as needed (notably for
             verbs)
          4. Build relationships
          5. Push relationships into temporary on-
             tology
      iv. Merge temporary ontology into main ontol-
          ogy
          1. Find matches
      v.  Generate new information based on struc-
          ture of main ontology
      vi. Clear temporary ontology
2. For the question follow steps 1.a.i-iv
3. Find an answer to the question yes/no/unknown by
   matching the temporary ontology to the main on-
   tology
```

Figure 1. High level view of methodology

The first step towards understanding English using our methodology is to acquire an annotated tree parse of the English statements. OpenNLP (Baldridge, 2005) and StanfordNLP (Toutanova, 2009) are used to acquire the annotated parse. Using them together we get a higher number of acceptable parses.

Given a grammar tree from the parsers mentioned above, pattern matching tells us the type of intermediate object we must instantiate. The intermediate object represents a sub-tree within the grammar tree. It holds information for that particular sub tree. Additional information will be added based on pre-determined rules derived from the language contained within the FraCaS Test Suite. The intermediate object specifies how words relate to one another.

Nouns and verbs are normalized, to assist in matching. All nouns become singular and a quantity attribute that indicates the number or range of elements is attributed to it. Depending on whether the noun was a proper noun or not helps indicate if it was an instance or a class as far as the ontology is concerned. All verbs become present tense and gain a time component, indicating if they occurred past, present, future, etc. A time component is attached to verb predicates is to maintain information as well as infer time based semantics.

Intermediate objects for verbs are similar to a predicate logic. Parameters for a predicate tuple can be either a reference to a noun object or a pointer to another predicate. If it is a pointer to another predicate, think of it as a way to link a verb phrase that has a noun with a prepositional phrase where the preposition is the predicate of another tuple. Other predicates are keywords that describe the action the system should take upon further analysis of said predicate. A unique identifier is added to instances and classes when created, to differentiate between similarly named instances and classes.

After a premise has been processed this temporary ontology is merged into the main ontology. If it was a question it stays as a temporary ontology for analysis in step 3 as shown in Figure 1. When there is no information in the main ontology, the temporary ontology becomes the main ontology. In a more interesting case, instances and classes must be matched against preexisting instances and classes that exist in the ontology. When a match is found, all elements that related to the instance or class in the tempo-

[1] A grammar tree is valid when all sub steps are completed successfully

[2] If there is a set of children where there is no match in the grammar tree restart loop starting on next grammar tree

[3] This information is maintained for nouns to keep track of the quantity, the information is needed for verbs to maintain a partial ordering on the information as it is presented

rary ontology is remapped to point to the item in the main ontology instead.

Step 1.a.v checks every element in the ontology to see if additional information can be generated that is factually true about the currently known information. For example; if there is an *instance contract* in the ontology that represents only 1 *contract* then clearly there is the class *contract* that should exist which represents the set of all instances of *contract*. If there exists a *class contract* with a quantity 1 that has no parent class then it would be true that there is another uniquely identified *class contract* that contains the quantity that is set to 'all' which represents all contracts that can exist.

The same process can be done for an instance that contains a property about the instance. Facts are generated similarly for *contract*; in addition there is also the set with the attribute propagating up the hierarchy where each parent that has the attribute is also a child of the same class without the attribute.

When a question is input to the system the previous steps are taken as indicated above except the temporary ontology isn't merged or cleared. The problem then becomes to find a satisfiable mapping from the temporary ontology to the main ontology. Every object in the temporary ontology tries to find the potential matches it has in the main ontology. For some matches, a temporary set of instances may need to be collected e.g. Figure 7. The system looks at each tuple and evaluates it to be true, false, or unknown depending on the information in the main ontology. The temporary ontology from the question is evaluated for every instance and class and all connections are formed to the main ontology. Using these connections, an attempt to replace the temporary ontology instance or class with each specific related term. At least as far as these problems are concerned, there is only one solution that can be found if it is either *true* or *false*.[4] *Unknown* is the case where no such replacement was found to satisfy a particular relation. The process is to evaluate every relation under this assumption. If a result of either true or false is produced then that is the answer to the question and it returns. However, if it returns unknown then it continues to change another term and repeats this process until no more configurations are possible in which case the answer is truly unknown.

Figure 2 shows one of the problems evaluated using the system, based on the methodology mentioned above.

[4] Some premises and questions can have multiple interpretations, our software picks one (has programmed bias).

Smith signed one contract.
Jones signed another contract.
Did Smith and Jones sign two contracts?

Figure 2. Problem 111 from the FraCas Test Suite

Starting with the first premise in Figure 2, the system generates the main ontology shown in Figure 3.

sign<past tense, t+1>(<Instance: QTY 1>SMITH_1, <Instance: QTY 1>CONTRACT_2)

Figure 3. Main Ontology for premise 1

Figure 4 shows new facts that are generated from the main ontology.

instance_of(<Instance: QTY 1>SMITH_1, <Class: QTY 1>SMITH_1)
instance_of(<Instance: QTY 1>CONTRACT_2, <Class: QTY 1>CONTRACT_2)
subset_of(<Class: QTY 1>SMITH_1, <Class: QTY ALL>SMITH_3)
subset_of(<Class: QTY 1>CONTRACT_2, <Class: QTY ALL>CONTRACT_4)

Figure 4. New facts generated from Main Ontology

The second premise from Figure 2 generates the following facts shown in Figure 5.

sign<past tense, t+2>(<Instance: QTY 1>JONES_3, <Instance: QTY 1>CONTRACT_4)

Figure 5. New facts added to main ontology from premise 2 seen from Figure 1

When generating new facts based on the now updated main ontology, everything follows as normal for Jones. However, for *instance contract*, there is a *class contract* in the main ontology with a quantity set to one, a direct match. No additional information is generated as it already exists.

instance_of(<Instance: QTY 1>JONES_3, <Class: QTY 1> JONES_5)
instance_of(<Instance: QTY 1>CONTRACT_4, <Class: QTY 1>CONTRACT_2)
subset_of(<Class: QTY 1>JONES_5>, <Class: QTY ALL>JONES_6)

Figure 6. New facts generated based on main ontology

sign<past tense, t+3>(<Instance: QTY 1>SMITH_5, <Instance: QTY 2>CONTRACT_6)
sign<past tense, t+3>(<Instance: QTY 1>JONES_6, <Instance: QTY 2>CONTRACT_6)

Figure 7. Facts in temporary ontology for question

Answering the question becomes an exercise in mapping ontologies and checking the predicates. Every instance/relation from Figure 7 must map to another instance/relation in the main ontology. In this case, each relation is satisfied if replacements for both instances can be found. Another condition on the relation must be satisfied by looking at the time component. Not only must there exist a relation *sign* that has both instances but, that relation has to hold true before time (t+3). When trying to find a match, it first attempts to match relation name, which it finds, then check to see if the time component matches, which in this case is satisfied. Next, it checks the first term in the tuple, which for both it finds a valid replacement. However, for the *contract* with QTY 2, no match is found. The process is then to generate all sets that contain instances that are subsets of the instance *contract* that add up to QTY 2, and then try to apply each element within the set to see if it is a valid replacement. All elements in this temporary set must be used. Since all relations were successfully evaluated to true the result to the question is therefore yes.

4 Evaluation

The FraCaS Test Suite contains 346 NLI problems, divided into nine sections, each focused on a specific category of semantic phenomena (Cooper, 1996; MacCartney et al., 2008). For comparison to previous work, we will not remove multiple-premise problems, or problems that are missing a hypothesis as done in (MacCartney et al., 2007; MacCartney et al., 2008). No modification to the test set has been made to accommodate my research. However, we do remove problems from the test suite that contain a bad parse on any one of the premises for the problem or the question. We will show a comparison based on percentage of problems that are answered correctly. This research focuses on six sections which represent Generalized Quantifiers, Plurals, Adjectives, Comparatives, Verbs and Attitudes respectively.

Table 1 show that the system performs exceptionally well. The accuracy is calculated based on the correct answer and remaining problems. There is one critical thing to be taken from this, that while this methodology is fully capable of solving these problems, obtaining a valid part of speech tree for each premise and question in each problem is paramount.

Section	Original Problems	Bad Parses	Remaining Problems	Correct Answer	Acc %
1	80	10	70	61[5]	87.00
2	33	11	22	21[6]	95.45
5	23	7	16	16	100.00
6	31	9	22	22	100.00
8	8	4	4	4	100.00
9	13	6	7	7	100.00
Total	188	47	141	131	92.90

Table 1. Results

When our methodology is compared against the semantic containment and exclusion method as seen in (MacCartney et al., 2008) we clearly see that when statements are analyzed in depth we gain greater accuracy overall, as shown in Table 2. With the notable exception to the first section, generalized quantifiers, where the system does not yet support the language contained in 9 of the problems despite it producing a valid parse. In addition to a higher accuracy rate on the FraCaS Test Suite we also are capable of working with problems that contain multiple premises.

	Problems	Acc%
Most common class 'yes'	178	51.68
MacCartney 07	108	75.00
Natlog	108	87.04
This system	137	**92.27**

Table 2. Performance on FraCaS problems on sections: 1, 2, 5, 6, 9 compared

In total, the results mean that where our system supports the language, the system works well. The exception is when multiple problems in the test suite are the same but can be interpreted differently.

5 Conclusion

Making machines understand natural language at any level is a challenging problem. We've developed a methodology that converts natural language into ontology while leveraging the ontology to help solve questions posed in natural language about the facts in the ontology. We've shown that our methodology which works around extending the semantics of language, by keeping track of inferences, quantities, inheritance, properties, and set related information, produces a high degree of accuracy. Using more information than is directly seen in the statements allows us to help match terms in a natural way, which allows for questions to be proved correct (yes or no) or unsolvable (unknown).

6 Future Work

The next logical step is to see how well our methodology adapts and performs to the other sections that are not addressed in this paper. Also, there is a maximum of just five premises in the largest problem in this problem set; analyzing a full page document is a direction that needs to be pursued.

[5] The system realized that it could not answer the 9 questions out of the 70 remaining problems for section 1 so it produces a null answer; we count null answers as wrong.

[6] It can solve problem 87 from the test suite but due to this it cannot solve problem 88 due to word play.

References

Baroni, Marco, and Roberto Zamparelli. "Nouns are vectors, adjectives are matrices: Representing adjective-noun constructions in semantic space." Proceedings of the 2010 Conference on Empirical Methods in Natural Language Processing. Association for Computational Linguistics, 2010.

Buitelaar, Paul, Philipp Cimiano, and Bernardo Magnini, eds. Ontology learning from text: methods, evaluation and applications. Vol. 123. IOS press, 2005.

Dagan, Ido, Oren Glickman, and Bernardo Magnini. "The pascal recognising textual entailment challenge." Machine Learning Challenges. Evaluating Predictive Uncertainty, Visual Object Classification, and Recognising Tectual Entailment. Springer Berlin Heidelberg, 2006. 177-190.

Giampiccolo, Danilo, et al. "The third pascal recognizing textual entailment challenge." Proceedings of the ACL-PASCAL workshop on textual entailment and paraphrasing. Association for Computational Linguistics, 2007.

Grefenstette, Edward, and Mehrnoosh Sadrzadeh. "Experimental support for a categorical compositional distributional model of meaning." Proceedings of the Conference on Empirical Methods in Natural Language Processing. Association for Computational Linguistics, 2011.

J. Baldridge. 2005. The OpenNLP project, http://opennlp.sourceforge.net/

J. Sukkarieh. 2003. Mind your Language! Controlled Language for Inference Purposes. Oral presentation, Presented at the Joint Conference of the Eighth International Workshop of the European Association for Machine Translation and the Fourth Controlled Language Applications Workshop, Dublin, Ireland.

K. Toutanova. 2009. The Stanford NLP Group Part-of-Speech Tagger, http://nlp.stanford.edu/software/tagger.shtml

MacCartney, Bill and Christopher D. Manning. 2007. Natural logic for textual inference, In ACL-07 Workshop on Textual Entailment and Paraphrasing, Prague.

MacCartney, B. and Manning, C. D. 2008. Modeling semantic containment and exclusion in natural language inference. In *Proceedings of the 22nd international Conference on Computational Linguistics - Volume 1* (Manchester, United Kingdom, August 18 - 22, 2008): 521-528.

Manning, C. D., and Schütze, H. 1999. Foundations of Statistical Natural Language Processing. Cambridge, MA: The MIT Press

Mitchell, Jeff, and Mirella Lapata. "Composition in distributional models of semantics." Cognitive Science 34.8 (2010): 1388-1429.

Nastase, Vivi, et al. "Learning noun-modifier semantic relations with corpus-based and WordNet-based features." Proceedings of the National Conference on Artificial Intelligence. Vol. 21. No. 1. Menlo Park, CA; Cambridge, MA; London; AAAI Press; MIT Press; 1999, 2006.

Pantel, Patrick, and Marco Pennacchiotti. "Espresso: Leveraging generic patterns for automatically harvesting semantic relations." Proceedings of the 21st International Conference on Computational Linguistics and the 44th annual meeting of the Association for Computational Linguistics. Association for Computational Linguistics, 2006.

R. Cooper, R. Crouch, J. Van Eijck, C. Fox, J. Van Genabith, J. Jaspars, H. Kamp, M. Pinkal, D. Milward, M. Poesio, and S. Pulman. 1996. Using the Framework. Technical report, FraCaS: A Framework for Computational Semantics, FraCaS deliverable D16.

Romano, Lorenza, et al. "Investigating a generic paraphrase-based approach for relation extraction." Proceedings of EACL. Vol. 2006. 2006.

Rosario, Barbara, and Marti Hearst. "Classifying the semantic relations in noun compounds via a domain-specific lexical hierarchy." Proceedings of the 2001 Conference on Empirical Methods in Natural Language Processing (EMNLP-01). 2001.

Schubert, Lenhart K., and Chung Hee Hwang. "Episodic Logic meets Little Red Riding Hood: A comprehensive, natural representation for language understanding." Natural Language Processing and Knowledge Representation: Language for Knowledge and Knowledge for Language (2000): 111-174.

Schubert, Lenhart K., Benjamin Van Durme, and Marzieh Bazrafshan. "Entailment inference in a natural logic–like general reasoner." Proc. of the AAAI 2010 Symp. on Commonsense Knowledge. 2010.

Turney, Peter D., and Patrick Pantel. "From frequency to meaning: Vector space models of semantics." Journal of artificial intelligence research 37.1 (2010): 141-188.

What Do We Drink? Automatically Extending Hungarian WordNet With Selectional Preference Relations

Márton Miháltz[1], Bálint Sass[1], Balázs Indig[2]
[1]MTA-PPKE Hungarian Language Technology Research Group, Budapest, Hungary
[2]Pázmány Péter Catholic University, Faculty of Information Technology and Bionics, Budapest, Hungary
{mihaltz.marton,sass.balint,indig.balazs}@itk.ppke.hu

Abstract

In this paper, we describe an ongoing experiment which aims to extend Hungarian WordNet with new verb-noun relations that specify selectional restrictions for various argument positions. We present an algorithm that uses frequency data from a representative corpus and information from a verb frame description database to generate sets of semantic classes, represented by WN hypernym sub-networks. The method intends to cover all possible argument positions of verbs found in the corpus which are marked by various case inflections or postposition particles. The new links in HuWN are assigned corpus-based probabilities. We present some preliminary results and discuss some of the arising issues.

1 Introduction

Since its first release in 1985, Princeton WordNet (PWN) (Fellbaum, 1998) has become a de facto standard lexical semantic resource for natural language processing research and applications. Its availability, vast lexical coverage and solid development over the years helped it achieve a prominent status.

Over its history, a number of possibilities for improvement of WN have become evident. From the NLP user's perspective, one of PWN's weaknesses lies in the low number of cross-part-of-speech semantic relationships it defines. Most of the existing relations across the different sub-networks for nouns, verbs, adjectives and adverbs are morphological (derivational) connections, e.g. research (verb)-researcher (noun), engage (verb)-engagement (noun) etc.

In this paper, we describe an ongoing experiment whose goal is to automatically extend Hungarian WordNet with verb-noun relations that reflect selectional preferences observed in a representative corpus. We try to automatically generalize classes of concepts (hyponym sub-graphs) that represent typical arguments for certain syntactic verb-noun relations, e.g. {to eat}-{food}, {to write}-{written material} etc. This information will be used, for example, in a project that aims to construct a novel parser for Hungarian that will in part rely on deep semantic processing of the input (Prószéky 2013).

Hungarian WordNet (HuWN) (Miháltz et al., 2008) follows the principles underlying the EuroWordNet and BalkaNet projects (Vossen, 1999, Tufiş et al., 2004). It uses Princeton Wordnet (version 2.0) as its inter-lingual index, meaning that the majority of Hungarian synsets are mapped to English WN synsets. HuWN contains localizations of the Balkanet Core Set synsets, plus additional concepts totaling 42,000 synsets. In addition to the standard semantic relations found in PWN it introduces new relations to reflect some intrinsic properties of Hungarian (Kuti et al., 2008).

The rest of this paper is organized as follows: in the next section, we briefly cover some points about verb argument syntax and semantics and present our goals. Section 3 presents related work, which is followed by the description of our proposed algorithm and the presentation of some preliminary results. The paper ends with a discussion of further work and our conclusions.

2 Background

In Hungarian, the syntactic roles of verb arguments (complements) are reflected by any of 18-34 different morphological case markings (exact number depending on the chosen linguistic theory) or by various postposition particles. Different verbs have different argument structures which impose different morphosyntactic constraints on their arguments. These in turn correspond to different semantic types of nominal concepts: *figyel valamire* (to pay attention to something[case=SUBL]), *elkezdődik valami* (something[case=NOM] begins), *odaéget valamit* (to burn something[case=ACC]), *érdeklődik valami után* (to show interest in something[postp='after']) etc.

Connections between verbs and their nominal arguments show a range of types. On the one extreme, there are idiomatic, non-compositional verb-argument relationships where a certain sense of a verb only accepts a specific lexical element in a certain argument position, e.g.: ***hangot*** *ad valaminek* ("to give **voice**[case=ACC] to something": express one's opinion about sg), *issza a* ***szavát*** ("to drink someonone's **words**": to listen closely to someone), ***tenyerén*** *hordoz* ("to carry someone around on the **palm** of one's hand": to pamper someone) etc. On the other extreme, there are verbs that impose semantic selectional restrictions on their preferred arguments. These arguments belong to (one or more) specific semantic classes: *to eat something (food), to write something (piece of writing), to spill something (liquid)* etc. These semantic classes can productively predict which lexical items these verbs will prefer in given argument positions.

The goal of the project described in this paper is to find automatic methods in order to extend Hungarian WordNet with instances of a new type of semantic relation that links verb synsets with their typical nominal argument classes. Each of these new relation instances will have two associated properties: morphosyntactic information (the case mark or postposition) identifying the given argument position, and the strength of the connection, expressed as a probability estimated from the corpus based on the frequency of usage. For instance, the connection *{to drink}–[case=acc, p=.87]–{liquid}* designates that the arguments of the verb *drink* carrying an accusative case mark (direct object position) will fall into the semantic class represented by *{liquid}* with 87% probability (as observed in the corpus.) The synset *{liquid}* here represents itself and all its direct and indirect hyponyms, thus it also represents a class of related concepts.

3 Related Work

Charting selectional preferences is a key step in the semantic processing of written language. It involves determining which word meanings are frequent and/or allowed in a specific syntactic context of another given word. Following work by Resnik (1996, 1998), several studies relied on WordNet in the detection of selectional preferences (Clark and Weir, 2002, Ye, 2004, Calvo et al., 2005).

While recent approaches have focused on Latent Dirichlet Allocation (LDA) methods (Ritter et al., 2010, Guo and Diab, 2013, Rink and Harabagiu, 2013), we present an approach that more closely resembles Resnik (1998). It is applied to resources in Hungarian, which has not been researched previously before. Our work does not only focus on the classic problem of verb-direct object selectional preferences but all possible syntactic types of arguments (20+ in Hungarian) are considered, as recommended by Brockmann and Lapata (2003).

In contrast to approaches that only aim to define which set of words are preferred as arguments of given verbs (e.g. Erk, 2007, Tian et al., 2013, Rink and Harabagiu, 2013), in line of the approach outlined by Resnik (1998) and also adapted by Guo and Diab (2013), our research attempts to assign semantic class labels to verb argument positions, which define selectional preferences. This enables us to accomplish our goal, extending Hungarian WordNet with a new type of verb-noun (verb-argument) relation.

4 Methods

We propose an algorithm which takes a set of words (frequency list of nouns in a certain argument position of a given verb from a representative corpus) and returns a weighted list of WordNet synsets that represent them (semantic classes/generalizations representing the argument position). The resulting synsets (and the hyponym sub-graphs that they represent) should satisfy the following conditions as much as possible:

Coverage: the synset and its hyponym descendants should contain as much input corpus words as possible.

Density: the hyponym sub-graph should cover as few words as possible which were not included in the input word list.

Meaningful generalizations: the output synset and its hyponym sub-graph should express a generalization of the meanings of the corpus words in the verb argument position, but it should not be too generous. For e.g. assigning *{entity}* to all verb arguments has little or no benefit as it does not give insights to the semantic preference characteristic of different verbs.

Automatic word sense disambiguation: if a word associated to a verb as an argument in the corpus has several meanings in WN, we expect the algorithm to yield relations that link the verb only to the sense(s) relevant for that argument position.

Our algorithm works as follows:

1. First, it generates all possible paths from all WN synsets that contain the input words to the root nodes in the hypernym hierarchies. All the synsets at all points in all these paths are considered as representatives of candidate semantic classes.

2. This is followed by filtering of the candidates: eliminate those candidate synsets that represent only a single corpus word and which are (1 or more degree) hypernyms of the synset that contain the word. This step is applied to omit some of the candidates that present no generalization information.

3. Next, the algorithm scores the remaining candidates based on two factors: *coverage* (how many input words they cover) and *density* (number of synsets representing input words covered by the sub-graph of a candidate to the total size of the sub-graph.) The following formula is used to calculate the score for candidate synset *c* (where *subgr(c)* is the hyponym subgraph starting from synset *c* and I_c is the subset of all input words that are covered by *subgr(c)*):

$$Score(c) = |I_c| \times \frac{|\{s \in subgr(c) : w \in s, w \in I_c\}|}{|subgr(c)|}$$

4. The top N candidate synsets are returned based on the ranking. To ensure disambiguation of input words with respect to the verb argument position, the following procedure is applied: if there are any 2 candidate synsets in the list that each contain different senses of the same input word, then the lower-ranked candidate is eliminated and the N+1. ranked candidate is added to the list. This is repeated until there are no more ambiguities.

New verb-noun relations can be added to the WN network in which the verb argument positions are semantic classes represented by the winning candidates. Link probabilities are calculated using the corpus frequencies of the input words covered by the classes (see Section 6.)

We used the database of the *Verb Argument Browser (VAB)* project (Sass, 2008), which was constructed from the 187 million-word Hungarian National Corpus (Váradi, 2002). In VAB, a simple rule-based parser was used to identify clauses, finite verbs and noun phrases (heads and their morphosyntactic properties: cases and postpositions) in all sentences of the corpus. From this, for each verb in the corpus, we extracted frequency lists of all the nouns it co-occurred with, grouped by different case markings and postpositions.

To determine the possible argument structures of each verb in the corpus (number of arguments and their morphosyntactic constraints), we relied on the lexical database of the *MetaMorpho* Hungarian-English machine translation system's syntactic parser (Prószéky et al., 2004). It contains 33,000 verb frame descriptions (argument structures for various senses) for more than 18,000 Hungarian verbs. During the construction of Hungarian Wordnet, verb synsets were linked to the corresponding verb frame descriptions in this database (Miháltz et al., 2008). This information can be used to unambiguously determine the verb synsets that will participate in the newly generated selectional preference relations.

We used a subset of the MetaMorpho syntactic analyzer's rules to identify verb argument structures in the 20.24 million sentence clauses that constitute the basis of the Verb Argument Browser database. This was done to refine the contents of the VAB database, because 1) it employed a less sophisticated parser, 2) it does not differentiate between verb complements and optional modifiers (adjuncts). By using the parser, we were able to focus on the true complements. We obtained 32,000 different verb argument frequency lists for 25,500 different verb frames to run our selectional preference class identification algorithm on.

5 Results and Discussion

Since we are still working on an evaluation methodology to compare the output of our algorithm against the judgments of human annotators, we demonstrate our results on some relevant examples.

Table 1 shows 6 selected verb argument positions (with argument cases indicated) along with the top ranked HuWN synsets that were identified as preferred semantic classes with our algorithm.

Verbal argument	Semantic class
iszik ACC	*{folyadék}*
to drink sg	{liquid}
kigombol ACC	*{ruha}*
to unbutton sg	{garment}
olvas ACC	*{könyv}*
to read sg	{book}
ül SUP	*{ülőbútor}*
to sit on sg	{seat}
vádol INS	*{bűncselekmény}*
to accuse (sy) with sg	{crime, ...}
megold ACC	*{nehézség}*
to overcome sg	{hindrance, ...}

Table 1: Automatically identified semantic classes for verb argument positions

We also present the top 5 semantic classes obtained from the nouns found in the accusative argument position of the verb *iszik* (to drink) with their calculated scores in Table 2 (for brevity, we only show the English WN equivalents).

Score	Class	c	d
9.1	{liquid}	26	.35
8.796	{beverage, drink, ...}	25	.351
4.888	{alcohol, alcoholic drink, ...}	16	.305
4.375	{liquor, spirits, ...}	7	.625
3.759	{food, nutrient}	28	.134

Table 2: Top 5 semantic classes identified as direct object arguments of *drink (*c: number of corpus words covered, d: density of the sub-network)

Looking at WN's hierarchy, we see that {liquid} subsumes {beverage, drink} which in turn subsumes {alcohol, alcoholic drink}. But which of these do we exactly want to link {drink} (verb) to? Selecting the most general and most highly ranked category will lead us to choose {liquid}. From a different point of view, however, {beverage, drink} could be more relevant, since not all liquids are drinkable. For some applications indicating the strong association with {alcohol, alcoholic drink} could also be important. By preserving the top *N* semantic classes representing arguments and their degrees of association in the proposed new links, we intend to give an opportunity for future users of our data to freely decide these questions according to their needs.

6 Future Work

Currently we are working on refining our methods. When an evaluation methodology becomes available, it will be possible to fine-tune the candidate scoring formula and to experiment with the best way to assign link probabilities. Additional information that can be used includes corpus frequencies of input words, the depths of the candidate synsets in the hypernym networks and the average distance of the corpus words' synsets from the sub-graphs' root nodes.

As we showed, our method assigns noun frequency lists to verbal argument positions and proposes WN synsets that are most likely to describe selectional preferences. However, argument positions within a verb frame are not independent of each other. It is often the case that binding one of the arguments (assigning a lexical item to that position) entails special selectional preference conditions on another argument position. Examples are *ad ACC* (give something) in the case of ***hírt*** *ad DEL* ("give **news** about sg": to report sg), or *húz ACC* (to pull something) with the argument ***hasznot*** *húz ELA* ("pull **profit** from sg": to profit from sg). As it is also stressed by de Cruys (2010), in the future it is important for us to advance towards a multi-argument model that is able to detect complex verbal units like *hírt ad, hasznot húz* etc. and able to identify selectional preferences for their additional arguments.

According to Mechura (2010), categories in WN do not completely correspond to selectional preferences, and asks the question: "what should an ontology actually look like if it were to reflect accurately the semantic types involved in selectional preferences?" Examining classes that our algorithm assigns with high probabilities may lead to the answer.

7 Conclusion

In this paper, we described a proposed method to automatically enrich Hungarian WordNet with new verb selectional preference relations, which could be useful for semantic text processing tasks. The results may also be beneficial for psycholinguistic research by giving insights to the nature of some of the cross-part-of-speech relationships within the mental lexicon.

Acknowledgments

This work was in part supported by the TÁMOP 4.2.2/B - 10/1-2010-0014 and the TÁMOP 4.2.1.B - 11/2/KMR-2011-0002 projects in the framework of the New Hungarian Development Plan, supported by the European Union, co-financed by the European Social Fund.

References

Brockmann, Carsten -- Lapata, Mirella 2003. Evaluating and combining approaches to selectional preference acquisition. In: Proceedings of EACL 2003, 27-34

Calvo, Hiram -- Gelbukh, Alexander -- Kilgarriff, Adam 2005. Distributional Thesaurus vs. WordNet: A Comparison of Backoff Techniques for Unsupervised PP Attachment. In: Proceedings of CICLing 2005, 177-188

Clark, Stephen -- Weir, David 2002. Class-Based Probability Estimation Using a Semantic Hierarchy. In: Computational Linguistics 28:2, 2002, 187-206

Erk, Katrin 2007. A simple, similarity-based model for selectional preferences. In: Proceedings of ACL 2007, 216-223

Fellbaum, Christiane (ed.) 1998. WordNet: An Electronic Lexical Database. MIT Press: Cambridge.

Guo, Weiwei -- Diab, Mona 2013. Improving Lexical Semantics for Sentential Semantics: Modeling Selectional Preference and Similar Words in a Latent Variable Model. In: Proceedings of NAACL-HLT 2013, 739-745

Kuti, Judit Károly Varasdi Ágnes Gyarmati Péter Vajda 2008. Language Independent and Language Dependent Innovations in the Hungarian WordNet. In Proc. of The Fourth Global WordNet Conference, Szeged, Hungary, 254–268.

Mechura, Michal Boleslav 2010. What WordNet does not know about selectional preferences. In: Dykstra, A. -- Schoonheim T. (eds.) 2010. Proceedings of the 14th Euralex International Congress, Ljouwert/Leeuwarden: Fryske Akademy, 431-436

Miháltz, Márton – Csaba Hatvani – Judit Kuti – György Szarvas – János Csirik – Gábor Prószéky – Tamás Váradi 2008. Methods and Results of the Hungarian WordNet Project. In: Attila Tanács – Dóra Csendes – Veronika Vincze – Christiane Fellbaum – Piek Vossen (szerk.) Proceedings of The Fourth Global WordNet Conference. Szeged: University of Szeged, 311–321.

Prószéky, Gábor 2013. Kutatások egy pszicholingvisztikai indíttatású számítógépes nyelvfeldolgozás irányában. In: Ladányi Mária — Vladár Zsuzsa (ed.) A XI. MANYE-konferencia előadásai (megjelenés alatt)

Prószéky, Gábor – László Tihanyi – Gábor Ugray 2004. Moose: a robust high-performance parser and generator. Proceedings of the 9th Workshop of the European Association for Machine Translation. La Valletta: Foundation for International Studies, 138–142.

Resnik, Philip 1996. Selectional constraints: an information-theoretic model and its computational realization. Cognition 61, 1996, 127-159

Resnik, Philip 1998. WordNet and Class-Based Probabilities. In: Fellbaum (1998a)

Rink, Bryan -- Harabagiu, Sanda 2013. The Impact of Selectional Preference Agreement on Semantic Relational Similarity. In: Proceedings of International Conference on Computational Semantics (IWCS) 2013

Ritter, Alan -- Mausam -- Etzioni, Oren 2010. A latent dirichlet allocation method for selectional preferences. In: Proceedings of ACL 2010, 424-434

Sass, Bálint 2008. The Verb Argument Browser. In: Sojka, P., Horák, A., Kopecek, I., Pala, K. (eds.): 11th International Conference on Text, Speech and Dialog (TSD), Brno, Czech Republic. Lecture Notes in Computer Science 5246, 187-192.

Tian, Zhenhua -- Xiang, Hengheng -- Liu, Ziqi -- Zheng, Qinghua 2013. A Random Walk Approach to Selectional Preferences Based on Preference Ranking and Propagation. In: Proceedings of ACL 2013, 1169-1179

Tufiş, Dan Dan Cristea Sofia Stamou 2004. Balka-Net: Aims, Methods, Results and Perspectives. A General Overview. In Romanian Journal of Information Science and Technology Special Issue, 7(12), 34.

van de Cruys, Tim 2010. A non-negative tensor factorization model for selectional preference induction. In: Natural Language Engineering 16:4, 2010, 417-437

Váradi, Tamás 2002. The Hungarian National Corpus. In: Zampolli, Antonio (ed.) Proceedings of the Second International Conference on Language Resources and Evaluation. Las Palmas: ELRA, 385-389.

Vossen, Piek 1999. EuroWordNet General Document, Version 3. University of Amsterdam.

Ye, Patrick 2004. Selectional Preference Based Verb Sense Disambiguation Using WordNet. In: Proceedings of the Australasian Language Technology Workshop 2004

Comparison pattern matching and creative simile recognition

Vlad Niculae
Université de Franche-Comté, Besançon
Center for Computational Linguistics, University of Bucharest
vlad@vene.ro

Abstract

Comparisons are phrases that express the likeness of two entities. They are usually marked by linguistic patterns, among which the most discussed are *X is like Y* and *as X as Y*. We propose a simple slot-based dependency-driven description of such patterns that refines the phrase structure approach of Niculae and Yaneva (2013). We introduce a simple similarity-based approach that proves useful for measuring the degree of figurativeness of a comparison and therefore in simile (figurative comparison) identification. We propose an evaluation method for this task on the VUAMC metaphor corpus.

1 Introduction

The comparison structure is a common linguistic pattern used to express similitude or distinction of two entities with respect to a property. When the comparison is not intended to be taken literally, it is called a *simile*. Identifying comparison structures is important for information extraction, as it is a way of asserting properties of entities. The simile, on the other hand, is interesting for the striking creative images it often produces:

> "Mrs. Cratchit entered: flushed, but smiling proudly: with the pudding, like a speckled cannon-ball, so hard and firm, (...)" (In "A Christmas Carol" by Charles Dickens)

The simile, as a figure of speech, is receiving an increasing amount of interest, after being historically discarded as a less interesting form of metaphor. To clarify that the expressive span of the metaphor and the simile overlap but are different, Israel et al. (2004) gives examples of metaphors that cannot be perfectly transformed into similes, and vice versa. Further supporting this point, Hanks (2012) identifies many cases where the simile is used creatively as a way of describing things by constructing images that surpass the realm of the possible and the experienced.

2 Corpora

The VU Amsterdam Metaphor Corpus (Steen et al., 2010), henceforth VUAMC, is a subset of British National Corpus (BNC) Baby (Burnard, 1995) annotated for phenomena related to linguistic metaphor. It consists of 16 202 sentences and 236 423 tokens. About half (50.7%) of the sentences have at least an *mrw* (metaphor-related word) annotated. Of more interest for our study is the *mFlag* (metaphor flag) annotation, which surrounds trigger phrases for figurativeness. Table 1 shows the most frequent *mFlag* tags. We investigate the use of this annotation for automatically evaluating simile identification. Given the underrepresentation of similes in the VUAMC, we chose to only present experiments using the comparison patterns involving *like*. The methods used are not pattern specific. Up to a degree of variation given by subtle language behaviour, they should apply to any comparison, as they only involve the contents of the comparison constituents that will be described in section 3.

In addition to the VUAMC, we used the collection of examples from (Hanks, 2012) and a subset of extracted matches from the BNC (Burnard, 1995). All text was tagged and parsed using TurboParser (Martins et al., 2010) using the basic projective model and lemmatized using `Treex`[1] (Popel and Žabokrtský, 2010).

3 Syntactic aspects

3.1 Characterisation of comparisons

[1] `http://ufal.mff.cuni.cz/treex/index.html`

flag	count	freq. per sentence
like	57	0.35%
as	28	0.17%
as if	7	0.04%
of	6	0.04%
other	45	0.28%
total	143	0.88%

Table 1: Metaphor flags in VUAMC

```
dict(slot='E',
     pos=lambda x: x.startswith('VB'),
     kids=[
          dict(slot='C',
               form='like',
               pos='IN',
               kids=[dict(slot='V',
                    deprel='PMOD')]),
          dict(slot='T',
               deprel='SUB',
               optional=True),
          dict(slot='P',
               optional=True,
               deprel='PRD'),
    ])
```

Listing 1: Python code representing the simple pattern for comparisons using *like* defined by Figure 1b.

Hanks (2012) identifies the following constituents of a comparison: the topic (T), the eventuality (E), the shared property (P), the comparator (C) and the vehicle (V). An example (adapted from the BNC) of a simile involving all of the above would be:

> [He ^{T}] [looked ^{E}] [like ^{C}] [a broiled frog ^{V}], [hunched ^{P}] over his desk, grinning and satisfied.

Niculae and Yaneva (2013) used constituent parsing with GLARF (Meyers et al., 2001) transformations in order to match several hand-written comparison patterns. While the normalizations performed by GLARF allow for more general patterns (constructions using auxiliary verbs such as *have been* are handled transparently), the tool is only available in English, and it proves error-prone in practice for complex sentences.

Dependency parsing, based on the formalism of Tesnière and Fourquet (1959), has been more

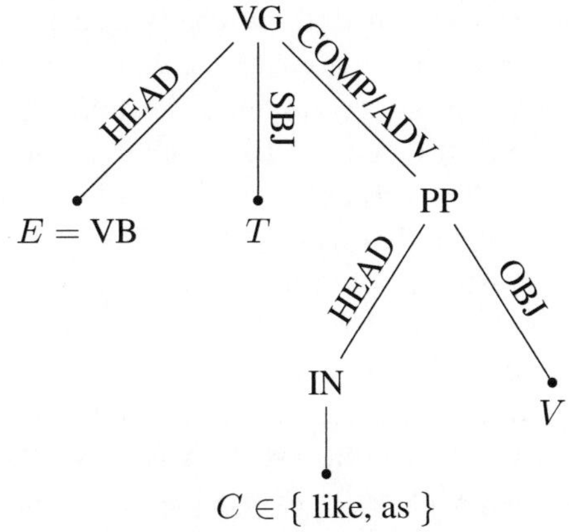

(a) GLARF-style pattern.

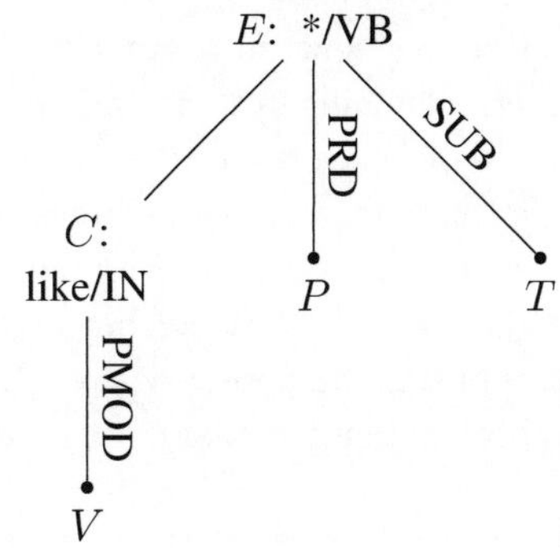

(b) DEP-style pattern. Its Python representation can be found in Listing 1.

Figure 1: Visualisation of the two types of approaches for encoding the *X is like Y* pattern.

actively developed recently. Compared to constituent parsing (phrase-structure grammars), dependency trees are easier to annotate, hence the availability of dependency treebanks and trained models for more languages. The space of possible dependency trees of a sentence is much smaller than the space of possible constituent trees, allowing for better models. Recent work in structured prediction includes the TurboParser (Martins et al., 2010), which we use in this work.

Figure 1 shows the GLARF-style pattern for comparisons using *like*, along with a corresponding dependency pattern.

3.2 Encoding and matching dependency patterns

In the case of phrase-structure treebanks, the powerful tools *Tgrep* and *Tgrep2*[2] permit fast extraction of trees sharing common patterns. Unfortunately, their formalism is inappropriate for query-

[2] http://tedlab.mit.edu/~dr/Tgrep2/

ing dependency trees. Additionally, while expressive, their syntax is arguably opaque and unwelcoming. We propose a simpler pattern matcher written in Python with patterns represented as Python code. The resulting patterns look similar to their graphical representation. This representation is a step closer to automatic construction of patterns, compared to hand-written pattern matching using conditionals. The implementation is currently available in the *comparison-pattern* package [3] under the permissive 3-clause BSD license. Like *Tgrep* works on parenthesised trees, common for representing constituent parses, our matcher takes CoNLL-style input.

For brevity, we henceforth refer to our dependency pattern matching system as DEP.

Listing 1 shows the code needed to represent the pattern. For certain underspecified patterns with symmetries, it's possible that several matches with the same root occur. Our matcher returns all of them and choosing the appropriate one is left as a separate problem that we do not treat in this work.

3.3 Comparison identification results

On the examples from (Hanks, 2012), DEP improves recall by identifying 6 additional matches, while losing only 2, one due to a POS tagging error and the other due to a parsing error. In cases when both systems match a sentence, it is sometimes the case that DEP provides more complete information, especially in the case of convoluted sentence structures.

On the subset from the BNC used by Niculae and Yaneva (2013), we examine only the points of disagreement between systems (sentences matched by one but dismissed by the other). Even though this analysis ignores the possibility of making qualitatively different matches for the same sentence, we opted for it for convenience, as evaluation needs to be manual. Contrary to Niculae and Yaneva (2013), we disregard matches that don't identify the vehicle of the comparison, as we are interested in finding common vehicles, for mining different comparators.

At first sight, DEP identifies 199 sentences that GLARF misses, while GLARF matches 36 instances missed by DEP. Upon going through the examples, we find that 43 matches out of the 199 are spurious because of preventable tagging or parsing errors, many of them in transcribed speech, where the word *like* functions as a filler word. However, 11 out of the GLARF-only matches were also spurious. Using dependency parsing is therefore a net gain for comparison identification.

[3] http://github.com/vene/comparison-pattern

System	P	R	F_1	count
LEXBL	0.166	1.00	0.284	320
GLARF	**0.303**	0.434	0.357	96
DEP	0.241	**0.717**	0.360	158
DEPSEM	0.252	**0.717**	**0.373**	151

Table 2: Simile identification performance, with respect to the 53 instances of *mFlag=like* annotation in VUAMC. LEXBL is the baseline that retrieves all sentences that contain the preposition *like*. The last column measures the number of retrieved instances.

3.4 Automatically evaluating simile retrieval

On VUAMC, we can use the *mFlag* annotation as ground truth for evaluating pattern matching. However, as the focus of the corpus is figurative language, literal comparison are not marked. Because pattern matching finds comparisons, without any semantic processing, the retrieval precision will be low (all literal comparisons would be seen as spurious simile matches). However, it passes the sanity check against the LEXBL baseline that simply returns all sentences containing the preposition *like* (after part-of-speech tagging). To our knowledge this is the first attempt at an automatic evaluation of simile retrieval performance. The results are presented in table 2. Even though raw extraction F_1 score is very close, DEP has much better recall and therefore leaves more way for improvement with semantic methods, as promised by our DEPSEM heuristic described in section 4.1. This heuristic manages to improve precision at no cost in recall.

4 Semantic approximations of figurativeness and creativeness

4.1 Approach

Though the setting imposed by the VUAMC annotation is to distinguish figurative from literal comparisons, the problem is much more nuanced. In addition, there exists a distinction between conventional and creative language, as discussed for example in (Hanks, 2013). We investigate the use of language conventionality as a proxy to negative

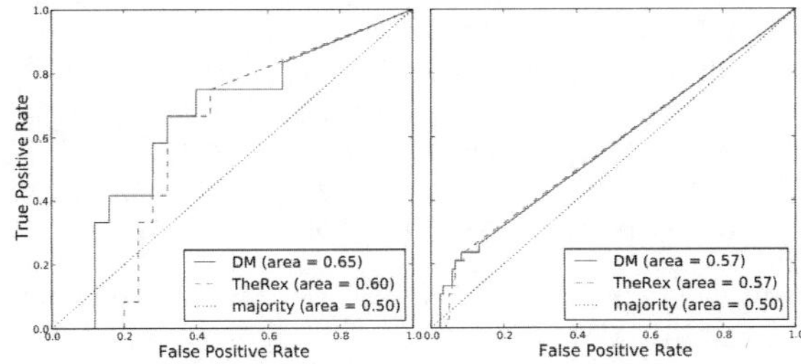

Figure 2: ROC curves for similarity as a predictor of comparison figurativeness measured on comparisons found in the semantic resources (left) and on all comparisons, assuming missing values are zero (right).

figurativeness. We approximate conventionality as similarity between the tagged lemmas of the head words of T and V. To this end, we make use of two precomputed, freely accessible resources. The DEPSEM heuristic filters out matched comparisons with similarity scores above a manually-set threshold, under the assumption that comparisons against highly similar things are unlikely to be figurative.

4.2 Resources

Distributional Memory (Baroni and Lenci, 2010), henceforth DM, is a general-purpose model of corpus-driven semantics. While it comes in a tensor form of *word-link-word*, we use the distributional word representations induced by random indexing, available online[4]. Shutova et al. (2010) used distributional verb-noun clusters in metaphor identification, suggesting that such methods can be adopted for measuring figurativeness. We measure similarity as the cosine between word vectors.

Thesaurus Rex (Veale and Li, 2013), henceforth THEREX[5] is a knowledge base of categories and stereotypes mined from the web using the patterns *as X as Y* and *X such as Y*. While less complete than a knowledge-cheaper distributional resource such as DM, THEREX contains structures that can be explored for simile simplification, by inferring the missing P as discussed in (Niculae and Yaneva, 2013). We measure similarity between noun pairs as a sum of the weights of all shared categories of the two words and categories of each of the word, derived from the other[6].

4.3 Evaluation

Figure 2 shows the ROC curves for the two methods, where the similarity scores are seen as predictors of the target variable that indicates whether *mFlag=like* is annotated within the sentence. It can be seen that these measures perform better than the baseline of always choosing the majority class.

For a qualitative evaluation and proof of concept, we point out several comparisons with low and high similarities, identified in the BNC.

> The piano ripples like patent leather. [DM(piano, leather) $= 0.076$]

> This is a vivid and funny production and their expertise makes the intricate puppetry go like a dream. [DM(puppetry, dream) $= 0.076$]

> Ink, like paint, uses subtractive colour mixing while the video monitor uses the additive colours; red, green and blue, to produce the same effect. [DM(ink, paint) $= 0.502$]

5 Conclusions and future work

We improve upon previous work in comparison pattern matching by using dependency parsing, and at the same time provide a more general interpretation of pattern matching. Our approach is much easier to adapt to other languages, as it needs a POS tagger and a dependency parser.

We show that there exists some negative correlation between lexical semantic similarity and figurativeness, that we exploit in a simple heuristic for simile identification. Such measures can be used as features for simile classifiers.

Obvious improvements include measuring similarity between children nodes and not just the head node of each argument, or measuring other arguments (E and V, for example). The shared categories of pairs of nouns and poetic categories of single nouns available in THEREX show promise for simile simplification. Measures of compositionality in distributional semantics as used by Vecchi et al. (2011) for identifying impossible constructions are expected to be better suited for our task than the representation based on simple co-occurrences.

[4] `http://clic.cimec.unitn.it/dm/`

[5] `http://ngrams.ucd.ie/therex2/`

[6] This strategy proved better than measuring just the shared categories, or than simply counting instead of adding weights. For brevity we omit the particular results.

References

Marco Baroni and Alessandro Lenci. 2010. Distributional memory: A general framework for corpus-based semantics. *Computational Linguistics*, 36(4):673–721.

Lou Burnard. 1995. *British National Corpus: Users Reference Guide British National Corpus Version 1.0.* Oxford Univ. Computing Service.

Patrick Hanks. 2012. The Roles and Structure of Comparisons, Similes, and Metaphors in Natural Language (An Analogical System). In *Presented at the Stockholm Metaphor Festival*, September 6-8.

Patrick Hanks. 2013. *Lexical Analysis: Norms and Exploitations*. Mit Press.

Michael Israel, Jennifer Riddle Harding, and Vera Tobin. 2004. On simile. *Language, Culture, and Mind. CSLI Publications.*

André FT Martins, Noah A Smith, Eric P Xing, Pedro MQ Aguiar, and Mário AT Figueiredo. 2010. Turbo parsers: Dependency parsing by approximate variational inference. In *Proceedings of the 2010 Conference on Empirical Methods in Natural Language Processing*, pages 34–44. Association for Computational Linguistics.

Adam Meyers, Ralph Grishman, Michiko Kosaka, and Shubin Zhao. 2001. Covering treebanks with glarf. In *Proceedings of the ACL 2001 Workshop on Sharing Tools and Resources - Volume 15*, STAR '01, pages 51–58, Stroudsburg, PA, USA. Association for Computational Linguistics.

Vlad Niculae and Victoria Yaneva. 2013. Computational considerations of comparisons and similes. In *51st Annual Meeting of the Association for Computational Linguistics Proceedings of the Student Research Workshop*, pages 89–95, Sofia, Bulgaria, August. Association for Computational Linguistics.

Martin Popel and Zdeněk Žabokrtskỳ. 2010. Tectomt: modular nlp framework. In *Advances in Natural Language Processing*, pages 293–304. Springer.

Ekaterina Shutova, Lin Sun, and Anna Korhonen. 2010. Metaphor identification using verb and noun clustering. In *Proceedings of the 23rd International Conference on Computational Linguistics*, pages 1002–1010. Association for Computational Linguistics.

G.J. Steen, A.G. Dorst, and J.B. Herrmann. 2010. *A Method for Linguistic Metaphor Identification: From Mip to Mipvu.* Converging evidence in language and communication research. Benjamins.

Lucien Tesnière and Jean Fourquet. 1959. *Eléments de syntaxe structurale*, volume 1965. Klincksieck Paris.

Tony Veale and Guofu Li. 2013. Creating similarity: Lateral thinking for vertical similarity judgments. In *Proceedings of the 51st Annual Meeting of the Association for Computational Linguistics (Volume 1: Long Papers)*, pages 660–670, Sofia, Bulgaria, August. Association for Computational Linguistics.

Eva Maria Vecchi, Marco Baroni, and Roberto Zamparelli. 2011. (linear) maps of the impossible: capturing semantic anomalies in distributional space. In *Proceedings of the Workshop on Distributional Semantics and Compositionality*, pages 1–9. Association for Computational Linguistics.

Determining *is-a* relationships for Textual Entailment

Vlad Niculae
Université de Franche-Comté, Besançon
Center for Computational Linguistics
University of Bucharest
vlad@vene.ro

Octavian Popescu
Fondazione Bruno Kessler
popescu@fbk.eu

Abstract

The Textual Entailment task has become influential in NLP and many researchers have become interested in applying it to other tasks. However, the two major issues emerging from this body of work are the fact that NLP applications need systems that (1) attain results which are not corpus dependent and (2) assume that the text for entailment cannot be incorrect or even contradictory. In this paper we propose a system which decomposes the text into chunks via a shallow text analysis, and determines the entailment relationship by matching the information contained in the $is - a$ pattern. The results show that the method is able to cope with the two requirements above.

1 Introduction

Given a pair of two text fragments, $\mathcal{T}$ and $\mathcal{H}$, the textual entailment task consists in deciding whether the information in $\mathcal{H}$ is entailed by the information in $\mathcal{T}$ (Dagan et al., 2006). Many and diverse systems participated in Recognizing Textual Entailment Challenges (RTE), which helped in pointing out interesting issues with an important impact in other NLP tasks. Under some assumptions, the papers published on this topic have proven that the TE methodology is useful for machine translation, text summarization, information retrieval, question answering, fact checking etc. (Padó et al., 2009; Lloret et al., 2008; Clinchant et al., 2006; Harabagiu and Hickl, 2006).

The two major issues emerging from this body of work are the fact that NLP applications need systems that (1) attain results which are not corpus dependent and (2) assume that the text for entailment may be incorrect or even contradictory. In this paper we propose a system which decomposes the text into chunks via a shallow text analysis, and determines the entailment relationship by matching the information contained in the $is - a$ pattern. The results show that the method is able to cope with the two requirements above.

Our system produces stable results on the RTE corpora and is little affected by the presupposed veridical value of the information in $\mathcal{T}$ and/or $\mathcal{H}$ and, therefore, it is instrumental in addressing the above enumerated issues. We focused on the pairs on which $\mathcal{H}$ has the form of an $is - a$ relation between an entity and a property. The method makes use of shallow text analysis, extracts the information contained in each chunk, and tries to find a match for the entity in $\mathcal{H}$ on the list of entities of $\mathcal{T}$. If the match is successful then the properties of the entities are compared in order to decide on the entailment.

In general, the information allowing the match is not found in a single chunk. The property of an entity expressed by the $is - a$ relation found in $\mathcal{H}$ may be not directly expressed in $\mathcal{T}$, the property and the entity being in separated chunks. The system resolves the coreference between the entities mentioned in each chunk by employing mostly techniques for inter-document coreference (Popescu et al., 2008; Ponzetto and Poesio, 2009).

To unify the information contained in each chunk we considered a set of heuristics which identifies syntactical fixed forms and expresses them as $is - a$ relations. For example, an apposition becomes a copula. We also recognized relations between entities which are typically expressed as a pattern, for example [[*e1 is known as e2*]], following the work of (Hearst, 1992; Pantel et al., 2004). The basic approach is extended by considering also synonyms/antonyms and negation mismatches. For comparison purposes we considered a set of features which extend the RTE feature set (MacCartney et al., 2006) and syntactic kernels (Moschitti, 2006) with SVM. The results we obtain support the statement that integration of syntactic and semantic information can yield better results over surface based features (Padó et al., 2009).

For a better understanding of the variance of the results according to the corpora, including robustness to noise and dependency of the veridical presupposition on the information in corpus, we used a technique of generating a scrambled corpus similar to the one described in (Yuret et al., 2010). The results we obtain confirm that the method is stable and overcome with a large margin other approaches. Unlike the methods based on logical forms and world knowledge, which many times are less efficient on noisy corpora, the proposed method maintains a shallow syntactic and semantic level while relevant information unification process takes part, a process which is mostly ignored by surface approaches.

The remainder of this paper is organized as follows: in Section 2 we review the relevant literature, in Section 3 we present the details of the methodology we employ and in Section 4 we present and discuss the experiments we carried on the RTE3, 4, and 5 corpora. The paper ends with the conclusions and further work section.

2 Relevant literature

Successful systems for recognizing textual entailment are usually complex and multi-tiered. The Stanford RTE system (MacCartney et al., 2006), for instance, has a linguistic analysis stage, an alignment stage and an entailment determination stage. The alignment stage, similar to (Haghighi et al., 2005), is based on dependency graph matching. The decision stage can be hand-tuned or learned, but the system did not perform significantly different in the two cases. In the RTE-5 competition, the best systems reach precisions up to 70% using rule-based methods (Iftene and Moruz, 2009) and distance-based approaches. Many systems are based on machine learning classifiers with lexical similarities (Castillo, 2010), non-symmetric causal metrics (Gaona et al., 2010) and syntactic features (Zanzotto et al., 2009). They attain competitive accuracy scores, but there is no report of precision.

3 Methodology

In this section we describe the main components of the strategy of finding a match between the information in $\mathcal{H}$ and $\mathcal{T}$. Usually the relevant information in $\mathcal{T}$ is not in a single chunk and it does not have a form directly comparable with the information in $\mathcal{H}$. Let us see an example:

$\mathcal{T}$: *Pop star Madonna has suffered "minor injuries" and bruises after falling from a startled horse on New York's Long Island on Saturday. According to her spokeswoman, the 50-year-old singer fell when her horse ...*

$\mathcal{H}$: *Madonna is 50 years old.*

The information in $\mathcal{H}$ assigns to the entity *Madonna* a certain attribute. In order to match this information in $\mathcal{T}$ we have to find the same entity and all its mentions and join the attributes of each mentions together in order to see if the attribute occurring in $\mathcal{H}$ is within all these. The general strategy of resolving the entailment is:

1. Match the [[X **be** α]] pattern in $\mathcal{H}$
2. Identify all entities $X_1, ..., X_n$ in $\mathcal{T}$
3. corefer X_i and join the attributes α_i in X_e and α_e
4. match X against each X_e and check the attribute α_e.

We use a parser to obtain the heads of all NPs. Most of the dependency parsers normalize the syntactic variant like passive, apposition, time expressions (De Marneffe et al., 2006; Meyers et al., 2009). Each head represents a possible entity and we extract as attributes all the heads of adjectival and nominal phrases which are under the respective head. For example in Figure 1, the entity *Bob Iger* has the attribute *CEO of Disney* in both cases. Notice that the dependency structures are very different and a direct comparison is likely to be of little help.

The coreference of heads is carried out using a local coreference engine based on multi-pass sieve coreference resolution (MacCartney et al., 2006). For attribute matching we also considered synonyms (Roget, 1911). For example, the system catches correctly the entailment relation in the example below:

$\mathcal{T}$: *The home at 7244 S. Prairie Ave. once owned by mobster Al Capone and his family has hit the market for $450,000.*

$\mathcal{H}$: *Al Capone was a ganster.*

because *gangster* and *mobster* are synonyms.

# +/-	RTE-3′ 104 / 91				RTE-4′ 90 / 102				RTE-5′ 134 / 131			
	A	P	R	F	A	P	R	F	A	P	R	F
BL1	.69	.71	.69	.70	.51	.49	.35	.40	.57	.56	.84	.67
BL2	.74	.71	.87	.78	.62	.62	.53	.57	.59	.59	.82	.68
BL3	.56	.61	.45	.52	.57	.53	.53	.53	.59	.59	.65	.61
NB	.57	.96	.21	.35	.62	.90	.21	.34	.44	.96	.18	.30
NA	.56	.92	.21	.34	.62	.88	.23	.37	.45	.96	.20	.34
SB	.56	.88	.22	.35	.62	.82	.26	.39	.44	.82	.21	.34
SA	.57	.86	.24	.38	.64	.81	.29	.43	.45	.78	.26	.39

Table 1: Results on RTE′ corpora.

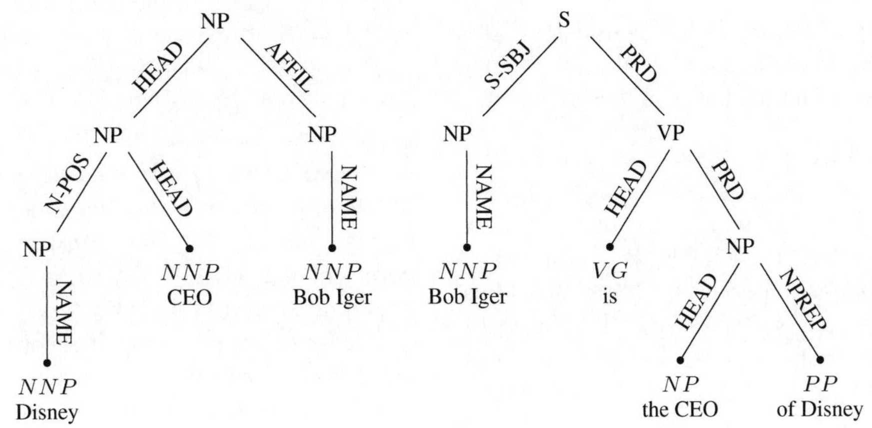

Figure 1: [[X is α]] pattern extraction.

An important improvement of the performances is obtained if before a transformation to $is - a$ relation is carried out for some fixed, strictly defined patterns. A very common pattern involving *as* phrases is:

$\mathcal{T}$: *During Reinsdorf's 24 seasons as chairman of the White Sox, the team ....*

$\mathcal{H}$: *Reinsdorf was the chairman of the White Sox for 24 seasons*

The pattern *[Person] as* α is equivalent with *[Person]* $is - a$ α. The following patterns are prototypical *as* usage as copula alternative: [[NP known as α]], [[NP served as α]], [[NP formed as α]], and [[NP work as α]].

Another common pattern is used for part of a whole or location: [[NP found in α]], [[NP located in α]], and [[NP in α]].

An example instantiation of such a pattern is:

$\mathcal{T}$: *The Gaspe is a North American peninsula (...) in Quebec.*

$\mathcal{H}$: *The Gaspe Peninsula is located in Quebec*

While the main strategy remains the same, using the transformation of these types of patterns increases the recall of the system significantly.

4 Experiments

We based our experiments on the freely available corpora from the Recognizing Textual Entailment competitions RTE-3, 4 and 5. All of the entailment pairs were parsed with the BLLIP parser (Charniak and Johnson, 2005) and subsequently processed with GLARF (Meyers et al., 2009). The copula pattern [[X **be** α]] was matched in all hypotheses, and only instances where the match was positive were kept, see Table 2. The method presented in the previous section does not require training. However, in order to have a direct comparison with other methods, we report only the results obtained on the gold corpus.

We employed three progressively complex baselines:

- **BL1**: Lexical overlap baseline with threshold determined by a linear SVM (Mehdad and Magnini, 2009)

	RTE3	*RTE4*	*RTE5*
copula gold	202	102	269
copula dev	204	101	246

Table 2: RTE corpora, only copula examples

- **BL2**: Linear SVM, features: number of common words, number of words exclusively in $\mathcal{H}$, number of common named entities, number of named entities exclusive to $\mathcal{H}$, number of negative words in $\mathcal{T}$ and respectively $\mathcal{H}$, and number of common parse subtrees
- **BL3**: Tree kernel SVM (Moschitti, 2006), each pair being encoded as the set of common parse subtrees between $\mathcal{T}$ and $\mathcal{H}$.

BL1 and **BL2** were trained using the *scikit-learn* machine learning library version 0.12 (Pedregosa et al., 2011), with the feature extraction from NLTK (Bird et al., 2009). **BL3** was trained using *svmlight-tk* (Moschitti, 2006; Joachims, 1999). In the case of RTE-3′ and RTE-5′ the provided train-test split was used, whereas for RTE-4′ we made a 50-50 split. The regularization parameters and the tree kernel parameters were optimized using grid-search with cross validation.

Four configurations of our system were evaluated, and were labelled with two-letter names. The first letter signifies whether synonym matching is used (**S**) or not (**N**). The second letter marks whether matching is performed at word boundaries (**B**) or anywhere (**A**).

Hypothesis scrambling. A cursory look at Table 1 shows that the baseline approaches vary significantly from corpus to corpus, while the attribute extraction is relatively invariable. Also, apparently, the BL3 using a tree kernel does not perform as well as BL1 or BL2. The difference may come from the typology of entailment pairs in RTE corpora. It seems that matching one entity from $\mathcal{H}$ with one entity from $\mathcal{T}$ is correlated with the entailment. However, this is not the case in general. On the one hand, this observation suggests that on a corpus with a lower degree of correlation, the results may be different. On the other hand, many NLP applications must make decisions when the relationship between $\mathcal{T}$ and $\mathcal{H}$ is more ambiguous than in RTE corpora. That is why we decided to apply the scrambling technique on RTE corpora for evaluation (Yuret et al., 2010).

	RTE3	RTE4	RTE5
#	673	315	418
BL1	.50	.75	.20
BL2	.15	.32	.18
BL3	.65	.60	.54
NB	.90	.95	.95
NA	.90	.94	.94
SB	.84	.91	.87
SA	.79	.85	.80

Table 3: Results on scrambled corpora

For each pair in an entailment relationship we replaced the name of the entities in $\mathcal{H}$ with entities from $\mathcal{T}$. For example the sentence *Bob Iger is Disney CEO* which originally was in entailmentship with *The puzzlement comes from video players who don't work at NBC, Fox or Hulu, and who can't see the upside in Disney CEO Bob Iger throwing in his lot with Hulu* was replaced with *Fox is Disney CEO, Hulu is Disney CEO*. On the corpus obtained in this way we run all thesystems obtaining the results in Table 3.

In absolute values, the performance of attribute extraction systems does not change too much, but the baseline systems have registered a serious drop in accuracy. Also the BL3 system was much better than the other baselines. This shows that the use of structural information pays off.

5 Conclusion and further research

In this paper we introduced a system for TE which identifies the entities in both $\mathcal{T}$ and $\mathcal{H}$ and determines the attributes which may match in order to infer the entailment relationship. The system uses a shallow text analysis. While the precision of this type of approach is very high, the experiments show that without the help of modules that cope with grammatical variance and synonymy correspondence, the recall remains very low. However, the method is stable and the scrambling experiment suggests that the presented approach is competitive for applications requiring unbiased results on heterogeneous corpora.

We think that pattern matching is a good solution to increase the recall. The mapping from fixed syntactic structures to an $is-a$ relation seems possible.

References

Steven Bird, Ewan Klein, and Edward Loper. 2009. *Natural language processing with Python*. O'Reilly Media.

Julio J Castillo. 2010. Using machine translation systems to expand a corpus in textual entailment. In *Advances in Natural Language Processing*, pages 97–102. Springer.

Eugene Charniak and Mark Johnson. 2005. Coarse-to-fine n-best parsing and maxent discriminative reranking. In *Proceedings of the 43rd Annual Meeting on Association for Computational Linguistics*, pages 173–180. Association for Computational Linguistics.

Stéphane Clinchant, Cyril Goutte, and Eric Gaussier. 2006. Lexical entailment for information retrieval. In *Advances in Information Retrieval*, pages 217–228. Springer.

Ido Dagan, Oren Glickman, and Bernardo Magnini. 2006. The pascal recognising textual entailment challenge. In *Machine Learning Challenges. Evaluating Predictive Uncertainty, Visual Object Classification, and Recognising Tectual Entailment*, pages 177–190. Springer.

Marie-Catherine De Marneffe, Bill MacCartney, and Christopher D Manning. 2006. Generating typed dependency parses from phrase structure parses. In *Proceedings of LREC*, volume 6, pages 449–454.

Miguel Angel Ríos Gaona, Alexander Gelbukh, and Sivaji Bandyopadhyay. 2010. Recognizing textual entailment using a machine learning approach. In *Advances in Soft Computing*, pages 177–185. Springer.

Aria D Haghighi, Andrew Y Ng, and Christopher D Manning. 2005. Robust textual inference via graph matching. In *Proceedings of the conference on Human Language Technology and Empirical Methods in Natural Language Processing*, pages 387–394. Association for Computational Linguistics.

Sanda Harabagiu and Andrew Hickl. 2006. Methods for using textual entailment in open-domain question answering. In *Proceedings of the 21st International Conference on Computational Linguistics and the 44th annual meeting of the Association for Computational Linguistics*, pages 905–912. Association for Computational Linguistics.

Marti A Hearst. 1992. Automatic acquisition of hyponyms from large text corpora. In *Proceedings of the 14th conference on Computational linguistics-Volume 2*, pages 539–545. Association for Computational Linguistics.

Adrian Iftene and Mihai-Alex Moruz. 2009. UAIC participation at RTE5. *Proceedings of TAC, Gaithersburg, Maryland.*

Thorsten Joachims. 1999. Advances in kernel methods. chapter Making large-scale support vector machine learning practical, pages 169–184. MIT Press, Cambridge, MA, USA.

Elena Lloret, Óscar Ferrández, Rafael Muñoz, and Manuel Palomar. 2008. A text summarization approach under the influence of textual entailment. In Bernadette Sharp and Michael Zock, editors, *NLPCS*, pages 22–31. INSTICC Press.

Bill MacCartney, Trond Grenager, Marie-Catherine de Marneffe, Daniel Cer, and Christopher D Manning. 2006. Learning to recognize features of valid textual entailments. In *Proceedings of the main conference on Human Language Technology Conference of the North American Chapter of the Association of Computational Linguistics*, pages 41–48. Association for Computational Linguistics.

Yashar Mehdad and Bernardo Magnini. 2009. A word overlap baseline for the recognizing textual entailment task.

Adam Meyers, Michiko Kosaka, Nianwen Xue, Heng Ji, Ang Sun, Shasha Liao, and Wei Xu. 2009. Automatic recognition of logical relations for english, chinese and japanese in the glarf framework. In *Proceedings of the Workshop on Semantic Evaluations: Recent Achievements and Future Directions*, pages 146–154. Association for Computational Linguistics.

Alessandro Moschitti. 2006. Making tree kernels practical for natural language learning. In *Proceedings of EACL*, volume 6, pages 113–120.

Sebastian Padó, Michel Galley, Dan Jurafsky, and Chris Manning. 2009. Robust machine translation evaluation with entailment features. In *Proceedings of the Joint Conference of the 47th Annual Meeting of the ACL and the 4th International Joint Conference on Natural Language Processing of the AFNLP: Volume 1-Volume 1*, pages 297–305. Association for Computational Linguistics.

Patrick Pantel, Deepak Ravichandran, and Eduard Hovy. 2004. Towards terascale knowledge acquisition. In *Proceedings of the 20th international conference on Computational Linguistics*, page 771. Association for Computational Linguistics.

F. Pedregosa, G. Varoquaux, A. Gramfort, V. Michel, B. Thirion, O. Grisel, M. Blondel, P. Prettenhofer, R. Weiss, V. Dubourg, J. Vanderplas, A. Passos, D. Cournapeau, M. Brucher, M. Perrot, and E. Duchesnay. 2011. Scikit-learn: Machine learning in Python. *Journal of Machine Learning Research*, 12:2825–2830.

Simone Paolo Ponzetto and Massimo Poesio. 2009. State-of-the-art nlp approaches to coreference resolution: theory and practical recipes. In *Tutorial Abstracts of ACL-IJCNLP 2009*, pages 6–6. Association for Computational Linguistics.

Octavian Popescu, Christian Girardi, Emanuele Pianta, and Bernardo Magnini. 2008. Improving cross document coreference. In *Proceedings of JADT*.

Peter Mark Roget. 1911. *Roget's Thesaurus of English Words and Phrases...* TY Crowell Company.

Deniz Yuret, Aydin Han, and Zehra Turgut. 2010. Semeval-2010 task 12: Parser evaluation using textual entailments. In *Proceedings of the 5th International Workshop on Semantic Evaluation*, pages 51–56. Association for Computational Linguistics.

Fabio Zanzotto, Marco Pennacchiotti, and Alessandro Moschitti. 2009. A machine learning approach to textual entailment recognition. *Natural Language Engineering*, 15(04):551–582.

Association for Computational Linguistics
209 N. Eighth Street
Stroudsburg, Pennsylvania 18360

CURRAN ASSOCIATES INC
proceedings.com